The Inability to Love

The Inability to Love

Jews, Gender, and America in Recent German Literature

✦

Agnes C. Mueller

NORTHWESTERN UNIVERSITY PRESS
EVANSTON, ILLINOIS

Northwestern University Press
www.nupress.northwestern.edu

Printed in the United States of America

ISBN 978-0-8101-3437-9

The Library of Congress has cataloged the original, hardcover edition as follows:

Mueller, Agnes C., 1968– author.
The inability to love : Jews, gender, and America in recent German literature / Agnes C. Mueller.
pages cm
Includes bibliographical references and index.
ISBN 978-0-8101-3017-3 (cloth : alk. paper)—ISBN 978-0-8101-6811-4 (ebook)
1. German literature—20th century—History and criticism. 2. German literature—21st century—History and criticism. 3. Jews in literature. 4. Memory in literature. 5. Antisemitism in literature. 6. Holocaust, Jewish (1939–1945), in literature. 7. Holocaust, Jewish (1939–1945)—Influence. I. Title.
PT149.J4M84 2014
830.93529924—dc23

2014026770

CONTENTS

ACKNOWLEDGMENTS

This is not a particularly long book within the realm of scholarship. Nevertheless, a number of institutions and individuals provided crucial help and support. The University of South Carolina supported work on this project in 2006, before it was even a book, with a Research and Productive Scholarship Grant that allowed me to conduct research at the archives of the Zentrum für Antisemitismusforschung (Center for Antisemitism Research) at the Technische Universität (TU) Berlin. I learned a lot from the archives, and also from the wonderful people associated with it, first and foremost Mona Körte. In 2007 I was the lucky recipient of a DAAD one-month summer research grant, permitting me to delve into the Berlin literary scene and to follow the invitation to present my work at TU Berlin. In 2010, I received a Promising Investigators Research Award from the University of South Carolina, once more bringing me to Berlin to conclude my scholarly explorations. In 2012 I was able to finish writing the manuscript thanks to the time afforded by a Provost's Humanities Grant. I am indebted to the University of South Carolina and its research support for the humanities, and particularly to Dean Mary Anne Fitzpatrick, who has been supportive of my work ever since her arrival at the university.

I would like to thank the *German Quarterly*, Universitätsverlag Winter, and Camden House Publishers for permission to use previously published ideas in this new context. The Jewish Museum in Berlin was helpful by putting me in touch with Menashe Kadishman, who kindly allowed me to use an image of his moving installation "Fallen Leaves," which is on permanent display at the Jewish Museum. My thanks also to Henry Carrigan at Northwestern University Press for believing in this project, and to all the superb staff.

Most instrumental are the wonderful and generous individuals who helped me see this project through, many from its tender beginnings. Mona Körte, Bill Donahue, Andy Gross, Sander Gilman, Steve Dowden, Stephen Brockman, Peter Höyng, Russell Berman, Hilene Flanzbaum, Greg Forter, Esther Frank, Yael Kupferberg, Yvonne Ivory, Birgit Tautz, Jonathan Skolnik, and Christoph Zeller were powerful as scholar-friends and/or friendly scholars, reading, listening, responding, commenting, sharing, provoking, and advancing my thoughts. Closer to home, Susan Courtney, Allen Miller, and Jill Frank offered friendship and support in many ways. In Germany, Harald Lazardzig, Xenia Frenkel, and Ute Wild are literally always there for me, even when I'm not. I have tremendous respect for the writers and artists I met on the way. Esther Dischereit and Anna Adam in particular were open and thoughtful in several conversations.

The book would not be what it is without my smart and engaging students. Among the graduate students in comparative literature, Kristina Stefanic Brown, now an accomplished teacher-scholar, Richard Sell, Catharina Wuetig Baker, Gregor Rehmer, and Isabel Meusen are inspirations in the classroom and beyond.

Above all I am thankful to my husband, Nicholas Vazsonyi, who was and is the most important source of love, comfort, and plain practical help. I am lucky to live with a partner who happily carves out precious time from his own research and work to share household chores more than equitably. Beyond this, his perspective as a Holocaust survivor immersed in German studies was probably the main inspiration for the project in the first place. Leah, Benjamin, and Cosima put up with one scatterbrained parent and with being dragged to and from Berlin frequently. For that, and for the joy and chaos that they bring to my life and to this project, I am grateful.

This book is dedicated to the memory of my parents, who were probably more affected by the "inability to love" than I fully realized while writing it.

A.C.M.
Columbia, S.C., April 2014

The Inability to Love

Introduction

> People are always shouting that they want to create a better
> future. It's not true.
> The future is an apathetic void of no interest
> to anyone. The past is full of life, eager to irritate us, provoke
> and insult us,
> tempt us to destroy or repaint it.
>
> —Milan Kundera, *The Book of Laughter and Forgetting*

The publication and reception of "Was gesagt werden muss" ("What Must Be Said"), the controversial "poem" that Günter Grass disseminated on April 4, 2012, in *Süddeutsche Zeitung*, *La Repubblica*, and *El Pais*, paradigmatically illustrates diverse and crucial issues surrounding the German memory of the past. Immediately following its simultaneous appearance in several European publications, this text provoked passionate responses from notables in German politics, academia, and the public arena, precipitating widespread commentary in ways that poems, even political poems, usually do not. The reasons for the intense attention seem obvious: Germany's most illustrious writer, often considered the Germans' moral conscience of the Nazi past, had published thinly veiled accusations against Israel. The extent to which a text that is void of any significant aesthetic or literary merit should elicit this kind of respect, especially considering that the aging and perhaps sentimental Grass is known for staging public debates (the well-placed excerpt of his autobiographical *Beim Häuten der Zwiebel* [*Peeling the Onion*, 2006] in the *Frankfurter Allgemeine Zeitung* of 2006 is the most notorious example), is perhaps more unexpected. The poetic persona, or narrator, of Grass's prose "poem"—which resembles an editorial more than a poem—accuses Israel of endangering world peace by threatening a first nuclear strike against Iran. The narrator then goes on to criticize the German government for delivering submarines to Israel. Perhaps most enraging to Grass's critics is the sixth verse, where the poetic persona or narrator explains that he had been silent for so long because of the implicit taboo imposed on any German wishing to express criticism towards Israel:

> Weil ich meinte, meine Herkunft,
> die von nie zu tilgendem Makel behaftet ist,
> verbiete, diese Tatsache als ausgesprochene Wahrheit

dem Land Israel, dem ich verbunden bin
und bleiben will, zuzumuten.[1]

But why was I silent for so long?
Because I thought my origin,
marked with an ineradicable stain,
forbade mention of this fact
as definite truth about Israel, a country
To which I am and remain attached.[2]

Leaving aside the petulant tone and lack of artistic effort visible in this single stanza, the relevance of the "poem" lies precisely in the widespread and violent debates ensuing, emphasizing the divisive nature of contemporary German discourse on the memories of the past. This kind of reception illustrates how public debates quickly turn painful when they recall the German Nazi period and the Holocaust, where questions concerning aesthetics or literary merit are immediately secondary to the apparently larger and more pressing discourse on the heritage of German guilt and anti-Semitism.[3] This is especially astonishing since today, decades after Adorno's famous and often misquoted dictum "to write poetry after Auschwitz is barbaric," the German and international community of intellectuals and critics should presumably have moved the debate on the poetics of German guilt and shame from its previously ingrained binary of acceptance or rejection of the notion of a successful *Vergangenheitsbewältigung* (dealing with the past) to a new level of a more differentiated view in which several discourses of the poetics and memory of the Shoah might coexist.[4] Furthermore, more than two decades after German unification, the new Berlin Republic might have incorporated both Eastern and Western models of addressing German guilt and shame.

More significantly for Grass's text, the poetic persona or narrator, could, conceivably, be read as a fictitious figure that is entirely separate from Günter Grass, the author. While, due to the lack of artistic finesse, such a reading is neither immediately anticipated nor seems to have been intended by Grass himself, it is noteworthy that it did not merit any consideration, consideration that could have toned down the fervor of the debate. Grass himself could easily have employed the argument that he, the author, is not simply to be substituted for the first-person narrator or poetic persona of the poem. Such a statement could indeed serve as a defense against the attacks on his person. The request to read his text as a work of literature that defies simplistic categorization into the voice of the author, a purposeful provocation where the poetic persona is an imaginary "I" that might have to be deconstructed, could have stopped any enraged critic in his or her tracks. The fact that neither Grass nor his defenders ever invoked this relatively obvious and simple strategy points to the fact that the poem was never meant to be read as a literary "poem" in the first place. In fact, it is doubtful if, considering this circumstance, the poem can be called poetry, or literature, at all. Instead, the key objective for its publication seems to have been the public outrage and antagonism that it promised. And, according to plan, the immediate responses to the piece, from writers, intellectuals, scholars, or politicians, culminating with Israel's Interior Minister Eli Yishai prohibiting Günter Grass from traveling to Israel, indicate that measured or discerning reactions were, indeed, not conceivable. Moreover, the text itself proclaims a "taboo" when it comes to addressing Israel and German history. Such a declaration of the prevalence of a "taboo" concerning the German past is familiar and reminiscent of the assertion of a "political correctness" that, likewise, prohibits Germans from speaking freely about their history.[5] The "poem's" implicit accusation against the German mainstream that "forbids" a renowned and reputable Nobel laureate from speaking the "truth" furthermore points to the extent to which the supposed taboo is, still in 2012, more than sixty-five years after the end of World War II, burdening public memories.

Rather than re-rehearsing the familiar and to a large extent predictable responses on both sides of the divide (with Marcel Reich-Ranicki staging the anti-Grass, Peter Schneider and politicians from Germany's Die Linke party speaking out in Grass's favor), this book is a study of the ways in which Jews, and with that, the memory of the Holocaust, are and are not represented in today's German literature. Identifying and understanding such contemporary literary representations reveals the motivations behind the ongoing public discourses that fuel the impulse for Günter Grass to articulate what could easily be read as an anti-Semitic tirade, and for the public to respond passionately either in his support or against him. As the reception indicated, Grass's "poem" is clearly not a work of literature with aesthetic merit that could render a multivalently coded interpretation essential. Thus, the questions that my analysis of unambiguously literary texts addresses are: How do present-day Germans feel about the Holocaust, and the Nazi past, and how are these emotions articulated in their representations of Jews and Judaism? Are (repressed) guilt and shame still the dominant modes of responding to the fathers' and grandfathers' crimes, as Alexander and Margarete Mitscherlich have formulated in their pivotal *Die Unfähigkeit zu trauern* (*The Inability to Mourn*, 1975) of 1967? The public spectacle created by Grass's pamphlet raises the question if anxiety and melancholia over German history are still, today, at the core of contemporary Germans' emotions, consistent with the Mitscherlichs' assertions four and a half decades ago. The inability to mourn seems to have, according to Grass's text and the reactions to it, turned into an inability to address the German past, at least when it concerns a German past that invokes Jews, Israel, and the Holocaust. Yet, apart from the possibly dated and clearly narcissistic ruminations of an aging literary icon, how do today's second, third, and following generations after World War II respond to the contested and divided German memory?[6] For these younger generations, have the forefathers' earlier sentiments been replaced with indifference, compassion, empathy—or secondary anti-Semitism? How do current Germans relate to representations of Jews in Germany, as they concern the legacies of German history and memory, and, more significantly, how do Germans view present-day Jewish life? Literature has the power to condense and even transform conditions in society. Importantly, literature, and the toolbox of literary analysis, can move beyond publicly staged spectacles, and thus has the capacity to reveal underlying and less openly visible currents in contemporary society. Literature—and the readers' interpretative work—can furthermore epitomize subversive and interstitial spaces in society that might be less visible to other fields in the humanities. The aim of this study is to shed light on pressing questions concerning German memories of the past, and on German images and imaginings of Jews in Germany, by interrogating numerous recently published literary texts, written by prominent contemporary German, non-Jewish writers.[7]

Importantly, not only Günter Grass and Martin Walser write literary texts and utter public remarks aimed at igniting by now familiar debates on the German memory of the Holocaust. Successful fictional texts by younger and prominent writers such as Bernhard Schlink, Peter Schneider, Susanne Riedel, Tanja Dückers, Katharina Hacker, Julia Franck, Thomas Hettche, and Thomas Meinecke contain anti-Semitic articulations that may not be immediately visible, but when carefully analyzed, turn out to be significant. While the history of anti-Semitism in Europe is exceedingly well studied, and sociologists and historians have gone to great lengths uncovering and describing the "new anti-Semitism" in Germany,[8] my readings of popular contemporary literary texts are different in that they show how and why the relationship between Jews and Germans today continues to be fraught, complex, and at times painful. In the works I will discuss, fictional fantasies, acted out in literature, exhibit how the Germans' relationship with their past is marred by the absence of Jews in dialogues over German guilt and shame (chapter 1), by demonstrations of gendered anti-Semitism (chapter 2), by conflations of masculinity and Germanness acted out against male Jews (chapter 3), and by imaginings of America as a location to conveniently displace anti-Semitic fantasies (chapter 4). In the works discussed, Judaism mostly appears as an undefined label for an unfamiliar, seemingly unknowable ethnic identity that is represented as "the other" vis-à-vis the German cultural heritage. Most of these texts furthermore display love relationships between Jewish and German protagonists that typically fail. Most consistently, these are between Jewish women and German men, or between homosexually coded males, but in some cases between Jewish mothers and daughters or Jewish mothers and German sons. The infamous German "inability to mourn" of the more immediate post-World War II era is thus transformed, so my thesis, into an "inability to love." "Love" is here meant to designate a type of emotional attachment that transcends erotic or familial love, and that includes notions of acceptance and embrace.[9] The title therefore also alludes to an "inability to love" extending to multiple ethnic "others."

For example, the election of Barack Obama as the first African American president of the United States in 2008 prompted widespread speculation in the German media as to whether a Turkish-German could stand a chance of being elected chancellor in Germany today. As desirable as such an outcome may be in the collective German imaginary, the suggestion is fundamentally misguided. A more appropriate counterpart to Obama's victory, to the extent that such a comparison can be considered, would be the election of a German-Jewish chancellor, because the guilt and shame white Americans typically associate with African Americans concerning the history of slavery more closely resonates with the guilt and shame non-Jewish Germans associate with German Nazi crimes committed during the Shoah. Interestingly, the German public imagination does not consider the election of a female chancellor as equally compelling or noteworthy as the election of a (presumably male) perceived ethnic "other." This indicates the extent to which ethnicity is essential and visible to contemporary Germans, yet gender remains more inconspicuous. Within this paradigm, however, Jewishness and/or Judaism, even though perceived as an ethnic more than a religious category, seem essentially absent from German public memory. This can partly be explained by the fact that none of the extensive reeducation efforts in either East or West Germany were directed at familiarizing Germans with Jews, or with their more personal ties to the Holocaust past. Another reason may be found in the fact that comparatively few Jews resided in either East or West Germany after 1945, and the few that did were not necessarily visible. Yet, as the texts expose, most of the virtual absence of any significant discourse on Jews and Judaism in Germany today relates to the Germans' repressed emotions concerning their past culpability and resulting embarrassment. Thus, my study reveals an evident blind spot—twice over—in contemporary German post-unification culture. As my close readings of selected popular texts argue, prominent German authors are writing works that contain articulations of anti-Semitic and gender stereotyping, in some cases acted out as murder fantasies involving Jews. Surprisingly, the critical press has ignored this phenomenon, despite extensive public demonstrations of mourning and remembrance, indicating the continued absence of meaningful dialogues in the public arena, even within the academy. Because many of the literary texts that contain stereotypical or racist language also invoke gender issues, largely obscured up to now, this book interrogates how and why such prejudices by contemporary Germans apparently intersect with gender stereotypes concerning Jews, and how those discourses are situated in German-American and transnational contexts. Beyond the German and Jewish perspective, this analysis, then, refers to other trans-generational discourses on the memory of ethnic prejudice and gender stereotyping.

Recent scholarship on generational divides and the German memory of dealing with the past (*Vergangenheitsbewältigung*) typically follows the chronological succession of generations after World War II, a practice that is inviting to literature scholars also because of the newly emergent *Generationenromane* (generational novels) by many contemporary writers.[10] When thinking about generational divides concerning the discourse of German memories of the past, and the ways in which forgetting and remembering interact trans-generationally, Sigrid Weigel's work is central, even though her approach requires some revision for this particular purpose.[11] Even if we contend, with Weigel, that the framework of "generation" is outdated and therefore obsolete, asserting that more recent new media-compatible social concepts now function for various groups to self-identify, we are nevertheless still referencing "generation" as a model that served as a long-standing meta-narrative. The reasons for this narrative to persist even to this day remain powerful and compelling, especially for West and East German debates after 1945, and are inexorably intertwined with the subject of this study. The concept of "generation" helps to maintain the notion of 1945 as a "zero hour," an idea that is enticing for East German history and memory since it marks a decisive break with the pre-socialist past, and it is equally appealing for West Germans since it signifies the beguiling view that National Socialism, and, by extension, Holocaust guilt, are a thing of the past. Helmut Kohl's contested proclamation of the "mercy of the late birth" ("Gnade der späten Geburt") furthermore aided in establishing "generation" as a model that can offer personal comfort and relief from former German guilt. In postwar history, therefore, both East and West German narratives rely on generational divides after the war, significant also since no one could earnestly deny the import of 1945 as a momentous caesura in German memory and history. Similarly, as Erin McGlothlin's study analyzes with exemplary acuity, the legacies of Holocaust survivors are referenced—and self-referenced—in generational terms. Eric Santner and others have observed the extent to which especially second-generation children of both Holocaust victims and perpetrators are defined by their parents and families' traumatic experiences that often remained silenced.[12] Ernestine Schlant's *The Language of Silence* accentuates this nexus, although her book seeks to deemphasize the import of the notion of "generation." My study operates thematically, yet in so doing, nevertheless refers back to generation as a meta-frame. This seems justified since the concept still looms large, particularly for contemporary German writers,[13] and deconstructing it entirely would remove valuable points of reference that are significant for writers, critics, and scholars alike to identify and self-identify key issues. As my interrogation will show, a more fluid conception of "generation" can serve to indicate how today's Germans, even as they are on the third or fourth echelons more concerned with their own German trauma, have also become less concerned with Jews and Jewish issues.[14] Close readings of several popular narratives offer unexpected and detailed answers to the emergence of anxieties uncovered by the complex process of dealing with German trauma throughout several postwar generations. To make these processes acutely visible, the texts under investigation are all by contemporary German writers who are still alive, and were published, roughly, since the turn of the millennium. The textual analyses reveal how and why German representations of the German Jewish experience have been largely eclipsed from German memory debates. Even if unexpected, this turns out to be the case in spite—or because—of the many collective and plainly visible demonstrations of public mourning and commemoration, such as the Berlin Holocaust Memorial, several concentration camp sites, and countless other sites of Holocaust remembrance.[15]

There are several concerns that any interrogation into the representation of stereotypes as analyzed in literary texts raises. This particular study has the added challenge of working within a web of assumptions, prejudices, and attitudes that are often easily deniable, or whose relevance can be dismissed, particularly when studying works of fiction. Textual indeterminacy can be used as a defense against any critical or moral argument, since fictional texts are by definition multivalent in ways that defy a seemingly one-sided interpretation. In such an intricate setting, textual interpretation wishing to make any claims about texts and their societal relevance therefore needs to operate exceedingly carefully about making general proclamations (about a people, a group or groups of people, or a particular location or identity). Accordingly, whenever my interrogation employs the labels "German" or "Jewish," I ask my reader to remain suspicious, and imagine quotation marks around those terms, meant to indicate that those markers signify fluid and unstable identities. Assignments of "German" and, even more so, of "Jewish," can hardly be made without the understanding that even if they are markers of self-identification, they are multifaceted, typically referring to some cultural or religious origin, and highly ambiguous in the ways in which they might or might not signal belonging or identity. Since all texts under discussion here are written more than one and a half decades after German unification, "German" is mostly meant to incorporate both East and West German memory, except in cases where "East" and "West" are themes in the texts, or, presumably inform the debate surrounding a text or its authors' biography.[16] Yet, in order to reveal and recognize some of the opinions, attitudes, and even emotions prevalent among many Germans living today, descriptive terminology does need to be used. This study moreover seeks to mount arguments that attempt to subvert common generalizations and widely dispersed stereotypes, yet as such itself of course runs the risk of generalizing and stereotyping in completely new ways. Hence, when writers, and writers' identities are concerned, I will mostly abide by their own claims about their self-identification, being mindful that they might be equivocal and multivalent, as already specified, for the case of Julia Franck. For textual representations of Jews, Germans, or other local, national, ethnic, or gendered identities, this study, as a *literary* inquiry, will investigate each case separately and base any claims ascribing Jewish or German identity on the close textual readings of that particular textual moment, or instance.

For this very reason, investigations into the authors' biographies, and their personal stories, can decidedly not be the subject of this study. While writers' identities and assertions about their texts always inform the public perception of their works, and thus need to be taken into consideration, (auto) biographical texts and statements can only comment on the emotions or attitudes of one specific person, and are thus limited in what they might reveal about larger discourses in society. The purposeful staging of the poem by Günter Grass serves as a reminder as to why inquiries into author personalities do not necessarily yield any substantial scholarly results. While such statements and proclamations do initiate public debates, and those debates are important in that they indicate an underlying societal concern, they rarely serve to either properly delineate the problem, nor do they typically help to resolve it directly, even though the ensuing debate, such as in the case of the Walser-Grass debate, or in the earlier phases of the *Historikerstreit*, (historians' quarrel) does often lead to discourse and a more common awareness of underlying themes. Ultimately, we cannot discern with any degree of reliability whether information related in author statements, also concerning their biographies, is "true." Even if such factual veracity can be corroborated, the question remains whether any predictions for authors' intentions yield relevant meaning for conditions in any given society. In other words, we may not be able to determine with certainty whether anti-Semitism in today's German society is virulent just because Martin Walser made statements that can be read as anti-Semitic. Consequently, while authors' biographies and identities inform the background of this study, in that they shape our, the readers', perceptions of said writers, they are not the subject of this analysis. Nor would psychoanalyzing the writers themselves provide us with relevant insights. Psychology as a discipline makes claims about individuals; a study that looks at the history of memory and the reception of literature, by its very definition, needs to ask questions about people more collectively. A distinct literary text and its reception are therefore more relevant than an individual writer's biography or psychology, the literary text more pertinent than the author who created it. Furthermore, if exploring conditions in society is the ultimate aim of this study, then the reader matters—more so than the identity or perceived identity of the author, even the celebrity author. Thinking back to the profoundly outdated reader response models by Wolfgang Iser and Hans Robert Jauss from the 1960s and 1970s, we know that we can only make vague proclamations with respect to individual and specific readers' reactions. This notwithstanding, we *can* say that novels that are more popular and that have a wider distribution than texts read by smaller audiences are more likely to have a greater impact on the public discourse and general reader perception. The conclusions we reach via close readings, especially from popular, widely read texts, allow us to gain insight into the situation of

German memory discourses today. Yet it also follows from the above that, since it is concerned with representations, this book is not intended to deliver an account on the attitudes or situations of actual living Jews in Germany.

Hence, we need to, by examining primary texts, determine each individual literary text's articulations that might reveal anti-Semitic or otherwise stereotyped emotions. Klaus-Michael Bogdal's introduction and Mona Körte's contribution to the key volume *Literarischer Antisemitismus nach Auschwitz* (Literary Anti-Semitism after Auschwitz) provide an important frame for such an investigation, in that they acknowledge both the problems and the opportunities intrinsic to the extrapolation of stereotypical speech in works of art. This is crucial since the kind of literature that, via the expression of stereotypical speech, instead of supporting and propagating such speech, is rather attempting to expose and undermine it, and hence Bogdal concludes that in highly developed aesthetic artworks, "analysis is not a ban. It designates and critiques what has been written just so and not any differently."[17] The question, therefore, is, how to evaluate anti-Semitic and stereotypical articulations that evoke discriminatory emotions, particularly when they occur in fiction. Bogdal summarizes a set of three distinct criteria that we can pose as questions to the individual works under investigation. He asserts that texts are anti-Semitic when they display either (1) manifest, subjectively intentioned anti-Semitism, (2) unintentional, negligent (conscious or subconscious) use of stereotypes, and (3) conscious, deconstructing risk-provoking play with anti-Semitic repertoires. Apart from the obvious problem with these categories, which is the indeterminate and unspoken authorial intention that seems to lurk behind each one of them (although Bogdal does not specify this), there are other issues that need to be addressed. While the first measure is easily recognizable but not likely to occur in contemporary German texts, the second and third ones are more difficult to analyze and evaluate. Particularly with respect to secondary or new anti-Semitism, a more recent form of anti-Semitism at least partly emergent from post-Holocaust guilt and shame, Bogdal contends that observing, with Foucault, aesthetic representations of anti-Semitism are complex to analyze since any attempt at a scholarly critique must be refuted by the aesthetics or fictionality of the text. It is therefore, Bogdal concludes, even more pressing to thoroughly analyze literature that might invoke anti-Semitic speech. Careful textual analysis that asks those questions of each individual text must thus lie at the center of this study. As Linda Hutcheon reminds us, the assignment to uncover textual irony is central, since "historiographic metafiction" can subvert and thus dramatically alter the direction and meaning of a text, turning it into a problematizing return to history.[18] Consequently, I would add, the ways in which we ask any questions pertaining to close textual readings must, ultimately, be directed at the reader. For it is the empathy of the reader, and the question of the direction of reader empathy and compassion, that can decide how texts are received. It makes an important difference if the text induces the reader to primarily empathize with the Jewish subjects, or with the German and non-Jewish protagonists, or if reader empathy is evoked in ways that are ambiguous or unstable. In many texts the direction of reader empathy is evident, and deconstructing it lays bare the problems of stereotypical and anti-Semitic articulation. Naming the problems that are thus apparent might alter the discourse to include the possibility to induce its own critical reflection.

The limitation implied in seeking to deconstruct texts on the German memories of the past lies in its unspoken and of course problematical demand for some "ideal" way of addressing German memory and trauma. As Dominick LaCapra's work has shown, "writing trauma" is relevant to both Jewish *and* German memories after 1945, as is thinking about how trauma in the post-Shoah context can even be written about. Marianne Hirsch's conception of a "postmemory" serves as an important reminder of how memories are transmitted from one generation to the next, and how they get distorted in the process, although her concept does need revision for the purpose of this analysis, as it hinges too much on the notion of the second generation's family narratives. Yet, her discussion does indicate how intergenerationally transmitted trauma deserves special consideration. It also specifies that the reverberations of the previous German "inability to mourn" still seem to hold true—for the memory of the German second generation and beyond.[19] By proxy, her reminder of the "post" to memory also alludes to the farcicality of the demand for this process to be further along than it apparently is. The mere wish for "normalization" in the Berlin Republic, understandable as it might be, does not immediately—or ever—produce a literature, or a discourse, that can do this desire justice.[20] LaCapra's idea of the "middle voice" as an acceptable and productive form of remembrance in both literary and historical texts, and the extent to which such a creative use of language is absent in contemporary German literature, helps illustrate the persistent narcissism and anxiety concerning Jews and Germans, emotions resulting from the void of the memory of Jews living in Germany. The absence of the representation of a middle voice thus indicates the lack of a vibrant discourse on the German past. Both absences contribute to create characters in contemporary German literature who, still today, display an inability to love, a direct result from previous generations' inability to mourn.

Since absence is such a central motif in all of the texts under investigation, the first chapter of the book is entitled "Absence: Guilt and Shame." The discussions of works by older, first-generation German writers set up the historical and metahistorical framework for understanding contemporary German discourses of the memory of guilt and shame. Günter Grass's and Martin Walser's texts indicate how the absence of an engagement with Jews in recent Germany, and of a German engagement with the Shoah, is discernible in fiction, and the seminal factor in present discourses on anti-Semitism. Grass's novella *Im Krebsgang* (*Crabwalk*, 2002) and Walser's novel *Tod eines Kritikers* (Death of a Critic), both published in 2002, each portray the killing of a Jew by a German, non-Jewish male. Both texts represent reductively a German male fantasy of prevailing over the past. My discussion illustrates how such fantasies, resulting from the inability to mourn (the past), may lead to an absence of the capability to love or accept the (Jewish) other, as well as the (German) self in contemporary German settings. Perhaps predictably, these texts from older, first-generation writers keenly expose a framework of emotional confusion among their German and not Jewish protagonists, yet the thematic cores of critically unchallenged and unmediated anti-Semitism resulting from unresolved past guilt and shame resonate similarly in Schlink's best seller *Der Vorleser* (1995; *The Reader*, 1998), some of his short stories from *Liebesfluchten* (2000; *Flights of Love*, 2002) as well as in third-generation writer Tanja Dückers's 2003 novel *Himmelskörper* (Heavenly Bodies). A. Dirk Moses asserts that there are two divergent ways in which Germans address their traumatic past, one that seeks to affirm and recover German national identity while essentially denying the possibility that there is still anti-Semitism and xenophobia in today's Germany (the German German, or Martin Walser), and the contrasting one that seeks to escape the German cultural heritage writ large in order to avoid the memory of the painful past (the non-German German, as for example Jürgen Habermas). Needless to say, both attitudes are dubious since neither one confronts the issues at hand. Still for the narratives by Schlink, and Dückers, the concept of a "German German" vs. "non-German German" memory culture, as Moses has exemplified utilizing the public figures Jürgen Habermas and Martin Walser, can be traced.[21] Remarkably, Moses's approach does hold out hope for the fourth generation who is no longer directly burdened with living family members implicated in the Nazi past, and therefore able to develop trust in the Federal Republic's political structures. However, while Moses's analysis is compelling, it also reinstates a binary oppositional structure of acceptance versus rejection that Leslie Adelson had, already in 1994, pointed out as problematic, given that observing and stating such binaries often results in inadvertently reinscribing them as scholarly analytical practice.[22] This book's aim is, therefore, focused on subverting any previously conceived binary oppositions, be it German vs. Jewish or German German vs. non-German German identities. The close textual readings in chapter 1 primarily display, for the first- and second-generation writers' narratives, an absence of the engagement with Jews and Germans. Yet, for the third generation, this nexus turns into a discernible memory void, a void of the German memory of the Jews—and the reverse of what Moses's more optimistic interpretations propose for future generations of Germans.

Referencing Susan Bordo's and Dominick LaCapra's work on the memories of gender and trauma, chapter 2 demonstrates how in multiple German texts, Jewish women are cast as dark, seductive, and sexually threatening to the German male, and often exploited to fantasize a liberation of Germans from their trans-generational guilt. For example, in Schlink's "Das

Mädchen mit der Eidechse" (2000; "Girl With Lizard," 2002), the unnamed German male narrator relates the story of a painting that belonged to his father, and that haunted him in ways that prevented a meaningful relationship with women, displaying an inability to love. The painting depicts a Jewish girl ("Judenmädchen") looking at a lizard. Although only a child, the girl in the painting exhibits traits of the *belle Juive*, the beautiful, virtuous, and erotically seductive Jewish woman, as they were conceived in pertinent anti-Semitic texts from the turn of the nineteenth to the twentieth century.[23] When Schlink's narrator-son learns of the history of the valuable painting, including his by now deceased father's guilt of persecuting the Jewish painter and his family, he also discovers his father's illicit affair with the Jewish wife of the painter, depicted as the girl in the painting. The protagonist's way of dealing with his feelings of guilt is to burn the artwork at the end of the story, a "happy end" to this narrative that, I contend, indicates what I identify as "gendered anti-Semitism." The conflation of unresolved guilt and shame with anti-Semitic fantasies on the part of the male, second-generation protagonist with clearly misogynist and miscegenist longings towards the—mostly absent—female Jewish subject is all the more disturbing since it is also paradigmatic in Peter Schneider's popular 1999 novel *Eduards Heimkehr* (*Eduard's Homecoming*, 2000), where the gendered anti-Semitism is set in a post-unification East-West scheme. Even the "divided memory" (Jeffrey Herf) of the two Germanies apparently lends itself to this particular inscription. Whether the female protagonists are Jewish, East German, or American, whether their characters are conceived as a *belle Juive* or as Jewish mothers, in several cases femininity is oppressed and mocked by misogynist anxieties of the (innocent, "good") German male who "acts out" (LaCapra) the transgenerational trauma of his Nazi past. Most astonishingly, in Julia Franck's more recent novel, winner of the German Book Prize, *Die Mittagsfrau* of 2007 (*The Blind Side of the Heart*, 2010), the male German's intense psychic need to overcome the troubled past again results in various forms of gendered, post-traumatic acting out. This text, particularly when contrasted with Gertrud Kolmar's 1931 novel *Die jüdische Mutter* (*The Jewish Mother*) indicates a reconfiguration of the traditional anti-Jewish stereotype of the "Jewish mother" that ultimately leads to an inability to love or to even accept *any* female others. Such a gendered and anti-Jewish conception of femininity in a prize-winning, best-selling novel by a third-generation female writer is indicative of the continued paradigmatic prevalence of sexist and anti-Semitic articulations in contemporary German discourse.

The third chapter shows how this gendered anti-Semitism is, in short stories by Bernhard Schlink, as well as in novels by Susanne Riedel (*Eine Frau aus Amerika* [A Woman from America], 2003) and Katharina Hacker (*Die Habenichtse*, 2006; *The Have-Nots*, 2008), winner of the acclaimed German Book Prize, inscribed onto the body (or penis) of the heterosexual male, leading to a homophobia that culminates in fantasies of self-mutilation

(Schlink, Hacker) or in the death of the female Jewish protagonist (Riedel). For example, in Schlink's "Die Beschneidung" (2000; 'The Circumcision," 2002), the third-person German male protagonist experiences increasing discomfort when confronted with the Judaism of his Jewish American girlfriend. He feels that, in order to overcome differences of opinion with this girlfriend, emerging from his trans-generational guilt as a German, he has to be circumcised. He has the operation performed by a befriended surgeon in Germany, without the accompanying ritual by a mohel that would render it a meaningful act. When he returns to the United States after his "wound is healed," the relationship ends. While the girlfriend is clearly marked as a Jewish female "other," and again displays traits similar to those of the aforementioned stereotypical *belle Juive*, the mark of Jewish femininity here additionally entails a direct physical threat to German masculinity. The German male feels that he must sacrifice his foreskin—the integrity of his penis—and mutilate his masculinity to please the Jewish woman. He incurs a self-inflicted visible wound that is meant to heal the invisible internal one. Susanne Riedel's and Katharina Hacker's novels display similar instances of threats to German masculinities. In Hacker's text, the love object of the German male protagonist is Jewish and homosexual. In Riedel's novel, the German male returns to Germany to salvage his German heritage after his female Jewish partner had died as a result of arguments over German Holocaust guilt. Hence, while German women function to legitimate non-Jewish victimhood, German men become sites to test the multiple anxieties (sexual, social, historical) that haunt traditional German conceptions of masculinity in the wake of the Holocaust. Jewish men, in the rare instances that they are portrayed from the German perspective, display emasculating physical traits on the one hand, and are at the same time marred by a Jewish self-hatred that puts them in a position of fragility or victim when compared with their German, non-Jewish counterparts. While cast less stereotypically in third-generation narratives than in those by Walser and Grass, male Jews are marginalized, or their Jewishness is suppressed, indicating a continued need in contemporary German society to pathologize and repress the presence of Jewish males.

In Thomas Hettche's novel *Woraus wir gemacht sind* (2006; *What We Are Made of*, 2010), the nexus of German guilt over the Holocaust is set in a phantasmagoric and cinematic display of post-9/11 America. Chapter 4 discusses how in this and other recent texts (the ones already cited by Riedel, Hacker, Schneider, as well as Thomas Meinecke's critical success *Hellblau* of 2002 (*Pale Blue*, 2012), America functions as a location where long-repressed German racist sentiments appear to be, in Dominick LaCapra's terms, "acted out," rather than "worked through." Moreover, the imagery of a German white male who finds himself threatened and physically attacked by African Americans and by German-heritage Jews evokes the notion of the American as an evil, threatening "other." Stuart Taberner, Mary Cosgrove, and others have considered German memory discourses in the context of post-unification and the "normalization" of the Berlin Republic. My readings explore how the fictional representation of Germans and Jews displaced to America (a long-standing site of German and European love/hate projections) directly undermines any claim that the Germans have effectively worked through and resolved the issues of their past. Instead, America serves as a convenient location for forgetting or, worse still, displacing the guilt of the past. The anti-Semitism on display here is reminiscent of the conflation of anti-Americanism and anti-Semitism prevalent during the Weimar Republic (Dan Diner). America as a specific and prominent location for anti-Jewish racism, especially visible in Hettche's depiction of African Americans, inadvertently utilizes concepts of the colonial and colonized "other" as they were common in German nineteenth-century colonial fantasies. This displacement of such racist articulations to the contested space of America, particularly when 9/11 looms large overshadowing these paradigms, reveals how much nineteenth-century anti-Semitic discourse is still, today, a prevailing if concealed feature of everyday German sentiment. While Meinecke's novel does indeed go to some length to undermine such discourse, his text is less popularly acclaimed, and thus not as widely read and distributed as the ones that follow the paradigm of displaced German anti-Semitism. This chapter is audacious also in its challenge of recent more optimistic assessments of German Jewish relations by Jeffrey Peck, for example, and in its assertion that other minorities (Muslims, in particular) in today's Germany are subject to similar subconscious and concealed instances of racism and discrimination.

As such, the generational framework that the first chapter sets up comes full circle: literary texts by third-generation writers and critics are still entangled within the issues of the German past, just as are the ones by first- and second-generation writers. The inability to address the past, and thus to accept the Jewish or ethnic other manifests itself in diverse textual articulations: in that of a memory void, in gendered anti-Semitism, and, ultimately, in displaced xenophobic racism. The ways in which those emotions are acted out in the various fictional texts point to emotions that, on the surface of the plots, display an inability to love in the specific personal (hi)stories between Germans and Jews, but ultimately reveal emotional trauma that results from trans-generational guilt and shame that has, still, not been appropriately worked through.

Chapter 1

Absence: Guilt and Shame

Historians and sociologists, especially in contemporary anti-Semitism studies, often regard the nexus of trans-generational guilt among Germans as an "either/or" paradigm, and much of the debate on contemporary anti-Semitism in Germany seems to follow this dualistic pattern. Either Germans are—still today—guilty, acknowledging this guilt, or they engage in total guilt rejection, which is then soon linked with secondary anti-Semitism. My literary analysis seeks to explore the tensions between the two extremes of ascribing guilt routinely versus seeking to deflect it. Literature, I contend, occupies a special position in the investigation of such cultural phenomena, since it has, via fiction and invention, the power to both condense and, in cases of successful texts, transform conditions in society. Since literature can, furthermore, both comment on and alter identity positions of individuals in a society, it also takes a uniquely important place in the formation of cultural identity. Moreover, as some of the recent postcolonial models have shown, literature, and the toolbox of literary analysis, can be particularly valuable in exploring the in-between spaces, the ambiguities, and the undecidability or indeterminacy of individual, collective, societal, and cultural moments in any given setting. In literature after the Holocaust, and particularly in texts referencing the aftermath of the Holocaust, as any text engaging representations of Jews and Germans in today's Germany does, we need to lend special consideration to the role of fictional texts. As Richard T. Gray reminds us, multiple problems arise in fiction *after* the Holocaust, and even more so, in fiction *about* the Holocaust, and not only in relation to Adorno's famous dictum, and not only because of the inherent dangers of revisionism.[1] According to Gray, documentary fiction in particular evades many of these problems and provides a "double strategy" of the imaginary wedded with mimetic accuracy, if such a thing even exists. Most importantly, Gray also reminds us that Adorno's dictum has become a watchword for Holocaust studies, even though he retracted it later. While Adorno's retraction in the first place indicates a move away from the formalist perspective of aesthetic enhancement and enjoyment of literature as a mode of therapeutic expression, it also points to the predicament of the range of expression in Holocaust literature writ large. Hence, even critical evaluations of Holocaust literature have been shaped by a mistrust of invention, experimentation, and fabulation, to evoke privileging of testimony and witnessing grounded in personal experience. Yet, as Primo Levi has pointed out most succinctly, such privileging, although understandable from the point of view of the desire to show empathy with the victims of the Shoah, is in and of itself a problem. Only the "saved," or the survivors of the camps, lived on to tell their stories, whereas the majority of those who perished (the "drowned") can of course no longer speak, and thus are not able to contribute to the articulation of testimonial victimhood, skewing the veracity of the vast literature of witnesses.[2] While I agree with Gray's observations for the case of W. G. Sebald's important novel on the history of memory, *Austerlitz*, I contend that most fiction, Holocaust or not, is, in fact, located somewhere within the space between the imaginary and a claim for mimetic accuracy or authenticity.[3] At the same time, fiction can be "true" in ways that documentary texts, autobiographical or witnessing accounts, might not be. The main question, therefore, especially in the cases of texts authored by non-Jewish Germans dealing with the German Holocaust past (produced by the descendants of those implicated as perpetrators) remains that of moral responsibility, even if this might sound archaic. Yet, particularly in cases of societal oppression or discrimination, not to mention genocidal murder, it is important to recognize and to underscore morally abject behavior or utterances. Thus, in order to avoid a *morally* ambiguous outcome of such textual analysis, psychoanalysis and trauma research offer supplementary tools when it comes to analyzing fictional works that engage with the Germans' assessment of their problematic past, and more useful models than theories emanating from a structuralist or postmodern framework. Because of the moral ambiguity that structuralist or deconstructionist approaches induce, when asking specifically about the emotions that narrative strategies in fictional texts evoke in readers, paying close attention to metafictional devices in texts and possible readers' responses to texts themselves becomes crucial—even though traditional reader response theory models as formulated by Wolfgang Iser and Hans Robert Jauss in the 1960s and 1970s are outdated and seem too static to be of use for these questions. Fabulative metafiction, if it is appropriately decoded by readers, may better acknowledge the gulf that separates verbal and narrative representation of reality from the real itself, so that fiction becomes a lens through which present and past reality can be brought into focus. Experimental metafiction can thus function as a kaleidoscope that helps configure and reconfigure the "data" of the "real" in ever changing ways. The aforementioned German-based volume *Literarischer Antisemitismus*, edited by Matthias N. Lorenz and Michael Bogdal, addresses some of the issues concerning literary techniques and anti-Semitism in literature. As I already indicated in my introduction, Klaus-Michael Bogdal distinguishes essentially three categories of literary anti-Semitism: first, a manifest, subjectively intended anti-Semitism; second, a "careless," conscious or subconscious use of stereotypical speech; and third, the consciously intended, deconstructive, risk-conscious play with anti-Semitic tropes in language.[4] While Bogdal's categories might be useful for analyzing many different texts, I find the categories to be too limited to the subject position of the author. In most texts, I contend, we cannot easily discern author intentionality. We thus need to look for *literary* devices, as Mona Körte's compelling piece on meta-narratives and literary anti-Semitism exemplifies. Even though her discussion centers on Lion Feuchtwanger and William Shakespeare, who clearly did not write after Auschwitz, her text-based approach identifies specific literary devices such as breaks, inversion, use of grotesque elements, and more, that can be used in close readings to discern the presence—or absence—of an engagement with Jews that either is or is not anti-Semitic. "We have to suspect a case of anti-Semitism," Körte writes, "whenever texts do not succeed—regardless of whether this is intentional or not—to subvert or at the very least suspend the very stereotypes and ideologies that they engage."[5] She then uses examples of recent texts by Bernhard Schlink, Walter Jens, Luise Rinser, and Martin Walser to show how this subversion and suspension of stereotypes does not occur. Hence, even though Mona Körte's analysis of literary anti-Semitism is, for this book, one of the most useful in the collection, Lorenz and Bogdal's collection overall still does not address or anticipate people's desires to "read" texts in ways that deny or distort fictional texts' uses of literary tropes. In other words, if we contend that literary texts have the power to both condense and transform conditions in society, we need to focus on potential readers' responses, and take those into consideration when thinking about textual analysis. Therefore, in addition to the questions of who writes texts, what do the texts present, we also need to ask who reads those texts, and with what individual memory, personal history, or expectation.

To address these questions for this chapter, I would like to shift the attention to two major works by prominent and controversial contemporary German and non-Jewish writers, Günter Grass and Martin Walser, because both of these texts have been read in a number of different ways. My reading will focus on how the absence of an engagement with Jews in recent Germany, and of a German engagement with the Shoah, is discernible in such fiction, and, therefore, still today a determining factor in contemporary discourses on anti-Semitism in German literature and beyond. The novella *Im Krebsgang* (Crabwalk, 2002) and the novel *Tod eines Kritikers* (Death of a Critic), both published in 2002,[6] each portray the killing of a Jew by a German, non-Jewish male. Both texts represent reductively a German male fantasy of prevailing over the past. And both were widely debated in German feuilletons, leading to a larger contest on the German memory of the past. I investigate to what extent trans-generational transmissions of guilt and shame are still playing an important role in contemporary German memory discourse, and how they help shape today's reader expectations. For this, exploring a short story by younger, second-generation, best-selling writer

Bernhard Schlink will shed new light onto established binaries of German guilt and shame. One important question here will be whether and to what extent there are generational divides in the ways in which the German past is memorialized, and whether these divides are reflected in the texts as a result of the variations in their respective writers' generational affiliations. My discussion will ultimately illustrate how German memories (and fantasies) of exterminating Jews, resulting from an inability to acknowledge or mourn (the past), may lead to an absence of the capacity to love or accept the (Jewish) other, as well as the (German) self in contemporary German settings. My analysis will also indicate how the "acting out" (Dominick LaCapra) of anti-Semitism in literary texts does not necessarily fall neatly into categories of "non-German" German or "German" German identities, as formulated by Dirk Moses, be it for writers' identities or the characters in their narratives. The novel *Himmelskörper* (2003; Celestial Bodies, not trans.) by Tanja Dückers, a third-generation writer, will illustrate this and more compellingly.[7]

Absence

Even before his notorious 2006 autobiographical "confession" about his deliberate membership in the Waffen-SS at a young age, much has been written on Günter Grass and "Vergangenheitsbewältigung."[8] His fictional magnum opus, *Die Blechtrommel* (1959; *The Tin Drum*) received the most significant attention with respect to the Germans' dealing with their past (or the absence of their dealing). Of the more critical voices, Ernestine Schlant's seminal *The Language of Silence* (1999) puts it most succinctly when she concludes that in Grass's writings, "there is an ingrained obtuseness and insensitivity to those who suffered and died, evident in a language where silence is veiled in verbal dexterity and a creative exuberance rooted in pre-Holocaust aesthetics."[9] I would not take issue with Grass's—or anyone's—"pre-Holocaust aesthetics," since, clearly, there is no such a thing as "post-Holocaust aesthetics," and even Adorno retracted his attempt to prescribe a normative post-Holocaust approach to literature. Yet, with respect to Grass's oeuvre, it is important to point out that, even more than silence and insensitivity, the representation of Sigismund Markus, the main Jewish protagonist in *The Tin Drum*, is outright anti-Semitic, and, hence, stifles any possibility for empathy with the Jewish victims of the Shoah on the part of the (in the first place postwar German) readers. In addition to obtuseness, therefore, we encounter unmediated and relentless anti-Semitic stereotyping. Other scholars, in this case Ruth Angress Kluger, had previously noted the highly problematic portrayal of Sigismund Markus: "Markus, like the typical Jew of the Nazi press, is unattractive as a man, though he lusts after an Aryan woman, and ludicrous as an individual, for he acts and looks like a dog. He is a harmless parasite, a Jew without a Jewish community or a family, without a background, or religious affiliation, but with business acumen of sorts."[10] What is, additionally, even more significant than the negative portrayal of Sigismund Markus is the increased anti-Semitic imagination of the Jew after the end of World War II, since it is here that the reader might have expected a first stocktaking on the atrocities of the Holocaust. Especially since we are experiencing the war and its aftermath from the picaresque perspective of the "little people" from below, including that of Poles and the disabled (other victims of German Nazi perpetrators), containing extensive commentary on the Catholic Church, an engagement with the Holocaust and the Jewish victims' perspectives would presumably complete this multifaceted view. Yet, not only does Grass's work of over 700 pages merely demonstrate one and a half pages of references to the Shoah, this particular depiction is also highly problematic: the only Holocaust witnessing is taking place via the Jew Fajngold, who survived Treblinka as a disinfector of the camps. While the specific trauma of the Jews perishing in the Holocaust is represented in Fajngold's mentally disturbed imagination of his wife and children still being alive, even though the reader learns quickly that they are not, Fajngold's particular mental derangement, depicted as endearing, if a bit odd, pales compared to the trauma of the Germans on display who are suffering much more profoundly (Oskar's physical pain and fever, Maria's pain of losing her husband, the torturous train ride during their migration to West Germany, etc.). Most significantly, however, Fajngold is portrayed as unlawfully gaining from the German war victim in that he financially profited from the deceased Alfred Mazerath's reservoir in groceries, which allowed him to exchange goods to jump-start his new business after the war. "Idyllic times" is what Fajngold supposedly experiences when he begins to deal with sewing machines.[11] In addition, he seems to have quickly forgotten about his wife and children who perished in Treblinka, instead proposing to Maria (again, the Jew lusting after the Aryan woman), a proposal she rejects, mirroring when Agnes Mazerath had earlier turned down Sigismund Markus's marriage offer. In both cases, the underlying assumption is that it is both men's Jewishness that precipitates the German women's negative responses. Both Jewish characters appear riddled with anti-Semitic stereotypes, and Fajngold is said to have "clapped his hands to his head in the same expressive gesture Oskar had seen his toy merchant, Sigismund Markus, make years ago."[12] This underscores the notion that the link between the only two Jewish characters in the text is explicit and immediate in its physicality. Thus, most disturbingly, *The Tin Drum*'s representation of a Holocaust survivor is that of a victim whose victim status pales in comparison with the much more profound suffering of the German, from whom the Jewish survivor also benefited materially. In other words, surviving Treblinka and losing one's entire family is a casualty that is quickly forgotten and, in the face of what can be gained in economic terms, not worth dwelling on. The German trauma, however, is portrayed as intense, deep, and long-lasting. We can thus conclude that, even though Grass's *The Tin Drum* contains multiple metafictional devices, and thus might offer more opportunities for the reader to engage with the problems of Germans and Jews after World War II, it actually does not provide sufficient material or appropriate depiction that attempt to convey Jewish suffering during the Holocaust. When we look at Grass's more contemporary work on this subject, we will see that this absence of a positive model for identification with Jews, and thus for empathy with the Jewish victims on the part of German gentiles in a work published in 1959, is noteworthy here insofar as it marks an absence that still dominates the discourse on German-Jewish relations after 1990, and, perhaps more surprising still, in Grass's work of 2002 and beyond.

Grass's 2002 novella *Im Krebsgang* (Crabwalk) was debated extensively in the German press shortly after its publication, and, along with W. G. Sebald's earlier (1999) volume *Luftkrieg und Literatur* (*On the Natural History of Destruction*, 2003) sparked a widespread dispute on the notion of German victimhood, essentially questioning whether and to what extent Germans could, in the face of the Shoah, legitimately mourn their own German losses of the Second World War. Many voices contended that Grass's engagement with German victimhood was a long-standing taboo in German memory discourse that needed to be broken down, enabling an honest and complete stocktaking that would eventually result in providing Germans with a less emotionally fraught bond with their past. Others argued that recognizing German victimhood was not a taboo as German wartime suffering had been identified all along, and that in any case, a preoccupation with Germans as victims could blur the still largely unacknowledged and unresolved issue of Germans dealing with the Holocaust, perhaps even affording Germans the fantasy of a victim/perpetrator reversal at the expense of the actual Jewish victims of the Shoah. Grass himself spoke of a self-inflicted taboo on the Left that his work sought to break, and his supporters applauded this move by pointing to an increasing and desirable "normalization" in the Berlin Republic, twelve years after unification, and facilitated by the "unaffected" generation of the "grandchildren."[13] Others, such as Uwe Wittstock, on the other hand, argue that *Crabwalk*'s enormous and immediate success points to the fact that there was no real taboo, instead indicating the Germans' mere wish for normalization. This debate went through several permutations, with the German one-time left-leaning magazine *Der Spiegel* in 2002 putting forth an entire series on "Germans as victims." The heated conversation eventually resulted, within the scholarly community, in a tacit agreement to ostensibly focus attention merely on the literary merits of the text itself.

With Aleida Assmann we might conclude that, ideally, various different memories can coexist in today's German memory discourse, including those that empathize with German wartime suffering.[14] This would, however, require an equally serious and emphatic engagement of German Holocaust guilt. Yet, largely eclipsed not only from this debate itself but also from the scholarship concerned with it is the question of how this particular novella deals with Jews, or with the Jewish question. For if we want to agree with Assmann and believe in the existence and sincerity of several different discourses in today's German memory culture, the issue of how a text recalls the notion of Germans as victims and whether or to what extent it juxtaposes this notion with the undeniable historical fact of Germans as perpetrators, becomes crucial. Looking at the literary and fictional text as primary evidence can be especially productive in the face of the many public debates surrounding the—to some extent constructed and imagined—persona of Günter Grass. One important scholarly response to Grass's text, and one that also contextualizes *Crabwalk* with earlier texts that seek to position Germans and Jews in a similar vein, is Gilad Margalit's important essay "Grass und das jüdische Alter Ego" ("Grass and the Jewish Alter Ego"), in which he demonstrates Grass's disregard for the Jewish experience as systemic to all of his fictional texts while comparing Grass's approaches to Jews and Judaism with those of Hans Werner Richter, Alfred Andersch, and Heinrich Böll.[15] According to Margalit, Grass's ambivalent position vis-à-vis the National Socialist past points to unresolved feelings of guilt and shame. Yet, author's statements, particularly when articulated by "celebrity writers" such as Günter Grass, are often staged and while they of course contribute to the reading public's perception of a particular text, they can be contradictory and misleading for reasons that have to do with the public construction of authorship, as Rebecca Braun recently argued lucidly.[16] Looking at the text itself will shed some more light on this nexus.

The novella *Crabwalk* displays and perhaps also exposes an anti-Semitic imagination, and one that is both much more recent and even more offensive than the representation of Sigismund Markus in *The Tin Drum*. Yet, it is not entirely clear that any (ideal or imagined) reader will indeed be compelled to object to most of these stereotypical articulations. While the fictional frame of the plot is set in contemporary Germany, contemporary Jews are entirely absent from the narrative. Furthermore, even the imagined fictional chimera of the historical figure of a Jew is, in this narrative, killed by the main protagonist, a German. The character of the historical persona David Frankfurter who assassinated Wilhelm Gustloff, a Nazi official in 1936, is on the level of the plot reincarnated in 1997 in the philo-Semitic character of Wolfgang Stremplin, who poses in an Internet chat room as a Jew with the name David Frankfurter. When the German and the imagined Jewish protagonists meet, the presumed Jew is shot dead by the German, the narrator's son Konny. He is murdered because of his—merely imagined—Jewish identity. The question of whether and to what extent Konny might be portrayed as a German with whom the reader is invited to feel compassion, and, hence, with how much critical distance we are to evaluate Konny's heinous crime is one important issue here. Even more central to evaluating this text, however, is the apparent German anti-Semitic reflex, evident in a setting where the "Jew" is just imagined, but nevertheless still killed.

Before investigating possible motives for the representation of such a disturbing reflex on the level of the plot, asking what this might mean for the ideal or actual readers and the conditions of contemporary German society, we need to analyze the circumstances of Konny's actions more carefully. The main question here, as in any work engaging with the German past, needs to be whether the repertoire from which such stereotypical and anti-Semitic articulations are borrowed is in any way questioned, or whether the readers are, via a narrative or other textual strategy, invited to question or critically assess such stereotypes. The narrative structure is, as one expects in a novella, set up as a fictional frame. The narrator, a second-rate journalist born in 1945 and clearly cast as a typical protagonist of the 1968 generation, recounts the history of David Frankfurter shooting the historical Wilhelm Gustloff, whose ostensible martyr status according to National Socialists leads to the naming of the *Wilhelm Gustloff* ship. The sinking of the *Gustloff* is what Tulla Pokriefke, the narrator's mother and Konny's grandmother, recounts numerous times as an important illustration of German wartime suffering, and this in turn fascinates the narrator's son Konny who turns into a neo-Nazi, ultimately shooting the imagined David Frankfurter (a youth his own age who had merely posed as the historical figure). Most unsettling about both the frame and the fictional setup of the narrator's character is his apparent and persistent indifference. To some extent, this indifference (or lack of empathy) can be attributed to his professional failure as a journalist, but this as well as his highly uninvolved stance in his son's upbringing actually seem to be rooted in the 1968ers' dilemma of suffering from the inherited transgenerational guilt and trauma of their Nazi parents as well as a resulting sense of loss of moral direction. The inability to love that this narrator-character displays seems symptomatic of second-generation Germans. The narrator's (self-)perception, then, turns him into a victim (both of his parents' unresolved guilt and of the Nazis themselves) and seems to legitimize his failure as a son, a spouse, and, ultimately, as a parent. "Gabi wasn't the only one; Mother too saw me as a typical failure," complains Paul, the narrator.[17] The birth of his son and his wife's subsequent return to her studies are therefore interpreted as the main cause of his professional mediocrity:

> Then Gabi stopped taking the pill without telling me, was soon pregnant, undeniably by me, and dragged me off to City Hall to get married. Once the squalling baby was there and the future educator had gone back to her studies, it was clear as day to me: From now on, don't expect much. The best you can do is hold up your end as a house-husband, changing diapers and vacuuming.[18]

In several instances, the narrator talks about his involvement with the Left as something he did mainly because it was expected of him (Gabi is exposed also as the main architect of this presumed societal expectation). Interestingly, in both cases, it is a female who prevents the German male from reaching his full potential, both in his career and in his political edification. For, once again, his possibilities for agency are limited by his mother's Nazi legacy and its contemporary fallout, namely a political correctness impersonated by Gabi that forces him into silence about his "true" feelings.[19] The most revealing indicator for this, and why this text is really about the second-generation's concerns with Jews and anti-Semitism, even though, on the surface, it is Konny as a third-generation representative who shoots the imagined Jew,[20] is when Paul admits after the shooting that his son had acted out what he himself had been fantasizing all along:

> What can be done when a son takes possession of his father's thoughts, thoughts that have been festering for years under a lid, and even translates them into action? All my life I have tried to take the right track, at least politically, not to say the wrong thing, to appear correct on the outside. . . . I steered a middle course. . . . Well, that probably had to do with the circumstances of my birth; that could explain almost everything.[21]

On the level of the plot, therefore, the second-generation German male clearly blames the circumstances of his birth, his mother, and his girlfriend for his sublimated anti-Semitism. The question, then, is whether the text invites the reader to step back, examine Paul's motives critically, and conclude that Paul would, even as the second-generation "victim" that he is portrayed as, have had a chance to confront and work through his repressed guilt and shame, and ultimately be able to overcome his inability to love. Yet, we are inclined to conclude that Paul did not have this ability, both because of the ingrained character weaknesses that he displays throughout his own narrative, but, on a meta-textual level, mostly due to the narrative structure itself: the title *Crabwalk* not only alludes to the time line of the German past that is here uncovered in a staggering backwards motion, but also to the narrative time line that recovers history by shifting from present to past and vice versa. At the same time, the voice of the narrator Paul alternates with that of an omniscient narrative voice that recurs throughout the text. Such a remarkable narrative perspective could force us to step out of the time line of history, and question the veracity of historical narrative altogether in a way that might be similar to Dominick LaCapra's invocation of the concept of the "middle voice." Instead of Paul's flawed and troubling recollection of the German past, we might then come up with our own construction of the past that oscillates between Paul's narrative, the omniscient voice, and our own imagination or recollection, thereby creating new cultural memory. Thus, at first glance, the narrative structure does seem to offer the reader a valuable critical tool, in that it could invite distancing and questioning. Yet, instead of being able to engage in such a productive reading, we are again and again drawn into Paul's thoughts and emotions, and are merely presented with excuses for his behavior. What prevents a more distanced engagement with the material is the unmediated representation of Paul's perspective. I therefore do not concur with Gary Baker's recent claim that Paul's voice represents a "middling" or middle-voiced perspective that mediates between generations and perpetrator-victim "fault lines."[22] Instead, my reading contends that Paul's voice is unmediated and active, while his actions remain astonishingly passive. Rather than making us, the readers, think about ways in which Paul could have acted differently, the text's active voice seeks to repeatedly sensitize us to Paul's plight. This is underscored through the implied fatalism that is projected even beyond Paul's own perspective: "Never will it end" ("Nie hört das auf"), the text concludes, referring to the trans-generational anti-Semitism that leads Konny to shoot the imaginary Jew. Hence, the chance that the interesting narrative structure offers to the reader, that is, to gain distance from the text, is obliterated by the over-imposition of Paul, whose character lacks any quality of a corrective function in the text, and by a narrative voice that suggests time and again that none of the characters could have acted any differently, much less be held responsible for any of their actions.

This finding confirms the notion that Aleida Assmann's suggestion of several different memory discourses that might peacefully coexist in today's Germany, as desirable as this might be, is neither represented nor, on the level of the individual reader's response, evoked in this text. Grass's novella is, instead, marked by absence on several levels: the absence of a narrative strategy that could allow the reader to remain skeptical towards Paul's perspective, the absence of the representation of any real living Jews, and, finally, the absence of an expression of empathy towards the Jewish (or other) victims of the Shoah by any of the characters, or by the narrative voice. While it is of course legitimate, even important, to point to the problems that can arise on the German side from the trans-generational memories of guilt and shame, and to remind readers how such unacknowledged German memories can have devastating consequences, it is less legitimate to excuse such acting out, even if it happens "only" in fiction. On one level, because of the ambiguities of the narrator-persona Paul, and because of the many absences in this text, a reading where Konny's actions are excused, even condoned, is at least possible. That very possibility is, in 2002, inexcusable, regardless of any other benefits and insights that Grass's text might provide. Adding such a stance to German cultural memory today might lend itself too easily to political instrumentalization, be it with a specific purpose or unintentional.

Similarly problematic as the text by Günter Grass is Martin Walser's novel of that same year, 2002, *Tod eines Kritikers* (Death of a Critic). Ever since the Walser-Bubis debate, and Frank Schirrmacher's open letter, the question of Walser's anti-Semitism has been debated extensively, both in the academy and in the feuilletons. Without reiterating what is by now widely accessible,[23] a few remarks on how Walser's text accompanies that of Grass will illustrate that even though images and imaginings of Jews are present in Walser's texts, here, too, we encounter a marked absence of empathy with the Jewish victims and their descendants. Strikingly, this absence was visible already in Walser's 1998 novel *Ein springender Brunnen* (A Gushing Fountain) to the extent that even anti-Semitic Germans are eradicated from the fictional representation of Wasserburg.[24] Kathrin Schödel recently showed compellingly how Walser's "falsifying interpretation of history" transcends the less important question of aesthetic autonomy that Martin Walser repeatedly invoked when questioned about his anti-Semitism.[25] My discussion of *Death of a Critic* will show how the fervor of some of the anti-Semitic stereotyping actually mimics a post-traumatic acting out against Jews in Germany today.

Unlike Grass's text, Walser's novel is primarily concerned with the representation of a Jew, as Marcel Reich-Ranicki, the famed critic and Jewish Holocaust survivor is only thinly disguised as the inspiration behind André Ehrl-König, the subject character of the text. In contrast to other fictional texts, and also to other texts by Walser, the resemblance between the "real" character and his textual representation is so extraordinarily obvious that this in and of itself caused a considerable stir among the German literary scene. In the narrative, we encounter yet another murder fantasy on the part of a German male: narrator Michael Landolf turns out to be the same person as the writer-suspect Hans Lach who is thought to have killed Ehrl-König. This very fantasy, which comprises the actual plot of the novel, is intrinsically anti-Semitic, since Ehrl-König alias Reich-Ranicki's Jewish background is an implicit theme of the book. The fact that Ehrl-König was never really murdered, even though Landolf/Lach was a suspect, does not alleviate the anti-Semitic imagination in the text. When Landolf, the narrator who also seeks to retrace Hans Lach's motif for murdering Ehrl-König, visits the famed publisher's spouse who is also his love interest, Julia Pelz-Pilgrim, she states: "Hans Lach is the tormented Christian, who can only satisfy himself at first with a delirium, then with the act. Ehrl-König was the operetta version of the Judeo-Christian West, the Anti-Saturn writ large."[26]

Such positioning of Christian versus Jewish ethics and existence recalls a fundamental and religious anti-Semitic imagination, but one that fits neither the fictional Reich-Ranicki nor the actual one, since both the novel's character and its real-life model are portrayed as entirely non-religious. In addition, the Jew is ridiculed as "operettenhaft," that is, not serious, benign, and laughable when compared with "real" Christian suffering. Therefore, both the implicit and here also explicit anti-Semitic articulation against the famed critic appear to be the result of a hateful fantasy against all Jews, rather than a specific case against Reich-Ranicki, as the novel has been defended as staking out. Apart from the statement quoted above, Ehrl-König's Judaism or his survivor past are barely referenced in the text, which constitutes a remarkable absence, since the plot concerns, presumably, the murder of a Jew by a non-Jewish German. Therefore, it seems odd that anti-Semitism as one possible murder motif is only mentioned once, and late in the text, especially considering the minute detail with which the investigation itself is described. On pages 144/145, after anti-Semitism as a possible motif is finally introduced, Wolfgang Leder, a writer for a prominent German weekly, states that if the murder of a Jew is judged more harshly than the murder of a non-Jew, that judgment reveals anti-Semitism, and he then goes on to question Ehrl-König's Judaism—recalled in the subjunctive, a mode employed to ostensibly convey uncertainty, but clearly used to deflect guilt and shame on the parts of the non-Jewish Germans: "Had Ehrl-König been murdered because he was Jewish, then the others would be correct. Yet, it apparently seems to be uncertain whether Ehrl-König was, indeed, Jewish. He, Leder, appreciated nothing more in Ehrl-König than his modesty concerning the question of his ethnicity. That the press again and again made much of this fact wasn't Ehrl-König's fault, but indicative of the state of German self-posturing journalism."[27] The text then goes on to mock the feuilletons for picking up on the term "self-posturing journalism" ("Gesinnungspresse"), but does not further discuss either anti-Semitism as a motif for Hans Lach or the similarly problematic statement by Wolfgang Leder. Interesting to note here is that when compared with the real-life Marcel Reich-Ranicki, questioning Ehrl-König's Jewish heritage seems altogether out of place, since Reich-Ranicki's autobiography *Mein Leben*, which appeared in 1999 and was an immediate critical and sales success,[28] details his Jewish heritage as well as his survivor history. Considering that in all other respects, Ehrl-König so closely resembles Reich-Ranicki, up to the description of physical features and a speech impediment, this particular detail seems to indicate a desire on the part of the German (here: Leder) to deny the Jewish heritage of those few survivors who are living in Germany today. On a meta-textual level, this denial turns out to occupy a significant portion of the book, since neither Wolfgang Leder, nor his statement, nor the themes of Judaism and anti-Semitism are discussed any further. The reader is thus left with the impression that Ehrl-König, and, by association, Reich-Ranicki, might not even really be Jewish after all.

As a consequence, the prevailing theme, even in a novel detailing the murder of a Jewish Holocaust survivor, is absence once again. Because, even though Jewishness and Judaism are implicitly represented, they are neither directly referenced nor made part of the plot in a way that would allow the reader's engagement with the Jewish question or with the status of Jews in Germany today. Empathy with "the Jew" is likewise impossible since Ehrl-König alias Reich-Ranicki is portrayed as altogether unlikable, chauvinistic, and power-hungry, in addition to being ridiculed, among others, for his appearance on his TV show and his speech impediments. Instead, veiled references to the main subject's Jewish background serve to allude to the real-world persona of Reich-Ranicki, and the anti-Semitism thus seems focused on Reich-Ranicki, the "real" person, rather than on the character in the novel. In other words, the pronounced absence and denial of direct references to Reich-Ranicki's alias Ehrl-König's Judaism in the text serve as catalysts for an explicit anti-Semitism that is directed mainly *beyond* the text, at the "real-life" persona Reich-Ranicki, and the effects associated with this signification seem therefore both concluded from and aimed at German society writ large. Even though the satirical gesturing, a primary narrative structure of this text, is directed against several "real-world" media personae from Germany's contemporary literary scene (e.g., the renowned Suhrkamp editor Ulla Berkewicz-Unseld is satirized as Julia Pelz-Pilgrim), no other figure is as well known and as easily identifiable as that of Ehrl-König/Reich-Ranicki. This again points to what some critics have already attested for Martin Walser's work, and for his work long before the publication of *Death of a Critic*: if Walser's Jew, the caricature of an easily identifiable media persona, seems to have a questionable, possibly non-Jewish background after all, and is presented as shameless and power-hungry, even displaying sexually obsessive practices in his public appearances, then it is significantly easier for Germans to overcome their shame, and to utter accusations that would otherwise be considered entirely taboo vis-à-vis a Holocaust survivor.[29]

Such problematic positioning of the fictional characters in the text and in German society after unification can best be attributed to the German desire to "act out" their anti-Semitic fantasies, that are, in Walser's text, centered on the murder of a Jew whose Judaism seems entirely absent. In both Grass's and Walser's texts, we encounter fantasies of Germans murdering Jews, and in both cases, the "Jews" are not "really" Jewish. The reasons for this curious absence of the Jews' Judaism—in one case it is merely an imagined Judaism, and in the other, the Jewish heritage is denied—might be found in a German anxiety or reluctance to confront Judaism directly, which again might be rooted in unresolved guilt and shame on the parts of non-Jewish Germans. The expectations of contemporary readers, who are, due to their prolonged repression of guilt and shame, largely unaware of this absence, help reinforce this very notion.

Transmission of Guilt and Shame

The examples of texts by Walser and Grass, both born in the late 1920s and belonging to a generation of German, non-Jewish writers who experienced the Third Reich as children, could account for anti-Semitic disarticulations that make it impossible to move past any stereotypical representations of Jews and the absence of a careful engagement with Judaism—however well-meaning and ostensibly critical of the German Nazi past the writers (and their defenders) might think themselves or their works. Even though we need to be cautious and circumspect of the acting out of anti-Semitic fantasies that is so prominent in their texts, especially considering Günter Grass's and

Martin Walser's celebrity status in the contemporary literary scene, we might also be inclined to excuse such articulations and acknowledge that their life experiences prevented these writers from engaging the memory of the Shoah on a level that younger writers might find more feasible. This is what some of the supporters of both Grass's and Walser's texts frequently argue: their perspective matters, needs to be understood, and younger generations, due to their more limited perception, simply do not have the capacity to fully comprehend that generation's viewpoints.

Yet, my arguments indicate the need to shift away from author (auto)biographies, or speculations pertaining to writers' intentions or motivations, even though there has been a recent trend towards more interest in author and artist memoirs and personalities. While the presumed identity of an author does shape the readers' expectations and perceptions of a particular work, especially in post-Holocaust texts (as evidenced most dramatically in the Binyamin Wilkomirski case, and more recently, in the case of the Herman Rosenblat memoir),[30] literary analysis needs to remain skeptical of either psychoanalyzing the writers themselves or of over-interpreting any of their nonfictional statements. The reasons for such skepticism are twofold: First of all, an authors' (auto)biography is always only that: one person's biography. We cannot necessarily draw conclusions as to the veracity of that person's feelings or attitudes for a majority of a given society, even if the author personality is a prominent figure. Secondly, we can never fully know what is and what is not "true" of an author's biography or memoir, especially when it comes to uncovering that which might be sublimated. The extent to which authors' directives and intentions can often be staged or misleading, is perhaps best illustrated when Martin Walser claimed in an interview in 2003 that he had only meant to portray Ehrl-König much bigger, more lovable, and more comical than his real-life example, and that none of the other characters in the text were modeled after real-life personae.[31] Yet, Mona Körte's excellent essay "Erlkönigs Kinder" points out specifically how problematic, in the case of Walser, the author's gesturing and positioning can be, and how a critical reading of the narrative strategy presented by *Death of a Critic* furthermore reveals a childish gesture of reactionary acting out on Walser's part.[32] According to Körte, this is mainly due to the fact that Walser uses traditional stereotypes and metaphors without any critical assessment of the repertoire and background from which they are borrowed. Walser's supposed astonishment at some of the reactions his provocations stir up is thus not entirely credible. Therefore, fictional texts, especially ones that are published, can be interpreted, and need to be interpreted as multifaceted works of art, and as such allow us to deduce and to better assess underlying conditions in society. Hence, the meaning of the text as an important part of the fabric of cultural memory has significantly more relevance than the presumed meaning of its author's biography, or of the bearing of an author's biography on his or her text. Nevertheless, a writer's generational affiliation does need to be taken into consideration, as does Jewish versus German, non-Jewish perspective, but all from the viewpoint of the textual analysis.

To return to the initial question of the effects of trans-generational trauma, and thinking about what attitudes and emotions might be at stake in discourses that emerge from these important texts, it may thus be more sensible to evaluate the characters and narrative structures in both texts under discussion, and to draw conclusions from textual analysis, rather than merely prescribing either a "non-German" German or a "German" German position to Günter Grass or to Martin Walser. For it is the fictional characters that seek to affect the readers' emotions in the first place, even if, as in the case of Walser's text, those characters are only thinly disguised caricatures of the contemporary literary scene. But Hans Lach/Michael Landolf and Paul Prokiefke, both main characters with narrative voice and authority, clearly display the generational affiliation and emotional mapping of second-generation Germans who are haunted by transmitted Holocaust guilt and shame, as formulated by the Mitscherlichs, by Vamik Volkan, and by A. Dirk Moses. Both characters furthermore clearly belong to the second generation in terms of their birth dates and their lived experiences. Both are also marked by an "inability to love" that is, ultimately, used to explain their defending or, in the case of Paul Prokiefke, even condoning, of the—real or imagined—killing of the Jew in the respective texts.

If we expect literature to merely represent conditions in society, we might find both texts important in that their analysis can show us where German society finds itself today, many decades after the end of World War II, and more than a decade after unification. Not unlike the second generation of Jewish Holocaust survivors, the second generation of non-Jewish Germans, with Erin McGlothlin, "finds itself left stranded on the other side of a history it does not know by an event it did not experience, cut off from the essential knowledge of what happened to their parents or what their parents did."[33] This is what both texts reiterate: there is so much that remains "unknown" to second-generation Germans about their parents' crimes and the German (victim) past that they cannot help it but must act out feelings of anger and hatred that have been handed down, of course unbeknownst to them. Hence, both characters turn out to be "German" Germans, in that they feel the need, perhaps even the urge, to defend, to condone, even to reenact the German past. Yet, if we assume that literature merely depicts and represents, is this an adequate explanation for excusing the second generations' inability to love, and, ultimately, for replaying an anti-Semitic acting out against Jews during their own lifetime? Is it a legitimate conclusion to state, as McGlothlin suggests, that second-generation Germans, victims of their own parents and their own past, could not help it but are simply destined to act out, due to all that is unknowable to them? What might their responsibilities be instead, especially towards the next generation? Does the very notion of trans-generational trauma and a psychoanalytic approach to these texts possibly aid in formulating such problematic excuses in that it, too, suggests the inevitability of trauma that is handed down inter-generationally? And, if we, the readers, expect literature to also hold the power to transform society in ways that are meaningful and productive, what might such a reading convey then?

To answer some of these questions it might be helpful to consider texts from the next generation of writers, and in this case one who is clearly identified as belonging to the second generation after the Holocaust. A number of publications point to the fact that Bernhard Schlink's bestseller *The Reader* (1995) is also concerned mostly with the second generation's feelings of guilt and shame towards the Holocaust, that is, with those who were not yet born or not yet aware of public life during World War II, a generational position figured in the text by Michael Berg, the male protagonist. William Collins Donahue explores the relevance of this generational link in depth, when he aptly analyzes Berg's revisionist conflation of his generation's "entrapment" in their parents' guilt with the '68ers' identification with Jewish victim status.[34] As became clear from the analysis of the texts by Walser and Grass, and especially considering the debates that emerged from their works, the cultural memories of each generation and their relationships with Nazi guilt are different and, of course, intrinsically intertwined with the collective and personal histories these people share. This applies to readers and critics of German descent as well as to readers and critics of non-German or Jewish descent, since, today, the transnational, indeed global, dimension of the discourse on the memory of the Shoah is significant.

In Schlink's short story "Das Mädchen mit der Eidechse" ("Girl with Lizard") of 2000, a male narrator who is a law student (as in *The Reader*) relates a personal narrative where issues of the German past and of his parents' guilt as Nazi perpetrators lead to his personal suffering.[35] His agony seems linked to a painting in his father's study that depicts a girl looking at a sunbathing lizard. The painting had already and mysteriously attracted the narrator as a young boy, but his investigations as an adult lead him to discoveries about the painting and about his father's past during World War II. The painting turns out to be by the well-known Jewish-French surrealist painter René Dalmann. The narrator-son discovers that his father may have had an affair with the Jewish wife of the painter (presumably the girl in the painting), and that as a Nazi judge in Strasbourg, he sentenced an officer to death for hiding Jews—apparently the painter and his family. However, neither the painting's history and origin nor his father's guilt as a judge in Strasbourg are ever fully revealed to the narrator or to the reader, despite some attempts on the part of the narrator-protagonist to question his mother about his father and to ascertain how the painting came into his father's possession. Finally, the narrator-protagonist decides to burn the painting in order to free himself from the awareness of his family's guilt, which the painting has come to represent. As the painting is burning, another layer is revealed which reverses the image: the lizard now looks at the girl, and this is the painting the narrator had identified earlier as the famous but lost painting by René Dalmann.

Interestingly, the "absence" we encountered in the works by Grass and Walser is reflected here, too: the only Jew in this text is the Jewish girl in the painting. There are also obvious resemblances between the short story and *The Reader*, although the differences are equally important to consider. Hanna, who functioned as the maternal and feminine Nazi perpetrator figure in *The Reader*, is replaced with the father of the—now nameless—male narrator. Curiously, this narrator only begins to ask questions about his father's role as a judge in Strasbourg once his father has died, just as Michael Berg only finds out about Hanna's Nazi past once she has left him. Yet, the short story appears to raise more questions about the repression of guilt and the reversal of victim and perpetrator status than Schlink's novel, because the narrator's mother, who would be in a position to reveal the father's deeds along with the history of the painting, only provides sparse information. Instead, she breaks down when her son—apparently correctly—assumes that he was conceived when his father raped her in frustration about the Jewish woman he possibly had an affair with: "'When you conceived me, did Father rape you? Was it while he was in Strasbourg, doing awful things, and having an affair with the Jewish girl? . . .' Then he saw that she was crying."[36] However, "Girl with Lizard" reveals one remarkably comparable textual strategy observed in *The Reader*: Donahue points to the "entrapment" of the second generation in their parents' guilt, which in *The Reader* "functions . . . to marshal sympathy for a 'victimized' generation."[37] In the short story, the narrator's mother falls victim to marital rape, and thereby—though this is never spelled out—becomes a victim of the Nazis, despite her presumed perpetrator-status due to her generational affiliation, and as a silent accomplice to her husband's alleged crimes against Jews in Strasbourg. The shame of being a rape victim (or, as in Hanna's case, of being illiterate) turns out to be instrumental in suspending any apparent association with Nazi guilt on the part of the mother, since it explains and even justifies her silence. Accordingly, while in the short story the father clearly remains the guilty party, who also suffered professionally, personally, and physically from that guilt, the mother's victim status seems to somewhat offset the father's terrible past (which is never fully revealed). The problems here are apparent: the father, who is dead and therefore can no longer be questioned or held accountable, is singled out as the Nazi perpetrator, whereas the mother, although not portrayed as altogether innocent, is redeemed by her status as a suppressed and submissive woman: "Surely you don't believe your father consulted me," she says to her son when questioned about whether she thought his father should have defended himself in public.[38] Additionally, she was "not there" with her husband in Strasbourg, and also claims that she did not care much for hearing about her husband's wartime experiences later, only admitting to the rape and to her husband's wrongdoings when pressed by her son, all of which serve to underscore her suffering not only from the direct impact of the war, but—in her role as repressed and disenfranchised woman—even more so from her husband's position as Nazi criminal.

Some of the questions arising at this point originate from the implied differences between Schlink's novel and short story, rendering the second generation's entanglement in guilt and shame even more acute. What does it mean that "Girl with Lizard" goes to such lengths to single out the guilt of the male parent, while at the same time using questionable strategies to redeem the female? This gendered "liberation" saves the nonpolitical mother and wife. Then, finally, why are the gender roles that Joseph Metz's essay had shown for Hanna completely reversed, that is, why does the—highly troubling—association of Nazism with the feminine in *The Reader* turn into the representation of the feminine as naive, passive, and submissive victim in the short story? At this point, we can say that in "Girl with Lizard" the text's performance of a seemingly progressive gender critique seems to mask conservative sexist and racial Nazi politics. Yet, on a meta-level, the short story may also convey a critique of the Nazis' cultural ideology of masculinity, not dissimilar to arguments already brought forward in Klaus Theweleit's 1977 *Männerphantasien* (*Male Fantasies*, 1987).[39]

Before exploring the apparent gender issues in more detail in chapter 2, I will here examine how the inversion of guilt and shame explicates the significance of textual indeterminacy that is central to many of Schlink's texts, and to the issues that are involved with the trans-generational transmission of guilt and shame. In both the novel and the short story, the first generation's recollection of guilt (or of guilt by association) is replaced with shame about a personal fate which is, in "Girl with Lizard," directly linked with the perpetrator's guilt. The mother is raped by her husband who becomes a perpetrator twice over. The mother feels shame as a rape victim rather than guilt because of her affiliation with Nazi crimes. This shame resulting from guilt (her husband's guilt) then leads to the first generation's silencing of the Nazi past. The second generation, represented by the narrator-son in "Girl with Lizard," suffers directly from this silencing, and indirectly from his mother's shame. This trope can be compared to the plight of Paul, the narrator-protagonist in *Crabwalk*, since he, too, is suffering from his mother (in that case not her silence, but her compliance with the Nazis). Schlink's narrator's suffering ultimately leads him to burn the painting of the girl and the lizard after an obsessive but inconclusive inquiry into its origins, since the painting itself and its mysterious origins had haunted him in ways that seemed to render meaningful relationships with women impossible, showcasing his inability to love. This suggests, then, that the second generation can liberate itself from its entanglement in guilt, shame, and silencing over the Shoah only by "burning" the image—and evidence—that could provide enlightenment of the actual Nazi crimes committed by the parent generation. One main problem here is that the mother's "shame" is not shame about her generation's guilt, yet the text still utilizes her "shame" as a strategy to cover up the father's crimes. Clearly, the image of the burning artwork where the figures of the (Jewish) girl and the lizard are inverted just before the flames fully consume the painting evokes this very inversion of shame and guilt, and of victim and perpetrator, but also, and this is even more disturbing, of the extermination of the Jews. For, at least emblematically, it is a Jewish girl ("Judenmädchen") that is burned. Even if we neglect this troubling metaphor since, admittedly, the lizard is also consumed by the flames, the narrator commits an act not dissimilar to the infamous book burnings of the Nazis, in that he deliberately burns a valuable artwork by a Jewish painter. Of course, this "resolution" to Schlink's short story also reflects the imagined extermination/killing of the Jews in Grass's and Walser's texts.

We could at this point argue, employing post-structuralist theory, that this short story presents a prime example of a text that performs its own deconstruction. Just as the painting is burned and the signification of the victim-perpetrator and guilt-shame discourses is erased, the text itself merely offers a void of decidable truth, or represents the very act of deconstruction of truth and meaning. We can no longer pinpoint what "truth" is, neither within the text, nor within the society it seeks to depict, and we may therefore point to the text's "indeterminacy" as the way out of a complicated moral quandary. The narrative stance of the nameless child-turned-adult protagonist could, furthermore, be read as a "middle-voiced" unavailability of clear-cut positions, as "[Roland] Barthes himself relates the middle voice to the problem of the relation between the present and the past."[40] Hence, we might argue, we cannot say for sure whether this short story functions to consign and solidify existing anti-Semitic, racist, and sexist undercurrents, or whether it in fact points to those problems in an attempt to alert the reader (and critic) that they persist in German society today, and that we must seek to overcome them. Such a post-structuralist reading seems legitimate, especially since the text itself does not provide any significant clues as to whether we are to identify with the nameless protagonist or maintain a critical distance. This kind of reading may be further supported by LaCapra's contention that "writing trauma is often seen in terms of enacting it, which may at times be equated with acting (or playing) it out in performative discourse or artistic practice."[41] LaCapra also points out that texts, when enacting trauma, "seem to engage in . . . indirection or veiled allusiveness" and he quotes, among others, Franz Kafka and Paul Celan as examples.[42] With respect to Schlink's short stories, and especially when we also consider Schlink's use of a thinly disguised Paul de Man figure in his later novel *Die Heimkehr* (2006; *Homecoming*, 2008), and furthermore thinking about both the Grass and Walser narratives and their huge public successes, indirection and allusiveness are not strategies any of these texts attempt to promote on a formal level. On the contrary, all three writers' works are clear-cut and highly readable narratives displaying mostly traditional narrative perspectives, structures, and plot constructions.

Nevertheless, the notions of indeterminacy and indirection are explicit in the narrative plots of the texts themselves. They do engage in writing trauma in that the (secondary) trauma of German guilt is a major theme and in that absence and loss are prevalent. However, these engagements need to be contested since the original trauma and the original loss—the Holocaust—is the meta-frame which, at least temporarily, is not visible. Visible, instead, is a seeming empathy with the perpetrator's loss—in Walser's, Grass's, and both of Schlink's narratives. This is why LaCapra reminds us that such texts "create an objectionable . . . kind of discomfort or unease in the reader or viewer by furthering fascination and a confused sense of identification with or involvement in certain figures."[43] Thus, recalling the 1987 scandal of Paul de Man's anti-Semitic writings may indeed point to the inherent problems of successfully employing post-structuralist readings when analyzing texts that deal with the German response to the Holocaust, no matter what the generational affiliation of the writer(s). The very notion of textual indeterminacy may preclude any clear positioning and may, instead, obfuscate the problems at hand, here the role reversal of victim and perpetrator or guilt and shame.

Yet, keeping in mind the generational perspective, the openness and indecisiveness that the texts present and the unease evoked in the reader with respect to the guilt-shame and perpetrator-victim complex could also, on a socio-historical level, be read as a constructed, wishful fantasy that carries appeal for second- and especially third- and fourth-generation (German) readers. We, today's Germans, would like to be able to choose whether and how we associate with the Nazi generation's guilt, with an—albeit constructed—victim status of either the Nazi generation or of the second generation. This affords us, today's (German) readers, feelings of shame that result only indirectly from the realization of our parents' and grandparents' guilt. Martin Swales's argument that, in *The Reader*, guilt is "contained by a statute of limitations," is certainly valid and can also apply to the father's guilt in "Girl with Lizard," or to that of Tulla Prokiefke in *Crabwalk*.[44] Likewise, it is true that "shame is more diffuse than guilt," and that shame, rather than guilt, is a "condition of self-consciousness."[45] Yet, the issue here is that while shame, be it for personal or other reasons, is not an altogether pleasant feeling, it is preferable to guilt, and certainly shame over a personal deficiency such as illiteracy (Hanna), poor parenting skills (Paul), or over the stigma of being a rape victim (the mother in "Girl with Lizard") is preferable to the guilt of complicity in the genocidal murder of millions of Jews. Accordingly, via the fiction of Schlink's short story and Grass's novella, we, today's German readers, can now imagine our first- and second-generation ancestors as victims, victims of the first generation's guilty "others" (such as the father in Schlink, Konny's grandmother in Grass), victims of the first generation's shame (the mother in Schlink and the entirety of the contemporary German literary scene in Walser), and victims of the silencing that took place as a result of shame. By means of this transference, we construct both first- and second-generation individuals as victims, since this provides us, the later generations, with an absolution from guilt, and from any "guilt by association," however remotely imagined. The burning of the painting by the nameless narrator in "Girl with Lizard" and the imagined killings of Jews in the texts by Walser and Grass thus reveal figuratively and much more blatantly what the—problematic—figure of Michael Berg in *The Reader* has only foreshadowed. We imagine our parents and grandparents as victims whose troubled silence actually indicates feelings of shame. Thus, we seek to erase the guilt of our painful past.

Furthermore, imagining feelings of shame for constructions of first- and second-generation "victims" and their silencing of the past affords the fantasy of a direct identification with Jewish Holocaust survivors. This fantasy might actually explain why—as Hartmut Steinecke has observed but not critically questioned—contemporary German, non-Jewish fiction about the Holocaust resembles more and more closely that of Jewish Holocaust survivors.[46] Gila Lustiger's recent fictionalized account of her father's recollections as a concentration camp survivor describes how her father had always wanted to be silent about the past, his past, and Lustiger describes how his need to be silent stems from his desire to protect his children—from himself.[47] Although Lustiger's novel—"a family novel" ("ein Familienroman")—only reveals at the end that it was at least in part the stigma and shame of being a "Holocaust survivor" that prompted his silencing ("So sind wir nicht, schrie es in mir auf"),[48] the text makes clear throughout that it was also the terrifying dimension of the experiences of the Holocaust that silenced her father, and that made it impossible to speak:

> As if we were always only this: predestined to suffer. But then I saw the photograph and I understood that factual and historical knowledge are nothing. That data are irrelevant, and facts a web of illusions, because no one can grasp the history of my family without relying on coincidence.[49]

Even though Lustiger's second-generation narrator herself makes the connection between the German's silencing and the silence in her family, the example of her novel renders the constructedness of the German silence out of shame as related in Schlink's and Grass's texts even more evident. Lustiger's novel reveals and recalls the painful history of her father's past by recounting specific details, whereas Schlink, Grass, and Walser avoid committing to any specific account of the fathers' generations' crimes and instead go to great lengths to eclipse the past. Schlink's narrators and Grass's protagonist, then, engage in the final act of eliminating family history when burning or murdering the only possible key to their past, whereas Lustiger's main character succeeds in unveiling her family's history in order to confront her father's past.

I will refrain from discussing the other, even more obvious differences between the texts by the German, non-Jewish writers and that of Lustiger. Yet the comparison with Lustiger's novel reveals that constructing a fantasy of Germans as victims does not, ultimately, aid second-generation Germans engage the past productively, regardless of whether the texts are written by first- or by second-generation Germans. Instead, "Girl with Lizard" evokes a construction of shame and victimhood that, when compared with the indisputable experiences of Holocaust victims, even if authenticity is not a category here either, falls short of "writing trauma." Rather than attempting to represent the painful past, the short story evades it once again, just as the Jewish girl in the painting is imagined to be exterminated—once again. Therefore, I do agree with Bill Niven that shame is an issue for the postwar generation, and that this has been overlooked by many who criticize *The Reader*, but I do not agree that Schlink's novel is "critical in its portrayal of Hanna."[50] Such a reading does not take into consideration what is even more evident from "Girl with Lizard" as well as the 2002 narratives by Grass and Walser: the extent of the desire of second and later generations to imagine their parents as victims. This may explain why representations of guilt and shame appear to obscure the actual trauma of real Holocaust victims, and why the real divide is not between generational affiliations, but between a German Jewish and a non-German Jewish perspective. Hence, a trans-generational transmission of guilt and shame is clearly at work in texts by Grass, Walser, and Schlink, but in all cases with the ultimate goal of guilt rejection or guilt deflection that is to serve third and later generations of German readers' needs.

The crucial question that remains from the readings of these texts is that of the actual responsibilities of the second-generation protagonists and their second- or third-generation (German) readers. In other words, how could the negative models that these writers seem to construct time and again be imagined to be more hopeful, productive, and positive? Exploring a "way out" of any "selbsverschuldete Unmündigkeit" so clearly at play in the avoidance strategies that all of these texts propagate might be more productive on both the textual and the meta-textual levels, not to mention more desirable from the perspective of what is morally appropriate given the context of the German history of perpetration and violent atrocities. It may be interesting to imagine second-generation "German" Germans who are, in the perhaps outdated manner of the *Bildungs-* or *Entwicklungsroman*, learning, gaining insights, and making progress in how they deal with their respective trans-generational traumata.[51] Interestingly, Grass's *The Tin Drum* still contained elements of the *Bildungsroman*, in that the figure of Oskar Mazerath clearly underwent a learning process. Instead of agreeing with *Crabwalk*'s dejected moan "never will it end" ("nie hört das auf") we, the readers, in our roles as (psycho)analysts, might prefer to read a hopeful "we are working on it." Instead of merely wishing for "normalization," remaining in a state of productivity and moral honesty could provide a positive model for second-, third-, and fourth-generation Germans who will—whether they like it or not—continue to be subject to scrutiny on how they are dealing with their perpetrator past. Such positive modeling is, it seems, currently more likely to be found in American literature that engages with the Holocaust and the Jewish past. Yet, if, instead of reiterating some form of the mantra of the "inability to love," Germans could engage in cognitive processes that shed light on their obfuscated past, such as, for example, modeled by the endearing protagonists of Nicole Krauss's novels, "working through" might indeed become possible.

The Legacy of Absence: Memory Void

According to Friederike Eigler and others seeking to examine more recent engagements of the memory of German guilt and shame, the second- and third-generation authors' representations after the war pay new critical attention to the public memory discourses engendered by the first generation of witnesses, perpetrators, and victims.[52] Yet, several of the multigenerational novels addressing Germans in World War II eclipse the Holocaust, or treat it only peripherally.[53] My discussion here is concerned with the texts that do seek to attend to German guilt and shame resulting from the Holocaust. Tanja Dückers's 2003 novel *Himmelskörper* (Celestial Bodies, not translated) is, in more than one way, a reprise of the themes in Grass's novel. Herself a "third-generation" writer, she admitted that when *Crabwalk* was published in 2002, she was in shock, and unable to write, due to the similarity of themes that Grass's and her own texts were engaged with.[54] Nevertheless, Dückers managed to publish her novel by the spring of 2003—proving once more that authors' statements need to be taken with a grain of salt.[55] She has, partly due to her own testimonies in interviews, been labeled as the new grandchildren's generation who are able to take a fresh and more candid look at the German past than even the previous generation of the 1968ers, who were still too caught up in their parents' culpability.[56] We might, furthermore, via the genre of *fictional* family narrative, achieve a more differentiated view on German culpability and Germans and Jews after the Holocaust than in the 2002 documentary *Opa war kein Nazi*, where the authors aptly found that it was common practice for children and grandchildren of National Socialists to view their families as victims.[57] Accordingly, Dückers's treatment of German memory discourses goes to greater lengths than that of Grass to illustrate not only Germans as victims, even though that is a central theme also in her text, but to also showcase German guilt. Indeed, the grandparents of the third-generation protagonist are revealed to be liable in several different ways, although much of the novel is spent circumventing the exact nature of the grandparent's culpability. The young female protagonist, Freia, relates how her grandmother Jo was proud of her, Freia's, braids, which induced Freia to wear a bald head since her teenage years.[58] More importantly, for the first time in a narrative engaging the German past, we encounter a female protagonist, and the grandmother's legacy that is related in this text is matrilineal (see Valerie Heffernan's piece on matrilineal family narratives; although she writes about Julia Franck, many of her observations of Matria history hold true also for this work).[59] In contrast to Grass's novella, in this novel we finally witness a case of female agency, and one where the female protagonist seeks to come to terms with her family's past of Nazi guilt and shame.[60] While the memories and imaginings of Germans as victims are reinforced relentlessly and awkwardly via the naming of the grandparents, in that Maximilian was, after his war injuries and resulting physical dependencies, renamed into "Mäxchen," and Johanna became "Jo," a mere fragment of herself, Freia (whose name is multiply overdetermined, referring to Richard Wagner's *Ring* while the text claims that it merely stems from a contraction of other names) is also shown to ask real and important questions of the past, especially when her Polish uncle Kazimierz is found to have committed suicide. Freia's questions center on the history of her family because she is pregnant, and she thus recognizes her own responsibility as a link to the future. While at first glance, the motivation for such an inquiry into her family history might be understandable, and as readers, we might react empathetically, it is important to identify that it is precisely her—egocentric—interest in her own, German, identity, history, and future that motivates her search. Just as her own—blonde, stereotypically German—braids were the physical object of her grandmother's delight, and later, her own source of dissent and rebellion, the reasons for her inquiries are motivated by a wish for a guilt-free German future.

While it is commendable that German guilt is, to some extent, named in Dückers's narrative, the narcissism inherent in this undertaking is all the more noticeable due to the painful and blatant absence of Jews—or any of the other victims of National Socialism. The Holocaust does not directly figure in Freia's questions about the German past, and about her grandparents' past. In fact, it is never mentioned. While the issue of Polish ethnicity and the victimization of the Poles is taken up, and undoubtedly Poles were, indeed, among the primary victims of German Nazi aggression during World War II, there is no concrete or immediate display of any—Polish or Jewish—characters in this text. I therefore have to disagree with Eigler's assessment that Dückers's *Celestial Bodies* appears "as forward-looking alternative(s) to a paralyzing focus on the past."[61] Instead, the focus on the German Jewish past, or on the past of Germans as perpetrators is replaced with a focus on the German German past that is nostalgic in its attempt to memorialize a "good" Germany. For, when Freia and her twin brother Paul attempt to access the grandparents' silenced memories, they are, also still as adults, mostly satisfied with the memories that represent their own family's point of view. The following fantasy of the furnishings of the *Wilhelm Gustloff* as related by the grandfather is constitutive of this one-sided approach.

> It was supposed to be furnished beautifully, with enticing banquet-sized rooms and salons, a cinema, a pool, a state of the art medical clinic, even a maternity ward, everything one could wish for . . . Of course they had lots of time to fantasize, those poor people, standing in front of the local headquarters' office, waiting for their tickets.[62]

This particular condescending and patronizing evaluation of the fantasy of what the *Gustloff* meant to many, by Mäxchen, Freia's and Paul's grandfather, sets up the narrative of suffering and expulsion that Freia's family experienced as a result of the war. It also serves to underscore how her grandparents were privileged in some way, although the exact nature of this privilege is not revealed until much later. Unlike Grass's recollection, where the historical relevance of the *Wilhelm Gustloff* marks the center of the narrative, and the account of the historical figure Gustloff is exposed, this perspective remains within the family and with *this* family alone. Even though Freia and Paul are presumed to disagree with their grandparents' point of view, we are not presented with an alternative vision. Freia's disagreement is merely expressed in her shaven head, but not in conversation with her grandparents, or with Paul. The one and only time that Mäxchen mentions Jews in an outrageously anti-Semitic reference comparing Jews to Cuckoo Bees, Paul and Freia exchange a "surprised glance" ("erstaunter Blick")—but neither the characters nor the ensuing narrative offer any further commentary, even though several long-standing anti-Semitic prejudices are enacted in Max's diatribe, and obviously negatively:

> Something like this apparently doesn't just exist with people: this homelessness, this nomadic state. To me, the Cuckoo Bees are the Jews of the bee population. They enrich themselves using the foundations of what other peoples had created. Exploiting. Calculating. But a strong Queen bee—at any rate she has an army of up to 60,000 worker bees at her side— . . . of course has the Cuckoo bees chased away.[63]

This short passage references three distinct anti-Semitic stereotypes: first, that of the nomadic Jew, second, the calculating and trickster Jew who seeks to gain from others, and third and finally, the Jew who is oppressed and ultimately defeated. Needless to say, this tirade represents a ruthless and callous fantasy, reminiscent of the anti-Semitic hatred expressed in Grass's text, and an articulation that begs to be deconstructed, yet in this text, it never is. While Freia's opinions are not congruent with those of her grandparents, she also is not seen to engage them critically, or to subvert their account in a dialogue. Freia and Paul's reaction to the rampant anti-Semitism of their grandfather evokes the exact same sentiment and adjective ("erstaunt," 179) as their discovery that he was passionate about keeping bees. Even more disconcerting, this passage comes shortly after we find out that Max is "weakened" and "diagnosed with prostate cancer," inducing empathy for him. When, after the grandparents' death, Freia finds a copy of *Mein Kampf* and other National Socialist propaganda among the estate, she again reacts with surprise, but never has a conversation about it, with anyone.[64] Taken together, these articulations indicate that Tanja Dückers's novel seeks to address the memory of the German past, and while accessing it via a matrilineal family history seems to yield considerable promise, the text itself does not make good on that promise.

As a result, this novel by a third-generation German, non-Jewish writer shows a pronounced absence of Jewish and other victims of Nazi persecution. By comparison, the texts by Grass, Walser, and Schlink invoke Jews and Jewish characters, even if remotely. Although they are represented with a Judaism or Jewishness that is marked as lacking, or that is portrayed as an "other," Jews are still cited or referenced in some way. Yet, in Dückers's text, there is a void so profound that even this absence of Jews, and with that, any representation of the Shoah, is no longer discernible. Hence, this particular deficiency is not just an absence, but rather a deep void of the memory of Jews. Seemingly, there are no memories of Jews that the Germans can even still refer to. Instead, there is an odd and disturbing replacement of German memory of German fate with that of the Jews. The hair (Freia's braids) and the teeth (false teeth of Jo, the grandmother) become objects of obsession for the first- and second-generation Germans (Jo, the grandmother, and Renate, the mother). The signification of "hair" and "teeth" is of course reminiscent of the many images that second- and third-generation Germans have seen of Jewish Holocaust victims. Many Holocaust documentaries portray piles of hair and teeth. Those images rely on the familiar perception that hair and teeth are what remain of a living body after its demise. The metonymic representation of "hair and teeth" for Jewish victims has thus become commonplace in the global vocabulary of referencing the Holocaust and German culpability. In the novel, the obsessive focus on those particular objects of memory and recollection (the hair is to remind Jo of Freia's childhood, and the teeth are to memorialize the dead grandmother for Renate) that the text attaches to the mother and grandmother metonymically showcases the void of the Jews as victims. Yet, it also presents the Germans as the new victims. Thus, represented in this text's focus on German hair and German teeth, Germans are now filling the memory void left by the Jews. This emblematic memory void, as opposed to the one so movingly represented in the image of the *Fallen Leaves* (*Shalechet*) at the Jewish Museum in Berlin by Menashe Kadishman, is not left as a void for the readers to see. Instead, it is filled with relatively benign German chatter about the Germans' flight from Poland—that is, representations of German victimhood. The notion of German victimhood replacing Jewish victims is reinforced when Freia's mother, Renate, commits suicide at the end of the narrative. Until this particular turn of events, the text does deliver an acknowledgment that the Polish uncle Kazimierz was a victim of the Nazis. Thus, the novel represents a victim that

Figure 1. Menashe Kadishman, Shalekhet (Fallen Leaves), installation, 1997–2001. © Jewish Museum Berlin. Photo: Marion Roßner.

is not German, even if he is not Jewish, and even in spite of the fact that Jewish victims are never mentioned. Yet, in the final turn, we are left with the trans-generational trauma of the second-generation German (Renate) that has become unbearable. Incidentally, both second-generation victims are victims of suicide, and in both cases, the inability to love in their current lives contributes to both of their decisions to end their own. Once again, this sudden and unmitigated conflation of (German) perpetrator with (Polish) victim serves to underscore the notion of Germans as victims.

Returning to the initial question regarding the role of reader expectations, we must therefore conclude that the reason why this novel by a third-generation young female German writer is so disconcerting is not because of its display of mixed literary skills, as most of the contemporary reviews propose. The problems that this text, upon critical inspection, alludes to are much more profound. We encounter a void of the memory of Jews so vast and intense that it leads not only to the erasure of the memory of the Jews in a text that seeks to address the German past, but it also propagates a filling of this void—with German memories. The replacement of German guilt with shame that we observed earlier in Schlink's texts is here replayed as a reversal of German and Jewish memory. This process of memory replacement also recalls Leslie Adelson's assessment, for a different purpose, and with Andreas Huyssen's terms, of the Holocaust as "a trope that migrates outward from Germany."[65] The Holocaust in Dückers's novel seems to have migrated away from Germany, not unlike the Cuckoo bees. While Adelson's invocation of the figure of Jewish suffering is slightly optimistic in its proclivity towards a productive discourse of taboo, and I'd argue with her observation that genocide history is palpable in present-day unified Germany, her argument describing how post-unification Germany sought to address a perceived taboo, the taboo of the trauma of Jewish suffering during the Nazi past, holds true. It is therefore not surprising that Adelson's comparison of the traumatic history of the suffering Jew with that of the Turkish immigrants to Germany culminates in a reading of Zafer Şenocak's *Gefährliche Verwandtschaft* (1998; Perilous Kinship). Relevant for my point is the last sentence of a paragraph that Adelson quotes from Şenocak's text. "Without the Jews the Turks stand in a dichotomous relation to the Germans. They tread in the footprint of the Jews of the past."[66] Adelson is concerned with the dismantling of an imaginary trialogue set up by Şenocak's text, since this particular imagination lays claim to a "mosaic of . . . multiculturalism" that neither Şenocak nor Adelson mean to propagate.[67] Yet, the image conjured up by Şenocak's *Perilous Kinship* is important since it pinpoints both the absence of the Jews in Germany, and the ways in which both groups, Jewish and Turkish minorities, are marginalized in contemporary German society to this day. The void of the German memory of the Jews, as Tanja Dückers's novel portrays it, is therefore central not only to German German memory discourses, but also to contemporary representations and imaginings of other marginalized groups in today's German landscape of multi-ethnicity.

In keeping with our initial frame of the ambiguity of writers' articulations and their role and impact in literary and cultural discourse, Tanja Dückers, the author, is not the one to blame. What her text signifies, instead, is what contemporary German readers have come to expect from previous German memory discourses. Once we have learned to accept the absence of Jews in discourses on the German past, and we are getting used to representations of replacing German guilt over the Nazi crimes with German shame over comparatively minor issues, as the novels by Walser, Grass, and Schlink reveal, we no longer expect an engagement of Jews and Judaism in a text seeking to address German Holocaust culpability. While this novel is earnest and sincere in its attempts to shed light onto the German past, and to address the trauma of the German past, it also eclipses an important part of it. Tanja Dückers's *Celestial Bodies* has therefore, within the troubled and disturbing logic of German guilt and shame reversal, and the recurring discourse of the absence of the Jews, after Grass, Walser, and Schlink, come full circle. This particular case of the transmission of German guilt and shame, resulting in a void of the memories of Jews, Judaism, and Jewishness, is witness to a post-traumatic German German memory discourse that can only reiterate its own narcissistic anxieties, while the Jews remain absent. The German identity position that contains a void of Jewish memory after Auschwitz is visible precisely in fictional texts that do not, outwardly, claim any documentary veracity. Yet, because of the possibilities of invention, these narratives are highly functional at revealing a different kind of truth—that is, the reality of the Germans' continued inability to love the self and the Jewish other. The implications for other minorities in contemporary Germany such as more recent Turkish immigrants are profound and, indeed, perilous.

Chapter 2

✦

Gendered Anti-Semitism: Femininity, the *Belle Juive*, and the "Jewish Mother"

Hilene Flanzbaum, a prominent American scholar of Jewish studies,[1] recently told me that she frequently utilizes Bernhard Schlink's *The Reader* (*Der Vorleser*, 1995) as teaching material in her Jewish studies Holocaust class.[2] Since this international bestseller was in 2008 released as a highly successful motion picture, the text no longer needs much of an introduction even to American college students. When I eagerly pointed out to my colleague why reading Schlink's works with a class of largely uninitiated undergraduate students might be problematic, she recognized that she doesn't necessarily think about the sexist and racist implications of the texts, or about the difficulties arising from representations of German guilt and shame, since, first and foremost, Schlink's texts do seem to acknowledge the Nazis' horrific crimes. Furthermore, for her purposes, the depiction of a Nazi perpetrator as a morally ambivalent figure and the victim-perpetrator reversal at work in Schlink's texts might help American students grasp the concept of ethically ambiguous war criminals, a notion that she finds especially relevant in the aftermath of the terrorist attacks of September 11, 2001. Her prudent justification thus illustrates that the differences between German and American audiences are significant, and that reader identity, expectation, and reception does, indeed, alter the meaning of the material itself. American college students might gain new insights into the morally ambivalent and challenging issue of German guilt and shame from *The Reader*'s positive and redeeming portrayal of a war criminal, whereas German readers, who themselves grapple with issues of trans-generational guilt and shame, might be able to use the victim-perpetrator reversal that is at work in Schlink's best-seller to escape a thorough engagement with their own Nazi past. By the same token, German and Jewish readers might respond differently to a text by Schlink than German non-Jewish readers, or than non-German Jewish audiences. As a result of *The Reader*'s popularity, Schlink's works, and *The Reader* in particular, rightfully received considerable attention among scholars concerning the issue of appropriate representation of the question of German guilt and shame. The latest and most differentiated contribution to this debate is by William Collins Donahue, whose *Holocaust as Fiction* considers Schlink's works as significant markers of popular cultural history, and *The Reader* in particular as an American—rather than German—text. This leads Donahue to important conclusions regarding Schlink's oeuvre.[3]

For my own analysis of this and other texts that engage with the history and memory of the Holocaust from a German perspective, what matters most is that, as Klaus-Michael Bogdal, one of the—German and male—authors of the 2007 volume *Literarischer Antisemitismus nach Auschwitz* (Literary Anti-Semitism after Auschwitz) appropriately concludes, scholarship in literary anti-Semitism deals with texts that can be analyzed, an observation previously made by Ruth Kluger, a German, Jewish, *and* American woman.[4] This chapter examines how multiple perspectives (of different generations, of different sexes) of German, non-Jewish writers consider representations of Jews and gender in relation to femininity, and how this might impact the perception of German reading audiences, and, thereby affect German memory discourses.

Gendered Anti-Semitism

In chapter 1, we saw in Schlink's 2000 (2002) short story "Girl with Lizard" ("Das Mädchen mit der Eidechse")[5] a male narrator who is a law student (as in *The Reader*) relate a personal narrative where issues of the German past and of his parents' guilt as Nazi perpetrators lead to his personal suffering. The unnamed narrator tells the story of a painting that belonged to his father and that haunted him in ways that prevented a meaningful relationship with women, displaying an inability to love. The painting depicts a Jewish girl ("Judenmädchen") looking at a lizard. The girl in the painting exhibits traits of the *belle Juive* (Sander Gilman)—in spite of being a child.[6] As the narrator-son learns of the history of the valuable painting, including his now deceased father's guilt of persecuting the Jewish painter and his family, he also discovers his father's illicit affair with the Jewish wife of the painter, who is depicted as the girl in the painting. The protagonist's way of dealing with trans-generational guilt, represented via the girl in the painting, is to burn the artwork at the end of the story. Hence, the "happy end" that this narrative presents results from sexist and anti-Semitic anxieties and disarticulations. The Jewish woman is sexually conquered by the German male (the father), and then her representation in a painting is burned, which of course raises the troubling imagery of the book burnings, not to mention the death camps. The conflation of anti-Semitic fantasies on the part of the male, second-generation protagonist with clearly misogynist and miscegenist longings towards the female Jewish subjects is all the more troubling since it is actually a child whom the narrator desires. Similarly to the other texts discussed, in Schlink's "Girl with Lizard," no actual Jewish characters appear (with the exception of the girl in the painting), and the anti-Semitism at work here is relegated to the absent females.

Yet, Schlink's "The Circumcision" ("Die Beschneidung"), another short story in the same 2000 collection,[7] is set in the midst of Jewish life in Manhattan, and only the male protagonist is German and not Jewish. Andi, a third-generation young German, visits New York City as a student and falls in love with Sarah, who is Jewish and American. He initially exhibits some minor discomfort with Sarah's Judaism and Jewish heritage when he feels that her family—in particular, her aunt and uncle, who are Auschwitz survivors—tell him too much about their Jewish background. When Sarah's sister Rachel explains that she would be devastated should her sons choose to marry a non-Jewish woman, Andi is taken aback since he assumes that she must then also disapprove of his relationship with Sarah, especially since he is German. However, he never asks Rachel about this, and avoids the issue with Sarah, observing instead the increasingly anti-German prejudices from Sarah's Jewish and American friends. When he takes Sarah to visit his native Heidelberg, he displays uneasiness when she questions his father about his whereabouts during the war, and they have an argument when Andi's uncle in Berlin suggests that it would be best to leave the long-gone German past alone. Their relationship becomes more complicated, and instead of openly addressing his discomfort and shame, he concludes that "we tolerate only those who are like us,"[8] and finally decides to get circumcised in order to prove his love for Sarah. However, he finds the idea of a ritual circumcision performed by a mohel embarrassing, and therefore travels to Germany, so that his German friend, who is a surgeon, may perform the clinical procedure in secret. Upon his return to New York three weeks later, Sarah does not even notice or care that he is circumcised, and their relationship ends by him leaving. The theme of this particular short story on the German, non-Jewish male's circumcision gains acute relevance especially now that, in 2012, a new debate ensued in Germany about whether or to what extent male circumcision is lawful. Even though the initial impetus for this debate was the misunderstanding pertaining to the case of a Muslim child, it of course extends to Jewish religious practice as well. In Berlin, after many months of confusion and heated debates, it was finally decided that in extenuating circumstances (including religious practice) it is, in fact, lawful to circumcise, yet the parameters for such circumstances are clearly defined by the "well-being" of the child in question.[9] As Wolfgang Thierse, former president of the Bundestag has criticized, the requirement of parents to "prove" their religious affiliation is a violation of Germany's freedom of religion, and the other requirement, that circumcision may only be carried out by a medical professional, discriminates against Jewish practice, where a mohel is usually carrying out the procedure. The difficulties arising from this debate indicate the extent to which Germans are unfamiliar with religious and cultural practices of Judaism.

To return to our texts, while the silence concerning the second generation's shame lies at the core of both short stories' representations of the German male, there is one important difference in the assignment of the first-generation female role. The German mother in "Girl with Lizard" represents the submissive and victimized maternal figure who is redeemed from her guilt via the rape. This type does not appear in "The Circumcision," where the mother of the protagonist seems altogether absent. In light of our earlier question as to why there is a role reversal from the identification of the female with Nazism in *The Reader* to the submissive, weak mother figure in "Girl with Lizard," this suggests that the female of the first generation is utilized solely for the purpose of constructing the fantasy of relieved German guilt and shame via victimhood, a construction that in *The Reader* finds its expression within the more complex, ambivalent figure of Hanna, but which in "Girl with Lizard" is neatly separated into a guilty father and a victimized mother figure. From the perspective of the third generation, as in "The Circumcision," females apparently no longer need to be divided into either victims or perpetrators. I would therefore contend that an additional reason for this particular representation of the German feminine (of Hanna and also of the mother figure in "Girl with Lizard") is the "identification with the phantasized [*sic*] maternal/feminine" that "offers men a form of psychic compensation that guards against the painful fragmentation of the self in the moment of traumatization," as Roy Jerome succinctly observed for other literary representations of postwar femininity.[10] Taken together with the guilt rejection reflexes described in chapter 1, the inability to love that both the title of the collection (*Liebesfluchten—Flights of Love)* and the emotions underlying these short stories put on prominent display, might here have been transferred to third-generation Germans.

Accordingly, on the surface, "The Circumcision" addresses a host of issues concerning third-generation Germans' dealing with Jews that "Girl with Lizard" evades. We finally get to know an actual relationship between a German man and a Jewish woman. The problems of German shame along with the inability to move beyond this shame over the Holocaust are once again core themes of a personal narrative. Concurrently, the similarities between both texts in their assignment of gender roles are striking. In both cases, a male third-person narrator reflects on his relationships with women, and in both texts his inability to maintain successful relationships is intrinsically linked with his inability to confront his German past. Also in both narratives, it is the *woman* as a Jew who prevents the German male from properly nourishing his relationships, be it in the form of the haunting representation of the Jewish girl in the painting, or in the form of the Judaism and Jewish heritage of the woman he loves in "The Circumcision." In "Girl with Lizard," the protagonist never engages in a serious attempt to understand and resolve the conflicts of his and his family's past, and while "The Circumcision" describes a—half-hearted—effort, here, too, the protagonist fails and leaves.

Yet, both texts ascribe to the Jewish woman the role of "the other." In "Girl with Lizard," the "otherness" of the Jewish woman is removed by her appearance as mere representation in the painting, underscoring the notion of imagined and constructed identities on the part of the German male observer. Here, the Jewish girl is the infantilized object of the narrator's gaze, and while presumably her real-life grown-up version was also that of love interest and, more importantly, victim of the perpetrator father, her representation in the painting is described as being about eight years old, and with a childlike face. Nevertheless, in that same paragraph, the girl in the painting is also imagined, at least for the narrator, in erotically seductive terms: "The shadow that her hair cast over her cheek and temple was a secret, and the darkness of the puffed sleeve into which the bare upper arm vanished, a temptation."[11] This notion of the Jewish girl as seductress and quintessential *belle Juive* finds itself uncomfortably exaggerated when the narrator encounters the original Dalmann painting, which, as we learn at the end of the story, is hidden beneath the surface image, revealing a huge lizard gazing at a small girl: "and it wasn't the lizard sunning on the rock but a tiny girl, adorable, with dark curls and pale face, bright bodice and dark skirt. She lay on one side, her head on her arm, half kittenish child, half seductive woman."[12]

The gaze of the lizard is conflated with the gaze of the observer, turning the (male) observer of the girl, but also of the painting, into a snake-like sexual predator. The immediate guilt of the first-generation father as sexual predator and exterminator of Jews is depicted—rather crudely—via the lizard/gaze of the observer in this inversion of the original image. The text, then, implies that the Jewish girl, who was the actual victim in the storyline and in the meta-narrative of the Holocaust discourse, is really a seductress who arouses the observer (presumably, as in the plot, the German male) and entices him to commit crimes. Considering the disturbing conflation of child/seductress in the painting with the timeworn anti-Jewish stereotype of the Jewish woman as (evil) seductress of the non-Jewish male, the burning of the painting at the end of the narrative might indeed come as a relief, as it does for the narrator, since it also erases this troubling imagery. Yet, the act of burning the painting resolves neither the narrator's entrapment in guilt and shame nor his discontented relationships with women, and the assignment of those gender roles thus merely serves to reproduce an anti-Semitic stereotype.

In "The Circumcision," on the other hand, we encounter in Sarah an adult, self-confident Jewish woman, who is involved in a progressive relationship with Andi. Her character, as depicted in the short story, assertively makes her own decisions and in no way invites any reduction to stereotypical love-object representations. However, the narrative raises important issues regarding the construction of her femininity and her Jewishness in opposition to Andi. First, Sarah is still portrayed as the (Jewish) seductress of the (non-Jewish) male, echoing the image of the *belle Juive* depicted in "Girl with Lizard:" "Sarah had bought flowers . . . She was waiting for him in a short-sleeved man's shirt that barely covered her butt. She looked seductive and she seduced him."[13] And, when Andi attempts to leave Sarah after an argument, he is not able to depart, because she seduces him: "He stayed. Sarah begged so hard he really couldn't leave. But he decided not to talk with her about his work ever again."[14] Thus, the conflation of Jewish woman and seductress still displays both anti-Semitic and misogynous tendencies as framed by Otto Weininger and others, especially when considered within the fin-de-siècle Salome discourse, as Sander Gilman explicates: "Being a seductress is contagious and marks one as a Jewess. But such seductresses are dangerous—they kill non-Jewish men like Holofernes."[15] Admittedly, Sarah is far from "killing" Andi. However, if we recall how her Jewishness causes difficulties in their relationship, she does represent a danger to Andi's German identity. Because of his entanglement in guilt and shame over the Holocaust, Sarah is ultimately the cause for his half-hearted and merely superficial circumcision. Given the context, it must be read as a mutilation of Andi's masculinity, which he, after the procedure, experiences as a loss of identity: "She looked at him, and he knew what she was thinking. But he realized that it didn't matter. He searched for his old sense of outrage, his old need to contradict and set things right, but found nothing."[16] Even if the male is not actually killed, his integrity is threatened, for "non-Jewish males are at risk when they are exposed to Jewish women."[17] As in common fin-de-siècle anti-Semitic discourse, the circumcised penis becomes a threat to the Aryan male's integrity.[18] The references to fin-de-siècle and early twentieth-century discourses are already forecast by some of the content material in "Girl with Lizard": Both Rene Dalmann, the painter, and the tragic circumstances of his life emulate the expressionist and impressionist periods in visual art.

Both short stories by Schlink thus showcase the ongoing catastrophic effects of failing to confront later generational implications in the sins of the earlier (first and second) generations. This is how both texts are linked, and how the representation of gender roles functions within the personal politics of generational guilt. From the narrative perspective of the male protagonist, the female is utilized to, first, confer absolution from guilt via the reversal of guilt and shame, or victim and perpetrator (the first generation mother in "Girl with Lizard"); second, recall the stereotype of the seductive *belle Juive* who is, at least partly, to blame (the Jewish girl in the painting as well as the figure of Sarah in "The Circumcision"); and third, represent the "other" who poses a literal and physical threat to German male integrity (Sarah in "The Circumcision"). Hence, the texts evoke the classic triad of the woman as protective mother figure, innocent virginal figure, and evil seductress. The texts' gender politics, though not consistently anti-Semitic, produce patterns within which a German male fantasy of absolution from guilt by association is dependent on those very gender politics. And this is why Schlink's short stories ultimately do exhibit what I would call "gendered anti-Semitism"—an all-too perfect example of the secondary anti-Semitism as defined by Gessler and others, which must be associated with both previous and current generations' inabilities to cope with the legacy of the Shoah. While in "Girl with Lizard," the second generation's relief from the Nazi past hinges on imagining a gendered isolation of male perpetrator and female victim, the instances of gendered anti-Semitism represented in both texts serve to reinforce the struggles of current, third-generation German male identities.

Gender and Totalitarianism

Judith Butler recalls from her visit to Germany in the mid-1990s that her persona (as an American feminist Jew) became a "vector" for "gender and sexual anxiety in the discourse on racial victimization."[19] Accordingly, when Eduard Hoffmann, the West German protagonist of Peter Schneider's 1999 novel *Eduard's Homecoming* (*Eduards Heimkehr*)[20] rides a Berlin subway, he muses whether women from the former East Germany are indeed significantly more likely to achieve orgasms than their West German counterparts, as the headline in a German tabloid claims. Whereas the "truth" claim (or truthiness) of the tabloid seems of little relevance at first, the plot of the novel itself reiterates this misogynist stereotype of the East German woman who can, free from capitalist consumer culture, hence more in tune with her body, reach orgasms more easily. Jenny, the Jewish American wife of the protagonist, who again displays formulaic gender stereotypes of the dark, threatening, seductive Jewish "other" (i.e., another *belle Juive*), cannot climax with Eduard, but Marina, his East German love interest, explodes in multiple peaks. Clearly, the theme of a female sexuality that is utilized to serve male political stereotyping is in itself problematic, especially since there are no distancing or subversive markers in this fiction that could code the text as satirical. We need not invoke Judith Butler to recognize that any assumption of the domination of the male as the sole keeper of female sexual pleasure is archaic and in need of revision.

Still, we might evaluate Judith Butler's observations as obsolete and overdrawn. Even though the theme of a female sexuality that is utilized to serve male political stereotyping even in contemporary settings is far from new, and, furthermore, here also marked as fiction, the unfolding of the plot where the Jewish and Western woman is positioned vis-à-vis a more abstract sexually charged Eastern femininity raises disturbing issues, since the narrative itself never questions this very paradigm, nor are there any distancing literary devices in the text, apart from the author's explicit claim of fictionality: "All the characters in this novel are fictitious."[21] Schneider's own deliberate and somewhat naive repudiation of anti-Semitic undercurrents in contemporary Germany by way of imagining "Jewish friends" and invoking other philo-Semitic rhetoric in his fiction does little to resolve the issue and has already been the subject of commentary for both *Eduard's Homecoming* and its less charged 1992 prequel, *Paarungen* (Couplings).[22] According to Colin Riordan, much of Schneider's attempts at defending his protagonists' stance towards the German past and any current anti-Semitic notions stem from the debate around the 1987 fictionalization of the Mengele case in his short story "Vati."[23] In this imagined account of the son of a Mengele-like Nazi perpetrator, Schneider drew heavily on materials published by the German tabloid *Bunte*, was later accused of plagiarism and, subsequently, of insensitivity to the Jewish communities, since the short story provides the Nazi father a platform to utter his anti-Semitic rants. The dispute was eventually resolved, and there is no need to reiterate either the debate or later findings already well accounted for elsewhere. Current theories of fictionality and aesthetic framing in literature after Auschwitz (Dominick LaCapra, Klaus-Michael Bogdal, Mona Körte), along with considerations of gender and minority discourse structure this exploration of mechanisms in contemporary German literature at overcoming totalitarianism at the cost of reinscribing gender stereotypes. Obviously, this novel again foregrounds the intense desire of contemporary Germans to prevail over feelings of guilt and shame resulting from both East German and particularly National Socialist totalitarianism. The Germans' denial reinforces stereotypical paradigms of East versus West, Jewish versus German, and female versus male, and the discrimination that results, because even post-unification Germans such as Eduard have not yet sufficiently addressed their entanglement with their history, and hence, with those very paradigms. Is this textual representation of stereotyping a reference to similar issues found in everyday life? And, if so, does the text, then, have the effect of enabling readers to work through those very issues with the ultimate goal of eliminating them, or does Schneider's novel rather function to confirm the stereotyping even further?

As Dominick LaCapra has shown in his pivotal *Writing History, Writing Trauma*, understanding the relationship between fiction and the non-textual reality a fictional text seeks to reference is both essential as well as complex, particularly when dealing with texts that address the implications of Holocaust trauma. Literary texts involving the psychological need of third- and fourth-generation contemporary Germans seeking to overcome this trauma also fall into this category. Even though LaCapra is mainly concerned with historiography, he argues for the structural similarity of literary and historical texts, and his examples include works of art and literature. He emphasizes the ability of fiction to evoke the reader's empathy, which he considers a critical category in addressing past trauma. After explaining his idea of a "discursive middle voice" that can appropriately relate trauma, LaCapra makes a stunningly convincing case for empathy to be of more import than the widely accepted notion of "experience."[24] This is relevant here because what follows from LaCapra is the next question, that is, where does the reader's empathy fall? Does the stereotyping evident in the tabloid quote and plot development in Schneider's text, then, represent an instance of "acting out" past guilt and repressed trauma, or do these signifiers represent provocations meant to stimulate opposition and "working through" on the part of the reader? Since, according to LaCapra, the referential relation that fiction versus historiography holds towards truth claims is a complicated and by no means binary one (i.e., we cannot say "history" = true versus "fiction" = untrue), the relationship between reader and text might provide a fruitful source to determine "truth" in texts, and perhaps more importantly, the text's ability to evoke empathy.[25]

German studies scholar Klaus-Michael Bogdal argues quite differently in his aforementioned introduction to *Literarischer Antisemitismus nach Auschwitz*. After differentiating between various instances of literary anti-Semitism (subconscious, unintentional, and intentionally deconstructive play with anti-Semitic imagery), he submits that criticism of a literary text for its use of anti-Semitic imagery (or, as I would contend, otherwise stereotyping/denigrating accounts) must fail precisely because of its aesthetic frame, which shields literature "wie ein Schutzwall" ("like a protective wall"). Bogdal invokes Pierre Bourdieu's theory of symbolic violence to uncover textual elements pertaining to a discourse of literary anti-Semitism.[26] Yet, while such an approach might be useful in instances where anti-Semitic metaphors, imagery, and figures are clearly decodable, it will be less successful in texts such as *Eduard's Homecoming* where more subtle anti-Semitic attitudes are presented alongside other discriminatory rhetoric, and where, moreover, prejudice is relegated to the plot level rather than more obviously discernible in metaphorical, metonymical, or otherwise textually coded form.

Mona Körte, a German studies and anti-Semitism studies scholar, suggests that stereotyping in literature poses serious problems for literary analysis, in particular as it pertains to anti-Semitism studies. Even in intercultural German studies, which concern themselves with shifting boundaries of self and other, there is so far no theoretical concept for examining stereotypes in literature. Yet, Körte determines that such a concept might not be desirable after all, since literary texts, owing to their indeterminacy, cannot easily be incorporated into a totalizing theory. Hence, the very analysis of literary anti-Semitism requires first and foremost a close textual reading, taking into account the (often unspoken) coding within literature as a system, while relying on the relationship between author intentionality and reader complicity. The suspicion that a text might indeed propagate anti-Semitism is usually warranted whenever a text does not succeed in obliterating or at least suspending stereotypes and discriminating rhetoric in poetic reflection, regardless of author intentionality.[27] Hence, according to Körte, we must ask questions such as "Who is speaking?" and "How do statements pertaining to Jews function within the text?" Do such statements rely on traditional imagery and inscription, thus reproducing it, or do they seek to undermine such imagery using literary or poetic techniques? Returning to LaCapra's call for the (literary) text to evoke empathy, the issue, then, is whether the evocation of empathy, as in so many texts after German unification, is limited to the notion of Germans as victims or whether, instead, the text induces compassion with the targets or victims of stereotypical discrimination. In the case of *Eduard's Homecoming*, this would mean empathy for "Ossies" (former East Germans), women, and Jews.

Despite most of the immediate responses to *Eduard's Homecoming* both in the feuilletons as well as some scholarly pieces that treat the work primarily as a novel of German reunification or a "Berlin novel," the issue of *Vergangenheitsbewältigung* (dealing with the past) is central to the text. Eduard inherits an apartment building from his Nazi grandfather Egon Hoffmann. At first, Egon appears to have confiscated the property from Jews during the Third Reich, but later in the text he emerges as a Schindler-like figure who had, with the purchase of the building, helped the former Jewish owners escape into exile. This revelation in the plot is, as Ulrich Baer succinctly notes, quite inappropriately crafted as a "surprise attack" by Eduard on Edita Marwitz, an elderly female Jewish Holocaust survivor in Florida. When Eduard suddenly and with little advance warning appears at her doorstep, the woman seems to instantly forget about German crimes and happily, in German, provides the information that equally instantly relieves Eduard from any trans-generational guilt. The text's imagination of a Jewish Holocaust survivor, that is, the victim, solving the German perpetrators' problems of guilt, shame, and forgiveness is, as Baer remarks, offensive, and, as I would add, invokes yet another stereotype, namely that of the "good German" amidst evil Nazis.[28] Susanne Rinner's reading thus overdraws the import of female agency when she observes that Edita's storytelling, "gendered as a female activity, is an important contribution to the writing of history."[29] Instead, Edita's deus ex machina-like appearance merely places the responsibility for addressing the past on the Jewish victim, and the mirroring of Edita and Eduard's grandfather's love affair with that of Jenny and Eduard underscores that very notion.

Yet, in order to ultimately determine whether this and other instances of stereotyping are to be read as strategic devices meant to stir reader criticism vis-à-vis incidents of totalitarianism, or merely as superficial attempts at *Gegenwartsbewältigung* (dealing with the present), close readings centering on the following three clusters of themes in *Eduard's Homecoming* will be revealing. This analysis will first and foremost explore the nexus of women and gender, which has not yet been the focus of any scholarly engagement with this text. From this, a discussion of Jewish identity and "literary anti-Semitism"—as it intersects with preconceptions about gender—will follow. At the same time, my reading will investigate the binary of East versus West, which is often considered the main theme of *Eduard's Homecoming*.

The three major female characters in Peter Schneider's text, Jenny, Marina, and Edita Marwitz, are merely depicted in their respective affiliations with the protagonist. Jenny, Eduard's wife, is introduced fleetingly in the second chapter, shortly after Eduard's musings over the tabloid headlines on East German women's higher orgasm rates, and, accordingly, the text shows her duly uninvolved during sexual intercourse.[30] We furthermore learn that the couple has children. Jenny is again mentioned in the text after Eduard's unsuccessful encounter with both the squatters in his apartment building and the "ossi"-fied police.[31] We now discover that Jenny's feelings concerning the images of the fall of the Berlin Wall had been much less enthusiastic than Eduard's. Together, these two encounters suggest a detachment and negativity of Jenny's character vis-à-vis both Eduard and unified Germany itself—a sentiment echoed in her decision to remain in California while Eduard leaves for Berlin, and one that becomes decisive in the plot when she is revealed to be Jewish. It is only in the fifth chapter that we learn more about her background, her Jewish identity, and her relationship with Eduard. Jenny's earlier reluctance to celebrate and embrace German unification seems to stem from her Italian-Jewish mother, whose family was deported in the Holocaust.[32] As a result, Jenny's opposition and ambivalence towards Germany come to the fore both in her pregnancy with her first child, where she identifies her family's history as a burden ("Last"), and in the threatening ways in which she perceives some imperative forms of the German language, such as "Halt!" "Stehenbleiben!" "Achtung!" and "Schnell, schnell!"[33] Yet, she seems to have chosen Germany as a place to study, and, moreover a German husband, as a mode of subversive resistance against her family, indicating a critical distance towards her own Jewish background.

Most remarkably, however, while we get to know Jenny as a Jew, and as the child of a Holocaust survivor who seeks to move beyond her family's tragic history, we also find one of the most disturbing anti-Semitic stereotypes attributed to her character. Eduard remarks the following about Jenny when describing her sitting seductively on his desk in black stockings: "Her complexion, a trifle darker than he'd known it in German latitudes, looked even darker and more exotic on the shadowy side of her face. . . . , and seemed eloquent of the sunlight and breezes of another continent."[34] This replica of the age-old anti-Semitic stereotype of the seductive Jewish woman or, again, *belle Juive*, is clearly misogynistic and seems altogether out of place considering Jenny's emancipated persona as a working mother who, as opposed to Eduard, during her visit in Berlin, has the courage to confront the squatters in Eduard's contested dwelling head-on. This episode is once again followed by yet another sexual encounter where Jenny remains ostensibly uninvolved. Taking this all into consideration, Jenny is here clearly pitted negatively as a Jewish "other" and "exotic/fremd" against the "German latitudes/deutsche[n] Breitengrade" along with a femininity that is at once enticing ("innocence plus intelligence plus perversion")[35] and threatening in her refusal or inability to succumb to Eduard's sexual advances. "Surrendering to one's libido meant swallowing one's pride and losing the contest," muses Eduard when sleeping with her,[36] and later in the text, Jenny declares that women want men to risk their lives in their pursuit of women. This notion corresponds directly with Jenny's refusal to embrace a unified Germany.

Hence, the gender politics of the text, inasmuch as they concern Jenny, suggest a gender identity that is tightly bound to a Jewish identity and that is laden with long-standing racist and sexist stereotypes. The notions that gender identity might also be a result of social representation (as formulated decades earlier by feminist and postcolonial theorists alike) or that Jenny's refusal to orgasm might actually be her own—feminist—assertion are entirely absent from the way in which Jenny's relationship with Eduard is portrayed. More troubling still, for significant portions of the text, Eduard even imagines Jenny as a former rape victim, alluding to the victimization of Jews by the Nazis, and a view that Jenny herself entirely rejects.[37] The character of Jenny thus epitomizes the traditional male sexual fantasy of the Jewish seductress, again evoking "gendered anti-Semitism" and one that is even more disturbing in its dubious constellation within what otherwise seems like a modern, enlightened, progressive female character. Most curiously, in the end, the *belle Juive* does achieve her orgasm as a result of Eduard falling out of the window of their bedroom: "When you disappeared into space like that, something snapped inside me," Jenny admits.[38] This, again, points to Jenny as the inferior sex, in that her sexuality is entirely dependent on the action of the male, and confirms the sexist statement from the tabloid, rendering the female "other" subject to the male's gaze. At the same time, it underscores the need of the German male to sacrifice (himself, his masculinity) in the face of Jewish femininity. Jenny as the Jewish seductress requires the sacrifice of the German male both literally and metaphorically, in order to save the relationship, and save Germany and the Germans from their transgenerational guilt.

Marina, on the other hand, the East German woman, is of course neither Jewish nor does she remain sexually aloof. As is foreshadowed in the tabloid headlines, her femininity is closely linked with her identity as an East German. Accordingly, Eduard first meets her when he is lost in the East German location of his workplace, the bowels of which resemble a "labyrinth," and at a time when Jenny has long been back in America (the West). Their encounters are predominantly for sexual pleasure, and Eduard enjoys the relief of being with a multi-orgasmic woman: "What bliss it was not to feel indebted to a woman. . . . Not to have to entertain the most ludicrous of all male self-doubts."[39] In what follows, the dispute over Eduard's inheritance turns violent and is made public by the squatters, and since it seems that Eduard's grandfather had "purchased" the apartment complex from Jews, the legitimacy of his inheritance—and, with that, the integrity of his German identity as the grandchild of a Nazi—is put into question. Parallel with this plot development, Eduard continues his joyful relationship with Marina, until she finally leaves him on a trip to Weimar of all places, the epitome of both German high culture and of East German backwardness. In the text, Weimar is cast as "the home of the new German Parsifals, the Camelot of those who invoked a better, more wholesome Germany," but also, for Eduard, "a health resort for his wounded manhood."[40] It may be one of the many idiosyncrasies of the text that the location where Eduard can finally cure his damaged masculinity also becomes the site of their breakup. Yet, this breakup in Weimar occurs only after Eduard has learned from archival materials that actually, his grandfather had purchased the property legitimately from the Jewish family, and had in fact fought for them to remain employed—against an "evil" German named Dahnke, the archetype of the anti-Semitic Nazi. Likewise, the breakup occurs after Eduard's wrecked masculinity has been restored. Hence, Marina, whom the reader does not become well acquainted with—we merely learn that she has a son with whom she has a relationship that Eduard deems inappropriately close—mainly serves to underscore both the East-West dichotomy set up by the text as well as the misogynist stereotypes of multi-orgasmic Eastern women. Her personality does not contribute directly to either the plot development around Eduard's inheritance, or to the resolution of Eduard's problems with Jenny. Marina only serves as a dummy for Eduard to temporarily escape his anxieties concerning his broken (German) masculinity. Once his German identity is rescued (he is no longer suspected to be the grandson of a Nazi), Eduard's masculinity no longer needs Marina's sexual affirmation—or the respite in Weimar.

This subservient role of Marina as the epitome of the East German woman is underscored when, instead of divulging more about Jenny's character, the fourth chapter of the first book introduces the reader to German studies in America, and the text mockingly refers to university German departments in the United States as strongholds of an outdated East German literature, where especially "the female authors of the other Germany" receive more attention than in Germany.[41] "Where, in West Germany, was their like?" the narrator asks rhetorically, and with not-too-subtle irony.[42] While again relying on gender stereotypes, once more pitching East against West, the narrator insinuates that East German literature by women is inferior, while implicitly suggesting that West Germany is not as patriarchal as commonly thought. In other words, this is a meta-textual instance where irony is used as a rhetorical tool, to undermine the notion that West Germans are more patriarchal than East Germans, but while maintaining—again via irony—that East German literature as a whole, and East German women writers in particular, are inferior to West German (male) writers. Hence, on a meta-level, the text does use distancing devices such as irony and rhetorical questions, yet they are not used to rebuke stereotypical depictions of women, of Jews, or even of East versus West. On the contrary, the narrator affirms those binary divisions via his rhetorical strategy.

Before returning to ask more pointedly what the function of these binary, stereotypical inscriptions is, and what effect they might have on the reader's evaluation of Nazi and East German totalitarianism, we must take a close look at the character of Edita Schlandt, aka Edita Marwitz.[43] As Eduard returns from his Weimar "Lustreise," his friend and lawyer Klott who had earlier lectured him on how East German functionaries had simply continued the exploitation and repossessing of Jewish property by the Nazis, thus creating an immediate link between Nazi and East German totalitarianism, had now found the original Jewish owner of Eduard's grandfather's property. Edita Marwitz now lives as Edita Schlandt in West Palm Beach, Florida. The reiteration of yet another anti-Semitic stereotype—a wealthy elderly Jew of course lives in Florida—is only superseded by the anti-Americanism of Eduard's clichéd description of American architecture as simulacrum (354). In what follows Eduard's aforementioned, ill-conceived "surprise attack" already criticized by Ulrich Baer, Edita Marwitz tells Eduard at length about his "good German" grandfather, who had been so decent as to buy the apartment in question from Edita's father after 1933 for more than the asking price. She also reveals why Eduard was often harassed in Berlin when he tried to claim his inheritance. He was simply mixed up with the grandson of one of the "evil Nazis." Thus far we encounter the copiously well-known pattern of a Jewish victim employed to help out a German perpetrator. However, and this is where both gender and Jewish identity come into play once again, Edita Marwitz is also revealed to have been the secret lover of Eduard's grandfather Egon. After her escape to America, her marriage to the businessman Schlandt turned out to be short-lived, and the love affair with Egon Hoffmann (a liaison between a Jewish Holocaust survivor and, at least on the face of it, a German Nazi) ultimately failed, not because she was Jewish and he German, and not because of the potential scorn of her parents, or the Nazis' racial politics, but because Egon Hoffmann was unfaithful to her, so she ended the relationship. This is reminiscent of the trajectory of the secret affair in Eduard's life, Marina, who also ends the relationship with Eduard. This subplot serves to underscore the role of the female gender as secondary and subservient to that of the—German—male. Moreover, Edita never mentions her own sufferings as a persecuted Jew in Nazi Germany, and then as a refugee in exile, doubtless harrowing experiences. Instead, she is repeatedly described as "spöttisch" (mocking) and "ironisch" (sarcastic) in her diction, alluding to yet another anti-Semitic prejudice.[44] While her silence over her fate as a Shoah survivor in the face of a German might be understandable, the fact that she is at the same time more than willing to divulge vast detail about Eduard's past seems odd, and together with the conjecture of an additional anti-Semitic stereotype is disturbing. Returning to the assignment of gender roles in the novel, while dominating and even intimidating in their sexuality, all three female characters are, on the level of the plot development, subordinate to Eduard, and are inscribed with sexist prejudice that is repeated throughout the plot.

The portrayal of Edita Marwitz's Jewish identity and the implications arising from her gender are thus exceedingly significant. First and foremost,

Eduard can now—via the assistance of a Jew and a woman—feel as the rightful owner of the inheritance, and as the descendant of a "good German." A survivor of the Shoah helps him reclaim his good conscience, his rightful German possession, and his German identity. In addition, because of the similarity in Eduard's and Edita's biographies—both had illicit affairs—and through the love between her and his grandfather, Eduard can fantasize himself as in various ways "related" to a Jew. Hence, Eduard may now also, particularly considering the recurrence of the liaison between a Jewish woman and a German man—feel reaffirmed in his relationship with another Jew, namely Jenny. And, unsurprisingly, Eduard not only sells the apartment building in mutual agreement to a consortium of the squatters, but at the very end of the novel he is also finally able to bring Jenny to an orgasm. Moreover, the character of Edita Marwitz seemingly serves as a female version of what Mona Körte has, for the "eternal Jew" in Lion Feuchtwanger, termed a *judaeus ex machina*. As Körte explains for Feuchtwanger's figure,

> The Jew embodies the "way out," where his entrance and exit appear to be determined by others; a mechanically reproduced missing link, he tightens and scews and glues the gaping speech of the anti-Semites and thus lends his own body to the mechanics of creating and reproducing stereotypes.[45]

Similarly, Edita appears as such a deus ex machina figure, but here on the level of the plot development: All seems lost, Eduard is losing his wife and his lover, in addition to his German inheritance, and his fateful and troubled identity as a German Nazi progeny appears sealed. But, with the emergence of Edita all that had seemed vanished is suddenly and unexpectedly salvaged—with the exception of Marina whom we never hear of again. But then, the East German woman—merely a dummy to begin with—seems even less important now that Jenny can have great orgasms and make Eduard feel like the man and the German he had longed to be, much like East Germany was subsumed into the larger West Germany in 1990—as though it was no longer needed. Edita, the *judaeus ex machina*, helps Eduard by lending herself physically as a subject of German anti-Semitic prejudice (living in Florida, displaying a mocking and ironic diction and appearance), and, perhaps more troubling still, she actually facilitates the anti-Semitic notion of German superiority and dominance over the Nazi past by allowing Eduard the fantasy of the "good (Nazi) German." Furthermore, the portrayal of her character evokes the perception that, for the Jewish Shoah victims, all is resolved in the end, as the Jew is alive and well, living in subtropical luxury.

There is obviously no doubt that the plot development in this text perpetuates stereotypes in all three areas: gender, anti-Semitism, and East versus West (Germany). Particularly after the comparison of the figure of Edita with that of Feuchtwanger's ironic and wittingly subversive invocation of the "eternal

Jew," we now need to explore how these speech acts and instances of stereotyping in Peter Schneider's novel function within the relationship between text and reader. While Feuchtwanger's use of stereotypes and anti-Semitic repetition is clearly used to comment on and critique the self-perpetuating traditions of anti-Semitic speech, their function in Peter Schneider's text is less obvious. If inscriptions of anti-Semitism in *Eduard's Homecoming* are perpetuating stereotypes in the extra-textual world, then the use of prejudiced speech on gender and on East versus West binaries might be read as problematic as well. Hence, our reading of all stereotypes that this text presents, and essentially, the question of whether or not the issue of Nazi and East German totalitarianism is "worked through" in today's German imagination, hinges on how the reader is to interpret the manner in which this text reiterates and references stereotypes.

We encounter in *Eduard's Homecoming* an omniscient third-person narrator who oscillates towards a personal narrator by inserting thought passages and reflections pertaining to current events, events within the plot, or to other characters in the text, but all from Eduard's perspective. There are occasional quotes that function to suggest historical authenticity, for example, the aforementioned tabloid headlines, quotations from a book on sexual desire disorders, and other characters' speech acts related in indirect speech, but we never fully gain any other characters' perspective. Hence, Eduard is at the same time clearly the protagonist around whom the plot is constructed, but also inseparable from the narrative authority. While there is considerable space between the narrator's stance and some of the other characters and events, there is almost no distance between the narrator and Eduard. Consequently, while the narrator is not entirely identical with Eduard, their mutual perspective links them closely, and the reader is via the minute display of Eduard's rhetorical questions, or musings, drawn into Eduard's world, and his thoughts and feelings, to primarily empathize with him (and not with any other character—male or female—in the text). Most of the stereotyping on the level of the plot is not set apart, or marked with any other rhetorical or literary device that might reference it as subversive, or ironic, and is therefore also to be taken as pertaining to Eduard's worldview. Hence, the reader is more likely drawn into the stereotyping that the protagonists' perspective in the text presents, and thus inclined to nod in agreement, rather than to stop and remain at a critical distance. This narrative technique is diametrically opposed to the one Körte references in Feuchtwanger, where disruptions and changes in the narrative perspective are used to cause poetic reflection, and a decisive break in the text reception on the part of the reader. Moreover, and this might put the narrative stance of *Eduard's Homecoming* even more into question than the reiteration of the stereotypes themselves, and might reveal the problematic link between the text and notions of totalitarianism, ironic diction and subversive mocking are strategies that the text uses. But, instead of using those rhetorical devices to *undermine* or *subvert* anti-Semitic speech (as in Feuchtwanger), they are used on a meta-textual level to *propagate* anti-East German sentiments and *affirm* Western (male) superiority. One striking example is when the narrator alias Eduard mocks the U.S. academic reception of East German women's writing. Consequently, instead of undermining prejudice by using irony and other rhetorical devices, the text uses them in order to characterize Edita Marwitz, thus employing them to reaffirm the flow of the plot and the anti-Jewish and anti-Semitic prejudice of the Jews' speech as mocking and ironic. Hence, while at first glance it seems as though we here encounter rhetorical strategies similar to those of Feuchtwanger's text, in that both texts are marked by irony and mocking, as well as a *judaeus ex machina* appearance, due to the narrative perspective in Schneider's text, these devices function in the exact opposite way. Instead of undermining anti-Semitism, sexism, and totalizing prejudices of East versus West, *Eduard's Homecoming* affirms all of those stereotypical inscriptions.

In order to understand more fully why this novel would employ such a problematical narrative stance with the stereotyping perspective presented unmediated by Eduard/the narrator, another work published by Schneider only two years later, this time nonfiction, might shed light. *"And If We Only Gain an Hour . . . :" A Jewish Musician Survives the Nazi Years* (my translation) impressively details the life of the German-Jewish musician Konrad Latte, and how he survived the Holocaust hiding in Berlin from 1943 to 1945.[46] Schneider's account emphasizes the important and largely neglected role of the many German helpers, seeking to work against the notion of guilt through generational affiliation, as it was most forcefully propagated by Daniel Jonah Goldhagen's notorious success *Hitler's Willing Executioners* (1996).[47] Schneider finds that subversive and silent acts of resistance by many Germans are still mostly unaccounted for, since, until the release of Spielberg's *Schindler's List* (1993), many of Germany's quiet helpers had not felt invited to speak publicly about their generosity because of a still Nazified post–World War II climate and, later, because so many Germans were competing to demonstrate their positive affiliations with Jews.

The story of those Germans brave enough to hide or in other ways knowingly support Jews in Germany, although well documented in the back of Schneider's book, was not fully written in 2001 (nor, indeed, is it today). And yet some of the conclusions Schneider draws raise questions. For example, in his introduction Schneider claims the following in his attempt to show how Germans—contrary to the (self-)perception of many who might have been willing to help Jews but saw no way to oppose the totalitarianism of the Nazi regime—did have a choice to resist: "To offer a piece of bread to a persecuted and abandoned victim, to let him sleep in one's home, to get him the next place to stay, for that one needed decency, cleverness, and courage, but not necessarily to be prepared to die [*Todesbereitschaft*]" (my translation).[48] And yet Schneider tells the story of one Heinrich List, one of Konrad Latte's helpers, who was discovered and deported to Dachau, where he was later murdered for aiding a Jew. This evidence is diametrically opposed Schneider's earlier claim: in order to help a Jew, List *did* need *Todesbereitschaft*, since he was actually killed for his actions.

The issue here is not the question of whether and how we best memorialize Nazi Germany's quiet resistance while also acknowledging the victims of Nazi persecution, since that belongs to an entirely different discussion. Rather, it is Schneider's passionate need to emphasize that it was not as difficult for Germans to help as many claimed after 1945, that Germans were in fact helping, and that Germans were not necessarily all guilty as Nazi perpetrators because of their generational affiliation. The intensity of this desire, which leads Schneider to go so far as to contradict his own evidence, while understandable, might therefore also be indexical of his powerful wish to overcome the memory of the vastly totalizing implications of Nazi crimes against Jews. This, in turn, might help explain how the desire to overcome memories of totalitarianism can lead to stereotyping, in the case of *Eduard's Homecoming* on the level of the plot, but also more broadly in the metatextual narrative stance of the work. Consequently, since the stereotyping at work here is not the result of poetic reflection (either on the part of the text or the reader), the reference to the stereotyping in extratextual everyday life that this text presents has the unfortunate effect of propagating those stereotypes rather than eliminating them. Dominick LaCapra has shown how such disarticulations can lead to post-traumatic acting out (*Writing History*), and while I would add that, in the case of Schneider's invocation of the past in both texts, these disarticulations might be entirely unintentional, they are no less problematic. As Primo Levi writes in his pivotal "The Memory of the Offense," "a memory evoked too often, and expressed in the form of a story, tends to become fixed in a stereotype, in a form tested by experience, crystallized, perfected, adorned, installing itself in the place of the raw memory and growing at its expense."[49] Just as the memory of a Shoah survivor or of a Nazi German can thus be abused, the memory of an entire generation is easily distorted by the intense psychic need to overcome, to fantasize one's past in a better light. Thus, *Eduard's Homecoming* has a totalizing effect—we are once again confirmed in our labeling of East-West, German-Jewish, and male-female stereotypes. There are no literary or other textual devices in the novel that could undermine such labeling; rather, the plot and narrative perspective serve to confirm the tabloid headlines, the gender prejudices, and the anti-Semitic imagery. The side effect of such disarticulation is that empathy, inasmuch as this text evokes it at all, is limited to the perspective of Eduard, or the narrator, and with that to the imagination of a "good German." Hence, the desire on the part of the novel to overcome totalitarianism—the totalitarianism of the Nazis and of the East Germans—directly corresponds to the desire of many of today's Germans to overcome their collective memories of Nazi and East German totalitarianism. More troubling, whether the female protagonists are Jewish, East German, or American, femininity is oppressed and mocked by misogynist anxieties of the (innocent, "good") German male who "acts out" (LaCapra) the trans-generational trauma of his Nazi past. I have shown elsewhere that, notwithstanding its premise of fictionality, Schneider's text perpetuates stereotypes in all three areas: gender, anti-Semitism, and representations of East versus West. As a consequence, we can conclude that this text put on display how Germans' intense psychic need to overcome their troubled past results in a form of gendered, post-traumatic acting out and, ultimately, in an inability to love or to accept others.

The Jewish Mother

The female typecast that we have merely encountered fleetingly thus far is that of the mother. In the texts discussed so far, we saw Jewish women as children and Jewish women as lovers. How, then, are mothers depicted, and how is a "Jewish mother" different from all the other, non-Jewish, mothers? For German readers, this question is perhaps best answered by looking at Raphael Seligmann's representations of Jewish mothers in *Die jiddische Mamme* (1990) (The Yiddish Mama) as well as his more recent novel *Der Musterjude* (1997) (The Perfect Jew).[50] Here, the stereotype of the overbearing, intrusive, and controlling yet also articulate and aggressive Jewish mother is (re)introduced to a German readership in satirical fiction. While this stereotype or typecast is of course well established in the American popular imagination, even amongst gentiles, a German audience might be less familiar and, hence, more in need of the introductions Seligmann's texts provide. A sociological study from 2000 about the American popular imagination of the Jewish mother stereotype reveals that, while a cultural construct by mostly male writers of the 1960s, triggering feminist reactions and engagements aimed to devalue the stereotypes' misogynistic negativity, recent images and imaginings have "defused the comic exaggerations of the overprotective mother."[51] According to the study, this change came about not because of the explicit aim to subvert the stereotype, but rather because of the altered life circumstances of contemporary Jewish mothers whose female identities expanded outside of their families and thus changed the stigmatized figure of the Jewish mother. A brief poll among Jewish mothers within my own circle, of course only anecdotally relevant, confirms these findings, also indicating that, to contemporary Jewish women, the "Jewish mother" stereotype is mostly associated with one's own family past, a nurturing/overbearing/anxious mother figure who incessantly prods (her) children to eat. Many feel that, in terms of the physical attributes (the big-bosomed feeder/nurturer), the stereotype seems to no longer apply to recent generations of mothers, but rather to today's mothers' grandparents' generation. This would then relegate the Jewish mother stereotype to a specific wartime feature where the anxiety over feeding is related to the food shortage resulting from the particular experiences of war, persecution, and exile. Those handed-down representations of Jewish mothers, hence, might not be significantly differently stereotyped from other, non-Jewish, wartime relicts of mothering anxieties, whether in German or American imaginings. A modern-day Jewish mother, then, might not be entirely dissimilar from other, non-Jewish, mothers, whereas previous generations' Jewish mothers were.

When Julia Franck was awarded the German Book Prize in 2007, she was well established in the contemporary literary scene. She had published three novels and two collections of short stories before her enormous success *Die Mittagsfrau* (literally: *The Midday Woman*; published in English as *The Blind Side of the Heart*, 2009)[52] earned her Germany's most prestigious literary award. In selecting Franck's novel, the jury members were unanimous in their praise of the novel's "vivid use of language, narrative power and psychological intensity."[53] Franck's depiction of Helene Würsich, later named Alice Sehmisch, a mother who, against the backdrop of war-torn Germany, comes to the decision to abandon her seven-year-old son at a railway station, provides two intertwined images of a "Jewish mother": once in the protagonist Helene, the mother of the abandoned Peter, and again, in the depiction of Helene's own Jewish mother Selma Würsich. Even though the generational affiliations of the mothers in this text render them that of the wartime grandparents' age group, Julia Franck's representation of the Jewish mothers in *The Blind Side* seems strikingly different from that of the popular imagination. Selma, mother to protagonist Helene and Helene's sister Martha, appears as mentally deranged, beautiful, seductive, animal-like with black hair, green eyes, and emitting a throaty, guttural cry. Especially when judged by the population of Bautzen of the 1920s and 30s, she is clearly marked as "other." When read in conjunction with the texts discussed in this chapter, she, too, is cast as a *belle Juive:*

> There stood Frau Selma in her nightdress, which was cut so low that it showed more of her breasts than surely she could like. . . . But her loose hair swirled in the air and fell in ringlets to her bare shoulders as if it were alive. The silver threads in it gleamed, winding over her breasts like worm trails.[54]

This obviously sexually coded representation is enhanced via the gaze of a German, non-Jewish male who is not her husband—Selma's figure thus clearly functions as that of a seductress, once again, to the German, non-Jewish male. Selma's enticing and threatening sexuality is even more pronounced in the German original, where the "worm trails" over her breasts are actually snake-like creatures ("Blindschleichen"). Yet, as opposed to other *belle Juives* in the other contemporary German texts, her Jewishness is at first referenced as more subdued in connection with her difference: "The people who lived in Tuchmacherstrasse spoke of her as 'the foreign woman.' . . . Rumors said she was ungodly."[55] Even though the terms "Jew" or "Jewish" are not yet used here, the reader's perception, along with that of the people of Bautzen, is directed towards this understated marker of Jewish identity as a gap or a question. It soon becomes apparent in the course of the narrative that Selma's otherness is, alongside her mental illness, in fact a direct consequence of her Jewishness. As Martha reveals, Selma first enticed her non-Jewish German husband with her stylish appearance, her extravagant hats, again reminding the reader of the *belle Juive*. Selma is furthermore described as devious and scheming when she faults her—German, non-Jewish—husband for participating in the Great War. "Do you think he minded her being Jewish?" Martha asks an incredulous Helene when they discuss their mother's past, for the first time revealing her Jewishness openly.[56] Martha, who is nine years older than Helene, doesn't answer this question, but instead proceeds to list their mother's idiosyncrasies as based in her—concealed—Jewishness: her "foreign" accent and use of "those words," presumably Hebrew or Yiddish, her refusal to go to church, and her avoidance of the people of Bautzen all turn out to be indications of her Jewish identity, even though she "doesn't wear a wig," doesn't go to synagogue, and doesn't keep separate sets of dishes.[57] In other words, she does not practice her religion, and it is not clear whether this is as a result of not believing, or of not having access to a congregation or a more informal minyan.

Unlike the stereotype of the Jewish mother, Selma's overbearing obsession is not with her children (she neglects both of her daughters to significant degrees), but instead, her attention has been diverted to inanimate objects, and this fixation turned her into a compulsive hoarder. While her isolation in Bautzen as a result of her Jewish heritage might explain her obsessive-compulsive disorder, the main reason for her trauma seems to relate to the loss of her sons: four boys were stillborn or miscarried, and her only living children are two girls, Martha and Helene, for whom she has no regard. It seems as if the emotionally domineering and compulsive mothering of the "Jewish mother" has, in Selma's case, turned into yet another anti-Semitic stereotype, namely that of the Jew who is obsessed with material possessions. Her curious fixation on *male* offspring is not referenced or explained in the narrative, leading the reader to suspect that this, too, must somehow relate to her conflicting identity as a German Jew. Most importantly, however, Selma is clearly cast as a negative, evil figure who neglects and abuses her daughters so thoroughly that Helene's act of abandoning her son, the center of the plot of the novel, can be explained almost entirely as a predictable consequence of the lack of motherly love she herself experienced.

It is particularly noteworthy in this context that Gertrud Kolmar (1894–1943) first introduces the subject of the Jewish mother before the Holocaust in her novel *Die jüdische Mutter* (The Jewish Mother; written 1930–31; first published as *Eine Mutter* [*A Mother*] in 1965).[58] In Kolmar's novel, the "insanity" of the mother is due to the loss of her—only—child, a girl, as a result of an atrocious rape, and not due to the unspecified (pregnancy) loss of male offspring. Here, the Jewish mother discovers that her five-year-old daughter had been brutally raped and will not recover from her severe physical and psychological trauma. Ending her daughter's life by administering poison, the mother searches for the rapist out of a desire for revenge, but in the end takes her own life when she recognizes that she is in fact her child's murderer. In addition, while Martha (!) Wolg, Kolmar's protagonist, is described as a Jewish "other," in terms of physical appearance as well as behavior, her mental instability, more introverted than extroverted like Selma's, is mostly constructed as a reaction to the loss of her child, while also foreshadowing the Nazis' horrific abuse of Jews. Kolmar's Jewish mother had a German, non-Jewish husband who died early, just like Selma, and she is reminiscent of a *belle Juive* when she is prostituting herself to entice another German man to find the murderer of her child. But her overabundant love is clearly and unambiguously directed towards her child, culminating in the poisoning of her daughter, her prostitution, and, ultimately, her suicide. Reading Julia Franck's revision of the interwar Jewish mother discourse thus points to the Jewish mother as a disturbing, negative, and deranged figure who seems caught in the irresolvable conflict between a dominant German masculinity (marked by her disappointed wish for a son) and Jewish femininity (troubled, mentally deranged). Selma appears to suffer from the trauma of her failure to bear boys significantly more than she suffers from her stillbirths and miscarriages. This suggests, with Dominick LaCapra, that, in the case of Selma as the Jewish mother, the structural trauma of not being able to bear male offspring is overshadowing and crowding out the personal and historical trauma of the actual, lived experiences of the miscarriages or stillbirths. The overwhelming fantasy of a superior German masculinity thus dominates not only Jewish femininity but also the discourse of the Jewish mother. Thus, as a (Jewish) mother and as a woman, Selma has failed in every respect. The stereotypical Jewish mother's overabundance of love, still visible in Gertrud Kolmar's beautifully unsettling narrative of 1930–31, has, with Selma, been turned into its disturbing opposite, a deranged and malevolent Jewish mother who is entirely unable to love.

Yet the protagonist of Franck's novel is, after all, Helene, and the plot as well as the title of the novel primarily center on Helene's shocking act of abandoning her seven-year-old son Peter *after* she survived the Nazi and war years as a single mother. Knowing Helene's mother's plight lets us comprehend why she abandoned Peter, entices our empathy for Helene, and also ties Helene and Selma together in their depictions as (Jewish) mothers. Rather than an excess of love, as in the popular stereotypical portrayal of the Jewish mother, and as Kolmar's text is still positively reminiscent of in spite of her tragic fate, Franck's Jewish mother figures both suffer from an absence or inability to love—their children. At the same time, the Jewish mother stereotype is still recalled, particularly in the representation of two mothers in one narrative. Yet, while Selma, who is cast as completely and unequivocally Jewish, is portrayed as wholly negative, Helene is the one we are to identify with. Not only is she less Jewish in her physical appearance as blonde and blue eyed, but she has a German, non-Jewish father and seems entirely divorced from any relic of the Jewish faith, while Selma's past is still ripe with material artifacts of her Judaism (such as a menorah, or Chanukkiah). The fact that Helene is given an alternate name by her German proto-Nazi husband Wilhelm, ostensibly to cover up her problematic Jewish heritage, referencing Kolmar's text once again, serves to underscore this shift from Jewish to German identity in Helene's generation. While Martha in Kolmar's text is renamed Mirjam by her German, vaguely anti-Semitic, lover, that is, she is given an alternate name that enhances and underscores her Jewishness, Helene is now known as Alice, further erasing any traces of Jewish memory from her persona. It is a thus cleansed, German, and almost non-Jewish woman whom we can identify with, whom we feel empathy for, and for whose bothersome act of child abandonment we can safely blame her deranged, dangerous, and entirely Jewish mother.

Since *The Blind Side* is a text that engages the German *memory* of Jews, Jewish femininity, and Jewish motherhood (rather than seeking to portray contemporary Jews and Germans as Peter Schneider, and most of Bernhard Schlink's texts undertake), we need to ask what this depiction of the Jewish mother before, during, and after World War II means for today's German memory discourse. When engaging the German memory of the war and its immediate aftermath, Peter Fritzsche reminds us of a vernacular narrative that avoided "much discussion of the Jews, the primary victims of the Nazis," on the occasion of reading sentimental narratives of the 1950s, obviously vastly different texts from the one under discussion here.[59] The identification of Germans as victims that quietly reproduced the elimination of Jewish life in Germany is a well-established concept that prevailed throughout much of the immediate postwar period and during Holocaust history and memory of the two divided Germanies. However, it does seem surprising that the avoidance of postwar Jews, here reconfigured by means of the vanishing Jewish traits of Helene, the protagonist, is still at present constitutive of German memory. If we take into consideration both Cathy Caruth's and Marianne Hirsch's theoretical underpinnings of the limits of historical experience and the idea of postmemory,[60] even as we are critical of their respective attempts to conceptualize the catastrophic effects of Holocaust trauma, it seems that in today's memory discourse, Germans should no longer depend on such obviously problematic revisions of historical memory, even if they are in fiction only. Separating out the Jewish traits, coding them negatively, tapping into the fin-de-siècle association of Jews with a destructive modernity, and relegating them to the memory of prewar or interwar history has the unfortunate effect of emphasizing German memory over Jewish memory, and of reestablishing the discourse of a German *versus* Jewish memory. Additionally, it—unwittingly—supports the notion of Germans as victims of the Jews (Helene and Peter are both clearly victims of Selma's mental illness), and, as such, is comparable to the 1950s' sentimental narratives of *Heimat*, where the figure of the Jew was typically written out of the text in order to construct a more usable national past. Moreover, thinking of the Jewish mother in relation to second-generation Holocaust memory almost immediately points to Cynthia Ozick's by now canonical work *The Shawl* (1980/1983), a powerful narrative that epitomizes the Jewish mother's love and unspeakable suffering in the face of her—half-Aryan—daughter's death in the camps. As Jessica Prinz points out in her recent contribution on the Jewish mother in America, Ozick was painfully aware of the double bind of second-generation Holocaust memory, and the inherent problems of the ethics of expression.[61] Franck's Jewish mothers' inability to love, by contrast, seems to eclipse the memory of pain and suffering that results from the trauma of the Shoah. Of course, it cannot be anyone's aim to suggest some kind of normative discourse on what German memory should be like. But if we uncover the narrative strategies at work here, we can see the ways in which today's German memory discourse is shaped, and how it works to occlude and conceal important aspects of past memories.

Consequently, regarding German and Jewish femininity, *The Blind Side* both confirms and exceeds this chapter's previous findings in the texts by Bernhard Schlink and Peter Schneider, even though Julia Franck is of a more recent generation of writers, and even though she is of course female. This underscores the notion that writer identity, or even generational affiliation, is not a pertinent indicator of the ways in which German memory discourse is created or disseminated. As we saw, Helene's mother Selma and Helene herself both embody the "Jewish mother," but, especially against the backdrop of the Jewish mother typecast, one who is "unable to love." Selma is described as an archetypal *belle Juive*, but also Helene is the Jewish woman who deceptively pretends to love the German, non-Jewish male. The victims of the Jewish women are often German males (Selma's husband, Helene's son). The character of Fanny, Helene and Martha's aunt in Berlin, accentuates the imagination of the Jewish woman as a flamboyant, wealthy woman of leisure, and of the Jewish female as a perpetrator (of men, of wealth, and of drugs). Her character is furthermore reminiscent of the Jewish Holocaust survivor's daughter in the movie rendition of *The Reader* (as William Donahue's aforementioned study excavates with acuity). Interestingly, both the Jewish mother and the daughter in Schlink's text are referenced as figures, but not given names or voices. Therefore, the "gendered anti-Semitism" in Franck's text is prevalent throughout the generations: Selma and Fanny, representing the memory of interwar Jewish femininity, are seductresses, *belle Juives*, "others," deranged, drug users, and, as such, dangerous. Of the prewar and war memories, Martha is lesbian, addicted to heroin, and even though

Helene is less Jewish, her otherness is still pertinent especially opposite her German husband Wilhelm. Helene's boyfriend Carl, the Jewish male in the book, is feminized, emasculated, and, most importantly, the *only* Jewish male visible in the entire narrative. He, too, hails from wealthy parents residing in a villa on the shore of the Wannsee, and he is eliminated—via a freak accident, and not via deportation. In fact, we do not actually witness any deportations of any of the Jewish characters, male or female, which is astonishing in a narrative centering on the history and memory of World War II and the Holocaust. We may thus think of Franck's text as a tribute to a kind of post-postmemory, referencing Marianne Hirsch's terms, whereby the experiences of those who grow up dominated by trauma narratives that precede their births cannot be understood by the current generation. It might, then, seem plausible that *The Blind Side* is characterized by the absence of Jewish suffering—an absence that also eclipses the Germans' atrocities, since second- and third-generation Germans cannot possibly know or understand the original trauma, the trauma of being implicated as a perpetrator in the Holocaust, in turn explaining the silencing of the Jewish mothers in Franck's narrative. However, even if we take this approach, thereby exculpating the lack of Jewish suffering in this novel, the representation and visual imagination of Germans as victims of—exclusively female—Jews is not at all elucidated, and much less justifiable. This is especially pertinent when we think back to Raphael Seligmann's mocking, yet lovingly cynical, self-conscious representations of classic Jewish mother types, or to Gertrud Kolmar's haunting, but ultimately redeeming portrayal of one tormented Jewish mother. This is why, as Katharina Gerstenberger rightly observes, in Franck's novel, the relationships "between the generations fail."[62] Yet, these failures are not only rooted in the de-ideologization and new sobriety that fiction on German Holocaust memory today requires, as Gerstenberger suggests, but rather in a partial eclipse of Jews in the discourse of the memory of German-Jewish relations.

To conclude, the readings assembled here suggest a German memory discourse that heavily relies on the Jew as female, and that, at the same time, casts those Jewish females in strikingly consistent negative terms. Even females who are not Jewish, as in the case of Schlink's German women (Hannah, Sarah, the women in "The Girl with Lizard"), are mostly given the task to help the male protagonist to escape his historical guilt and shame. Whether they are partners, mothers, children, or unrelated to the respective protagonists, the Jewish women are depicted as harmful and damaging, often invoking a stereotypical discourse that originates in fin-de-siècle and nineteenth-century representations of female Jews. As reading those texts in combination makes evident, they disturbingly recall the discourse that Otto Weininger, among others, found so appealing that he wrote entire treatises on how Judaism and femininity are intrinsically linked opposite the Aryan male, establishing a "psychology of sexes."[63] While to today's readers such an undertaking of course seems altogether absurd, we need to keep in mind how influential such a seductively reductive binary theory with scientific pretension was, and what catastrophic effects it helped produce. It is therefore particularly unsettling that these anti-Semitic and negatively stereotyped accounts resurface in contemporary German fiction. Whereas the stereotype of the Jewish mother is, in and of itself, not unambiguously negative (the nurturing and loving aspects can and are often read as positive qualities), the imagination of the *belle Juive* does not offer any redeeming qualities, since those that might suggest aesthetic beauty are usually undermined via the implied threat that emanates from such—clearly eroticized and exoticized—"beauty." Yet, as we have seen in Franck's depictions of mothers, the Jewish mother typecast is only raised as a foil—against the much more off-putting, disturbed, mentally ill, and overall evil depiction of the Jewish mothers in Franck's novel. And while we do encounter another Jewish mother in Peter Schneider's best-selling *Eduard's Homecoming*, any representation of Jenny's mothering is entirely omitted from the narrative, and we merely see her opposite Eduard—as his sexual and life partner, whose fantasies express and dominate Jenny's persona. Thus, the conflation of anti-Semitic fantasies on the part of the male, second-generation protagonist with clearly misogynist and miscegenist longings towards the female Jewish subjects is prominent in Schneider's text, where the gendered anti-Semitism is set in a post-unification East-West scheme. In Schneider's novel, whether the female protagonists are Jewish, East German, or American, femininity is oppressed and mocked by misogynist anxieties of the (innocent, "good") German male who "acts out" (LaCapra) the trans-generational trauma of his Nazi past. In Bernhard Schlink's short stories, the male Germans' intense psychic need to overcome the troubled past results in toxic forms of gendered, post-traumatic acting out against the German or Jewish females, and, ultimately, in an inability to love or to accept others. Schlink's texts utilize German females as mothers to fantasize German victimhood. But even Julia Franck's more recent and, taken author identity and narrative perspective into consideration, *female* accounts work along similar lines of eclipsing the German past: Jewish women are at fault for the neglect and abandonment of the—primarily German—male, who is victimized by the war and the memory thereof. Franck's text inadvertently goes so far as to link Jewishness almost exclusively with femininity, as German women are either not visible or not ascribed any agency in her novel. It seems that the unmitigated negative representation of *female* Jews serves to tacitly reaffirm the imagination of a damaged German masculinity.

We may not intend to go as far as to engage a Lacanian reading that assumes psychosexual dynamics pointing towards the inexorable link between German patrocentric, phallocentric, and anti-Semitic culture that seems to still dominate Germans today. Such a reading, while enticing, might overdraw the issue. Yet, it has now been established fairly consistently that all the texts discussed here engage in more or less severe forms of anti-Semitic speech that, ultimately, functions to whitewash the German past while imagining German males (and, in Schlink's texts, females) as victims. On the other hand, could we not also read those same texts as uncovering the problems of Germans and Jewish femininity before, during, and after the Holocaust? Could the gendered anti-Semitism at work here also be read to alert us to sexist and racist speech elsewhere, discursively undermining the very stereotypical depiction it seems to elicit? Instead of criticizing the narratives and the problems they create or perpetuate, could we read this discourse as an elucidating, helpful, and vital part of working through to overcome any such memories of the past? Any work of art of course lends itself to multiple interpretations, as is evident from the wide and divergent discussion concerning Schlink's texts. Reader responses can and should be diverse and contradictory. Yet literary texts themselves generally contain some textual or meta-textual indicators as to how they are to be read and received. Looking closely at the narrative structures of the three texts will thus deliver some insight, as will analyzing the reviews of the texts.

The void of a persuasive narrative technique in Peter Schneider's novel has already been established in this chapter, with the conclusion that the uncomplicated narrative structure serves to reinforce the binary, stereotypical depictions of Jews, women, and East versus West. Similarly, Bernhard Schlink's short stories and *The Reader* are straightforward third-person narratives where the reader consistently retains the perspective of the third-person male narrator, referred to as "he" or by name. To the extent that there is reflection within the personal narrator's point of view in both Schlink's and Schneider's fiction, it primarily centers on the introspection of the narrator himself. For example, Eduard muses about the possibility of East German women achieving orgasms more easily, and the nameless narrator in "Girl with Lizard" acknowledges his hurt feelings when he had to remove the painting before making love with his girlfriend. Yet we do not encounter another point of view than that of the narrator, rendering those texts conventional examples of the omniscient authorial narrator's voice. No frames set up the narratives, no changes or breaks occur in their respective narrative perspectives. While some of the secondary literature on *Eduard's Homecoming*, most recently Susanne Rinner, asserts that the "third-person narrator creates a reflective and self-reflective story that is marked by distance and irony toward his protagonist," the alleged irony is never directly referred to, analyzed, or quoted.[64] Presumably, Rinner reads the exaggerations of the tabloid headlines that the narrator enumerates when discussing women as "irony." This is, however, not a reading that can be substantiated. Irony in literature is a rhetorical device or discursive element illuminating a discrepancy or opposition between that which is said and that which is meant. Yet, Eduard's misogynistic assertions concerning East German women's ability to orgasm more easily[65] does not actually allude to any discrepancy, since the text goes on to confirm the assertion by introducing the character of Marina, an East German woman—who orgasms easily. Hence, irony as a textual strategy—if, indeed, it was to be one—is undermined by the story line itself, and the overall narrative turns out to be unambiguously sexist. While we might surmise that Schneider meant for the entirety of the sexist, misogynist, and racist assertions that are made by Eduard in the course of the novel to be read as "irony," this would defer the reader to mere interpretative speculation and not offer any hermeneutically valid readings.

The Blind Side functions according to a similar set of narrative conventions, this time maintaining the omniscient third-person perspective of Helene, the female protagonist. The only exceptions to this are the prologue and the epilogue, both of which present the, again, conventional third-person narrative of Peter, Helene's son, that is, a German male. We see glimpses of his perspective from when he was just abandoned at the railway station (prologue), and when he is seventeen years old and refuses to meet with Helene when she attempts to visit him (epilogue). The comparatively simplistic narrative technique in Schlink's and Franck's texts has the unfortunate effect of merely reproducing—rather than employing poetic techniques that could undermine, question, or suspend (Körte/Bogdal)—the Jewish attributes and anti-Semitic stereotypes, thereby unwittingly solidifying the unquestioned and unquestionable authority of the memory that is represented. In order to locate any discernible effort to discursively defer, or question, the gendered anti-Semitism, we would need to see either a break in the narrative perspective, a more complex or multifaceted narrative perspective, or any other literary or rhetorical devices that could serve as markers to otherwise shatter the unbroken third-person narration. In this respect, W. G. Sebald's 2001 novel *Austerlitz* could serve as an example where a complex narrative structure functions to both authenticate that which is being narrated (by suspending the narrator) and, at the same time, to gesture towards the unreliability of fictional accounts writ large (by pointing out that the narrative is mediated via the memory of two—possibly untrustworthy—narrators).[66] In *Austerlitz*, the entire "plot" of the story is related via a nameless narrator who, as a result of—fictitious—conversations with the protagonist Austerlitz, relates Austerlitz's search for his past, exposing the veracity of the genre of Holocaust memoir as unstable and problematic, and counteracting any notion of a dominant memory discourse or stereotypical inscriptions. Again, the aim here is not to suggest any kind of normative benchmark category to be employed by German memory discourses, and even Sebald's technique is not without problems, but his texts indicate that there are other, more complicated and self-conscious ways of telling the German past than via a naive third-person narrator.

Accordingly, most likely due to this clear-cut, uncomplicated narrative style that seems to be rooted in the movement of "Neue Lesbarkeit" (new readability), the texts under discussion mostly received positive reviews that were geared to entice a general, wide readership upon their publication. In fact, none of the daily or weekly venues that published reviews for a lay readership contained any significant references to the clichéd stereotypical inscriptions, or to the gendered anti-Semitism, nor did any, even of the more critical, reviewers take note of the misogyny at work in the texts. Schneider's novel, as already noted, was mostly received as a "Berlin novel," and even a more subdued appraisal in the reputable *Frankfurter Allgemeine Zeitung* does not mention the problematic depiction of German memory or of Jewish women—or of the entirely inappropriate misogyny towards East German women.[67] Moreover, Bernhard Schlink's collection *Liebesfluchten* (*Flights of Love*), also mostly positively reviewed, spurred almost exclusively references to *The Reader*, and emphasized Schlink's training as a lawyer, which, according to Thomas Wirtz, makes him particularly adept at dealing with questions of German guilt and responsibility.[68] The review by Verena Auferman is symptomatic of many in that it touches upon the responsibility of Germans in relation to their past ("Schlink lässt Walsers Wegsehen nicht gelten"), but then glosses over the problematic ways in which the narratives present German guilt and shame.[69] On the other hand, notwithstanding its critical success as the 2007 winner of the German Book Prize, some of the initial reviews of Franck's novel were rather mixed. The *Frankfurter Allgemeine Zeitung*'s Edo Reents enthusiastically reads the novel as an unsettling family drama where the scandal of child abandonment helps contextualize current German family discourses. It is thus appropriate, he concludes, that war, history, and ideology (!) remain on the periphery.[70] On the other hand, the main complaint of a more negative review by Kristina Maidt-Zinke concerns precisely the treatment of history: too much information, she states, makes the reader quite uninterested in the clichéd scenes of the troubled family life, the bohemian Berlin scenes, and, especially the melodrama of the relationship between Helene and Carl. Since much of the plot is set on the edge of what is still credible, Maidt-Zinke finds, and the metaphors are overabundant with an unwieldy and over-the-top colorful language, she suggests that the text would have been stronger if the prologue and epilogue had been fused into a short story, leaving the substance of the novel up to the reader's imagination. This is an interesting proposition, specifically when considering a female reviewer suggesting that a text on the memory of World War I and World War II that is—finally—presented from a female point of view be replaced, again, with the predominantly German male point of view. This very notion implies, once more, the imagination of German memory as masculine. Most importantly, however, Maidt-Zinke does note, even if in passing, that apart from the building of the first German autobahn, Nazi atrocities are eclipsed from this narrative—in spite of the overabundance of corny historical clichés.[71] Ultimately, even the more thoughtful reviews on all of these texts indicate that the one-dimensional narrative techniques do not promote a subversive, critical, or distant view of the issues at hand. While reviews in feuilletons can and should of course not be mistaken for all possible readers' responses, they do provide a glimpse into the range of reception among educated, but lay reading audiences. In sum, gendered anti-Semitism of varying degrees is dominant in all the narratives, and almost in all cases where women, particularly Jewish women (but also German, non-Jewish women), are represented in their inability to love.

Chapter 3

Masculinities and the Body

> I take the psychopathologies that develop within a culture, far from being anomalies or aberrations, as characteristic expressions of that culture, of the crystallization, indeed, of much that is wrong with it.
>
> —Susan Bordo

As Kaja Silverman so poignantly reminds us in her seminal *Male Subjectivity at the Margins*, there is nothing "natural" or culturally innocent about sexuality.[1] This is particularly true when sexuality is represented alongside additional markers of cultural or ethnic "otherness." Gender studies, and, for this chapter, masculinity studies in particular, can thus deliver important tools to decipher the meaning of such cultural inscriptions, indicating pathologies that otherwise remain hidden within a society. Although Silverman's thrust is different from mine, in that her book is dedicated to exploring "deviant" sexual behavior, her investigation of the politics of desire serves as an important source of inspiration here. Susan Bordo's notion of the spectrum of psychopathological behavior as a marker for cultural pathologies aids this inquiry into representations of German and Jewish masculinities in contemporary German society. Taking the conclusions of gendered anti-Semitism and femininity from chapter 2 one step further, I now shift the attention to the masculinities presented by some of those same texts, and, more importantly, some additional ones, while resisting to presume a simple binary opposition of the German male versus Jewish female. In other words, my investigation of masculinities is not to be understood as reading the "other side" of femininity, since I do not presume male versus female as a binary structure. Rather, my inquiry seeks to take the gender politics so clearly at work in many contemporary texts as a grid against which the society from which they emanate and which they inform is poignantly displayed.

Utilizing a rather basic model for exploring "masculinities," my analysis refers back to Robert Connell's theory of "hegemonic" masculinities.[2] "Their interrelation [of femininity and masculinity] is centered on a single structural fact, the global dominance of men over women."[3] This particular premise is useful because, while acknowledging the changing and shifting cultural fabric that, ever since the onset of modernity, has conjured up the notion of "masculinity in crisis," and the plurality of masculinities, it keeps its focus on dominant ideological markers and lets us see the power structures at work in a given society. Furthermore, the notion that various different masculinities, along with femininities, are subordinated to hegemonic, patriarchal forms of domination helps keep in perspective the particular subset of issues arising from reactionary and exaggerated masculinities prevalent during National Socialism. Connell's model also brings into view the marginalized and subordinated forms of masculinities (such as effeminate or homosexual males), and their relationship to the hegemonic power structure at work at any given time and place. Again, this analysis will focus on popular texts by German, primarily non-Jewish writers, in order to determine what many read and think about, yet seek to deflect the writers' (male or female) subjectivities in favor of observing the texts' impact on the larger contemporary German reading discourse.

As we saw in Schlink's aforementioned short story, "The Circumcision" (2000), the third-person German male protagonist named Andi experiences increasing discomfort when confronted with the Judaism of his Jewish American girlfriend, Sarah. Andi feels that, in order to overcome mounting differences of opinion with Sarah that emerge from his inherited guilt over the Holocaust, he has to be circumcised. Eventually, he has the operation performed by a befriended surgeon in Germany, without Sarah's knowledge, and without the accompanying ritual by a mohel that would render it a meaningful and sacred act. When he returns to New York City after his penile "wound is healed," the relationship ends. While Sarah is clearly marked as a Jewish female "other," and displays traits similar to those reinscribing the notion of the *belle Juive*, the mark of Jewish femininity here additionally entails a direct physical threat to German masculinity. Andi feels that he must sacrifice his foreskin—the integrity of his penis—and mutilate his masculinity to please Sarah. He incurs a self-inflicted visible and physical wound that is meant to heal the invisible, internal, psychological one. Paradoxically, Sarah never requested this. Instead, she wanted to resolve their conflicts—the perceived taboo of acknowledging Nazi atrocities while accepting her Judaism—by talking about their differences, a plea Andi never acknowledges.

The questions that this chapter addresses concern the meaning of the representation of masculinity as it relates to either German or Jewish identities, or both. In particular, is German masculinity, in its traditional hegemonic form, regularly represented opposite Jewish femininity? If so, how does this representation, often tied to physical accounts of the male body, correspond to the stereotypical depiction of femininity? Do the texts under consideration escape the—all too obvious—binary of German masculinity versus Jewish femininity that the Schlink short story sets up? This is particularly significant in the face of the vastly exaggerated, celebratory masculinity cults that both the era of Kaiser Wilhelm and, most importantly, Nazi ideologies induced. Susan Bordo's important distinction between the Penis as the physical object, the signified, and the Phallus as the representational power structure that induces chauvinistic hyper-masculinities (the signifier) will help shed light on these questions. Today's German culture should, presumably, have long moved past signifiers of such über-hegemonic images and imaginings of masculinities, as, on the face of it, representations of contemporary German men no longer seem to propagate any such notions. On the contrary, Anne Fuchs has shown convincingly how "Väterliteratur" (Fathers' literature) by Christoph Meckel, Uwe Timm, Ulla Hahn, and Dagmar Leupold successfully deconstructed the dominant German masculinity discourse of earlier periods, and above all, the "völkisch" ideology.[4] I squabble with some of her findings and argue that this particular deconstruction and emphatic embrace of a more critical stance towards the fathers' generation also served the construction of the "good German," as well as that of the "German as victim," particularly in the absence of any engagement with the Holocaust victims, thus feeding into the dominant narrative discourse on gender. Undoubtedly, these writers (as well as Heinrich Böll and Hans Erich Nossak, for example) helped to redirect the German memory discourse towards that of a new, and "less masculine," image of the German male of the past. Yet, in terms of hegemonic affiliation, the weaker German males on display here might implicitly be subordinated to previous patriarchal modes of representation. How does this new direction in German memory discourses, then, correspond with the inscription of German masculinities opposite Jewish femininity? Alongside the more obviously coded German masculinities, are Jewish males, inasmuch as they appear in popular texts by younger German writers, also represented stereotypically, that is, is the body of the male Jew cast in terms that emanate from the late nineteenth and early twentieth-century discourse of the effeminate male Jew?

Damaged German Masculinities

Focusing on the representation of the gender of the male body in "The Circumcision," while keeping in mind the obvious marker for cultural pathology that is on display via Andi's behavior further exposes the cultural meaning of Schlink's representation of the male body and its signified. As opposed to the Jewish protagonist in Maxim Biller's short story "Betrayal," who seeks to come to terms with his Judaism via a circumcision of his uncircumcised penis (i.e., circumcision will help him become "more Jewish"), Andi does not seem to want to understand Judaism or how Sarah relates to his German identity, nor does he seem to be sincere in his peculiar philo-Semitic desire to become Jewish. Niehouss, the uncircumcised Jewish character in Biller's short story, demonstrates the opposite when he decides to get circumcised, for "if one feels like a Jew, one's body had to be marked, had to be different—especially as it revealed the Jew within."[5] Andi's inability to rationally address issues of a male Jewish identity, or to reflect upon what circumcision might mean within Judaism, or for himself, can be read as a sign of his intense but unconscious identification with Sarah's Judaism that grows out of his memories of unreflected German guilt. The act of deciding to have his body—the exterior—physically marked is thus indicative of his psychopathological need to cover up the opposite, his true feelings—the interior. Hence, the external physical mark, rather than revealing the Jew within, reveals this German's anti-Semitism. Andi's German friend who is to perform the surgical procedure addresses this directly when he states: "You want to become a Jew for Sarah, but you want to wriggle your way out of what it actually takes to become a Jew. You find it embarrassing, it might hurt more than necessary—and you don't want that."[6]

Thus, Andi's desire for a "circumcision," a marking of his body, is merely a superficial, empty gesture which, once again, exposes his anxieties about Jews and the ways in which Germans may feel a deep psychic need to convey, but not openly pronounce, their responsibility towards Jews. The fact that they are, apparently, vaguely aware, but still not able to directly address their past guilt, is here acted out via a desired physical erasure of a part of the—German—male body, where the body is turned into an "other," a damaged imitation of itself. Just as Rachel never actually says that she would object to Sarah's and Andi's relationship, and, in fact, may not be against it at all, as far as we learn via the story's plot, Sarah also does not expect Andi to convert to Judaism, much less be circumcised. Instead, she asks him to never stop talking to her, a plea he completely neglects: "Ticklish subjects not to be talked about were: their families, Germany, Israel, Germans and Jews."[7] In fact, he does the opposite by getting "circumcised" without telling her, exposing an openly philo-Semitic desire to appease Sarah that is meant to cover up the concealed anti-Semitic anxieties concerning his German masculinity. Accordingly, it is not simply the anxiety of the physical pain of the operation that prevents Andi from having the procedure performed by a mohel, or even the embarrassment of having to expose himself in a ceremony. Rather, Andi never takes any steps towards trying to understand either Sarah's particular stake in her faith (which the text describes as different from that of her sister Rachel) or to explore Judaism itself, suggesting that underlying anxieties about both his masculinity and his German identity are really at the core of his decision. Andi's thus mislaid conception of what circumcision means in Judaism and the extent to which his decision evades any engagement with religion is emphasized if we consider the touching and genuine account by Michael Kimmel of what it meant to not circumcise his newborn son—even though he and his wife are Jewish.[8] While certainly not all reform or secular Jews would agree with Kimmel, his personal story showcases the thought and consideration that usually accompanies the decision to circumcise or not to circumcise, whereas Andi's conflicts merely revolve around his German identity. As a result of an argument over Andi's German identity, he asks Sarah, "How would you feel if I were to say that I love you even though you are Jewish? That my friends look for what is Jewish about you?" and he later states, "I don't know whether I can handle being liked or loved even though I'm German."[9] Andi's—entirely rhetorical—questions once again attempt an inversion of German guilt and Jewish victimhood: by reversing German and Jewish distress, Andi presumes that his suffering from Sarah's and her family's perceived harassment of him as a German is equivalent, indeed interchangeable, with her Jewish identity. In the end, and after his "operation," Andi escapes from the relationship with Sarah, seeking to "rescue" his German male identity. Of course, he incurred the physical "wound" of a damaged penis from the relationship with a Jewish woman. Incidentally, even today's discourse among Jewish parents when deciding for or against circumcision on behalf of their sons views circumcision in terms of damage or violation of the wholeness of the male body and penis (see Kimmel, "The Kindest Un-Cut"), prompting various national organizations and advocacy groups arguing for the wholeness of the male body.[10] In Andi's imagination, in order to fit Jewish expectations, the German male has to emasculate himself and become "less German" as well as "less masculine"—but even in spite of his self-mutilation and self-victimization, this endeavor fails, too. In the end, he has to break off the relationship with Sarah because, as a German (male), he cannot resolve his problems with the Jewish (female) "other." Thus, a damaged German male projects his unresolved German past onto a relationship with a Jewish woman, and, his masculinity must prevail in the face of femininity and Jewishness, in spite of the physical wound that the Jewish woman incurred. The previously hegemonic German male is, via the Jewish female, turned into a subordinate, damaged, less powerful male. Returning to Susan Bordo's terms, it is the penis that is mutilated—with the aim to (re)construct a phallus, a German phallus. For the underlying assumption of Andi's act is that the mutilation is painful, indeed masochistic, and needs to be undertaken as a form of repentance. Yet, this kind of atonement is entirely misplaced since it is neither expected nor helpful to the contemporary German-Jewish relationship at stake.

It is particularly interesting that, apart from the psychological damage and the physical wound of the "mutilated" penis, we do not encounter any physical description of Andi. This omission makes the link between the psychic condition of German guilt and shame and the physical wound or damaged masculinity even more pertinent. The anti-Semitic reflex that associates the bris, or the Brit Milah, the Jewish religious custom of circumcising boys, with the Christian pre-World War I view that circumcision is practiced merely because it is lucrative is vividly on display via Andi's tortured misgivings. Marc Shell describes in his fascinating account of the Christian obsession with Jesus's foreskin, as reflected in an Austrian caricature of a Jewish mohel,

"'The Circumcision' projects onto the Jewish practice the characteristic foreskin adoration that modern Christians repress, or fear to recognize, in Christianity itself."[11] The same can, accordingly, be said about the German projection of a thus weakened and damaged masculinity as it is illustrated in Schlink's story. The masculinity adoration and fantasy of phallic reconstruction that third-generation Germans purportedly repress, is here visibly and palpably exposed in German anxieties when Germans—like Andi—are confronted with Jewish religious practice. Since the foreskin is—literally and figuratively—at the heart of German and Christian masculinity, circumcision is revealed to present an insurmountable threat to both German-Christian identity and German male identity. As such, the misguided bris also exposes Andi's massive homophobia.

Notwithstanding this nexus of German identity and masculinity, the controversy even among Orthodox Jews as to whether or not to perform the Brit Milah dates back to the nineteenth century (Theodore Herzl, most notoriously, was against performing it). While the medical community in the United States has, most recently, confirmed newborn male circumcision to be not only a safe but also a recommended practice for entirely non-religious reasons,[12] the question immediately takes on a different cultural meaning when raised in the cultural and political minefield of postwar contemporary Germany. In 2012, the case of an allegedly botched circumcision of a Muslim boy made headlines, as it subsequently led Cologne's State Court to outlaw the practice. Immediately following, a debate ensued that involved religious leaders of both Islam and Judaism, and a final verdict by the Supreme Court is still outstanding. However, in August 2012, an elected commission on ethics recommended to allow circumcision with local anesthetics.[13] What the debate around this issue showcases is the extent to which practices that originate from non-Christian and non-German religious and cultural identities are contested, and seem impossible to discuss rationally. For the initial misunderstanding leading the court in Cologne to its troubling verdict was, as it turned out, entirely manufactured by insufficient knowledge and prejudice. The mother noticed some bleeding after a circumcision and went to the local hospital, which then accused the physician who had performed the surgery of malpractice. It took two years to determine that some bleeding after surgery is common and not an indicator that the operation was botched. Here again, German anxieties, even though not specifically anti-Semitic, over a "damaged penis" seem to have contributed to the fateful misinterpretation on the parts of several professionals.[14]

Consequently, we must ask how the gendered anti-Semitism alongside the imagination of a damaged German masculinity on display here functions within the cultural memory of German history, and today's Germany. Are today's Germans actively thinking about the implications of the psychopathology that so obviously affect Schlink's troubled protagonist? What does this mean for the German discourse of masculinity and anti-Semitism? This matter is especially fraught since the representation of gendered anti-Semitism and damaged German masculinity exposes male anxieties that are linked not only to the second generation with its closer tie to the nexus of guilt and shame associated with the Nazi perpetrators, but also to third-generation Germans, who, as my earlier analysis has shown, fantasize themselves as no longer entangled in matters of guilt and shame.[15] Just as the missing name for the second-generation protagonist in "Girl with Lizard" suggests that he can also stand for his entire generation of German males and their memories, the lack of a clear generational perspective in "The Circumcision," where the protagonist seems oddly in-between generations, further adds to the suspicion of an intergenerational transmission of Holocaust trauma, but also of unresolved issues with German guilt and shame. In other words, the previous model of the absent (German) fathers, or constructions of fathers as victims along with the deceptive concept of the "zero hour" of 1945 in texts of the 1980s (as described by Barbara Kosta, among others),[16] is here superseded with representations of masculinity that may not do justice to the problematic relationship between gender and history. The third-generation protagonists' acting out of guilt and anxiety is, still, exacerbated by a lack of experience with Jews and Jewish heritage, due to the apparent absence of Jews in present-day German society. This absence is glaringly illustrated in "Girl with Lizard," where the Jewish woman is reduced to a mere representation in a painting, and in "The Circumcision," by her removal to America, as the readings in chapter 4 will expose in more detail. Thus, while the fictional representation of Andi's decision to be "circumcised," and of the protagonist's burning of a famous painting may seem overly constructed on the plot level, the texts perform problematic appropriations of Jewishness that refer to anxieties and gendered fantasies that are still to be found in Germany today. The importance of the stories, therefore, lies in their capacity to reveal how tropes of (secondary) anti-Semitism, Judeophobia, homophobia, and misogyny persist. Merely labeling the protagonists of Schlink's short stories as "anti-Semitic" or even "anti-Jewish" both overstates the case and prevents a fruitful recognition of past traumas and present attitudes to Jews. Nor would ascribing "anti-Semitic traits" to the main protagonists be helpful, even though this has been suggested in some of the literature on *The Reader*. Yet, as the close reading of the two short stories in *Flights of Love* reveals, gendered textual politics—within which the characters are deeply embedded—display disturbing performances of secondary anti-Semitism that originate in long-standing anti-Semitic discourse and in fantasies and imaginings of unresolved transgenerational German trauma. Although the nameless narrator in "Girl with Lizard" does attempt to confront his parents' troubled past, Andi seeks to avoid any real confrontation in his contemporary life that might reference his past, while simultaneously desiring a guilt-free identification with Jews and Judaism. In the end, both characters fail in every respect. They cannot maintain their love relationships because of their fear that they must sacrifice a piece of themselves. The narrator in "Girl with Lizard" burns the painting that means so much to him, and Andi cuts off a part of his penis, of his masculinity. Similarly, while both males fantasize about liberation from Nazi guilt, their sacrifices ultimately do not deliver on those fantasies, since they relieve neither the problems in their love relationships nor their feelings of guilt and shame. These German male protagonists also never attempt or learn to empathize with the actual victims of the Holocaust.

The question, then, is, whether the damaged German masculinities that Schlink's stories depict resonate in other works, too. Only if similar representations appear in other contemporary texts that are at least somewhat popular can we speak of important societal trends, rather than just one author's inscription or passion. While it is, as William C. Donahue's work shows convincingly, of course completely legitimate to carefully dissect and interpret one author's work, particularly when he or she is as popular as Bernhard Schlink, my claims are better substantiated if similar traits can be found in other texts, too.

It is important here to recognize that the injured bodies represented in Schlink's accounts are not in any way comparable to the damaged bodies or identities that art and literature so masterfully produced in the discourse of modernity and beyond, such as in the visual representations of Georg Grosz, for example. The main difference lies, as evident from the comparison of Mona Körte's discussion of Feuchtwanger with the text by Peter Schneider in my chapter 2, in the unbroken, naive, and linear narrative perspective and representational aesthetics, as well as in the striking absence of any subversive or experimental narrative traits that mark both Schlink's and also Peter Schneider's texts. Hence, the damaged bodies in Schlink's or Schneider's works are not to be understood as representations of a damaged outside world that is reflected within, but rather serve to induce compassion on the part of the reader who is enticed to empathize with the German and non-Jewish protagonists. Perhaps all too plainly, Schneider's male protagonist Eduard displays anxieties that are similar to those of Andi, where the sexual and gendered injury to his masculinity is mostly caused by Jenny, the Jewish-American and female "other." Although some of Eduard's additional, non-sexual troubles are partly a result of the actions and articulations of Germans (the East German squatters, the extreme and militant Left, the inert East German police), it is the damage to his male sexual identity that Eduard perceives as most destructive to his endeavor of restoring an untainted German national identity. This is further underscored by the fact that the purely sex-driven affair with Marina is dedicated to repairing this particular blow to his male gender identity. The very notion that Jenny's orgasm is entirely dependent on Eduard's performance, and that his masculinity is therefore at stake when she doesn't orgasm, is consequently profoundly disturbing from a gender studies perspective. More importantly, however, it indicates the extent of Eduard's psychopathological injury, an injury that runs much deeper than what one might acquire as a result of a failed love relationship. This wound is clearly caused by intense anxiety over Jenny's Jewishness. Thus, the cultural meaning of Eduard's sexuality that is so visibly suffering from the Jewish woman is, again, that of a damaged German masculinity, and not at all dissimilar to that of Andi. The hegemony of German masculinity rests, once again, with an imagined previous state where the male is in control of female orgasms, and subordination is relegated to the female that functions as its binary opposite.

Some of these imaginings of damaged German masculinities are evident in a text not yet discussed, namely Susanne Riedel's 2003 *Eine Frau aus Amerika* (A Woman From America).[17] This novel by a popular female writer of a younger generation (born in 1959) was not well received in the feuilletons, but the criticism was mainly directed against her overbearing style and flawed character development. Riedel's previous success among critics with *Kains Töchter* (2000; Daughters of Cain) lead to especially bitter disappointment, the reviews suggest. Petra Kohse in *Frankfurter Rundschau* wrote the only consistently positive review of this text; all others display varying degrees of disappointment with Riedel's third novel. Yet, every single one of the reviews, positive or not, is overlooking disturbing issues of gender, anti-Semitism, and anti-Americanism, this time set in the immediate aftermath of 9/11.[18] Hannes, the German protagonist, and Sharon, his beautiful American partner of thirty years, live in Philadelphia, both professors in their sixties at a renowned university. Their conversations, centering on rather unoriginal and predictable German-American cultural and historical differences (American superficiality, German guilt of the Holocaust and inability to work through that guilt), become increasingly heated after the events of 9/11. After Sharon invites other German academics as part of a cultural exchange, she suddenly dies of heart failure at the concluding dinner. Sharon's abrupt death, which followed another argument, where Sharon had pointedly asked the Germans present to break the taboo of their past and ask difficult questions, prompts Hannes to visit Berlin again after more than thirty years. It is there that, by pure coincidence, he stumbles across a Holocaust chronicle that reveals to him and to the reader that Sharon had actually been a German-Jewish Holocaust survivor who was adopted by Americans when she was five years old. Replaying Sharon's death with this new information, we have the image of a Jewish woman brought to her death by an unrepentant German male on the transnational stage, where post 9/11 America becomes the locus of both Jewish postwar survival and unprecedented vulnerability. So it is no surprise that a now liberated Hannes returns to Germany, safe, relieved of the burdens of a Jewish woman and with America shattered. As in Schneider's text, we encounter the conflation of Jewish, American, and female, and again, the German protagonist, who is in search of an untainted German identity, engages in sexist, anti-American, and, as it turns out, anti-Semitic rhetoric.

Akin to *Eduard's Homecoming*, the diction of the female and Jewish protagonist comes across as mocking and ironic, in that Sharon's frequent rhetorical assaults against Hannes and the other Germans are scathing in their sarcasm, yet postmodern irony is absent from the narrative as a whole. Similarly absent as in Schlink's and Schneider's texts are any breaks or disturbances of the linear and naive narrative time line and male perspective, with virtually no dissident or subversive elements. The only feature that Riedel's text presents that differs from Schneider's and Schlink's approach is the narrative frame that intersperses the flow of the core narrative with Hannes's reflections of his later visit to Berlin. Accordingly, the main or core narrative is related in present tense as diary entries (complete with dates and places), whereas the Berlin frame reflections are all narrated in the past tense. Yet the impression of linearity remains, since the overall time line does not get broken, and also the sections on the Berlin visit are told in successive, linear fashion. Furthermore, Hannes's first-person narration is never changed or questioned, not even via the frame technique. Much of the fabric of the main text is related in dialogues, but the narrative stance consistently remains that of Hannes, which, especially against the backdrop of the frame which is also from his viewpoint, serves to reinforce that male perspective. The narrative point of view is, thus, once again, decidedly that of the German male, which is particularly interesting, given that the author of this novel is a woman. Even if we refrain from overemphasizing the significance of the author's identity, this suggests that the German imagination that codes "German" as "male" and "Jewish/American" as "female" is both a trans-generational and a trans-gendered perception. This, in turn, means that not only German males of the second generation (such as Bernhard Schlink and Peter Schneider) implicitly code their texts in this way, but instead, the discourse of German masculinity versus Jewish femininity is prevalent in Germany, regardless of generational or gender affiliation.

Even though this novel by Susanne Riedel was not a significant popular hit, or even a major success among literary critics, as evidenced by the numerous reviews, it transmits important material concerning the Germans' perceptions of German masculinity when faced with female Jews. More recently, the novel was lauded as a successful post-9/11 text, but merely insofar as it stands out from among the other, less complex examples of the same genre.[19] Yet none of the reviews address the gender grid that is set up here. Accounts of gender and sexuality that intersect with national and cultural identities and their stereotypical representations are pronounced. This is evidenced by the fact that the other characters who are participating in the "cultural exchange" that Sharon set up, presumably for Hannes, although she never spells this out, are all German, two male and one female, yet appear pale and hollow compared to Sharon and Hannes. Their particular idiosyncrasies are to reflect national identities and cultural prejudice: Ria is a successful writer, Jo-Hannes a self-indulgent journalist, and Michael a shy, admiring political sciences professor. All display predictable attitudes and preconceptions vis-à-vis America, life at an American university, and German-American relations.

While their ideas are less predictably organized along the lines of gender binaries than Sharon's and Hannes's, they, too, principally serve as carriers for various expressions of sentimental German nationalism. As one reviewer remarked, the Germans who are part of the cultural exchange resemble guests at a mediocre TV talk show, and the idea of the Holocaust orphan that was so movingly presented in W. G. Sebald's *Austerlitz* here merely functions as a cheap shot to evoke German "Feierlichkeit."[20] As the focal centerpiece of this strained staging, however, this text directly and unabashedly posits a German male (Hannes) *against* an American woman (Sharon). Sharon's arguments with Hannes and the other Germans about German-American differences after 9/11 oddly contribute to her sudden death. For it is at the height of their differences of opinion that Sharon, who is showing the symptoms of increasing psychopathological mental illness, suddenly collapses from heart (!) failure. It seems equally significant that Hannes learns only in Berlin, and only after Sharon's death, that she had been a Jewish-German Holocaust survivor. Again, the narrative perspective of the German male and his damaged German identity are confirmed and emphasized in the encounter with a Jewish woman. The twist that she is actually a German Jew adds to the Judeophobic and anti-Semitic notion of a German masculinity that must prevail when threatened by the Jewish female. Hannes's damaged German identity seems, at first glance, less pronounced than that of Schlink's heroes, but he is uncomfortable when he is reminded of his German origins, and had not visited Germany in over thirty years. Moreover, Sharon's persistently mocking attacks directly point towards his German identity. Thus, his particular discomfort seems more directly tied to the specificity of German history than in the cases of Schlink's and Schneiders' protagonists, where the uneasiness concerning Germany was more diffuse.

Hence, the threat coming from this Jewish woman, while not directly a physical threat to the males in attendance (as with Andi), still centers on bodily images and imaginings: the males are, in all cases, described as flawed and deficient in their physical appearance, whereas Sharon's beauty is uncontested and almost surreal in her artificial presence. "Jo-Hannes is standing up, his entire body flopping, the limbs of a marionette,"[21] and "lost in thought, he rubs his chin, where there must have been a beard once, as a sign of an elevated level of male hormones. The empty space that he encounters irritates him," all point to his feelings of male inferiority.[22] Not only does Jo-Hannes seem like a marionette in that he is not in control of himself, but he is also hormonally deficient, that is, deficient in his masculinity. Michael is repeatedly described as having a head that is too big, and accordingly, his recurring and continual statement of the "Eros of teaching" that he supposedly evokes when in close contact with younger female students renders him both ridiculous and impotent as a male. In other words, these particular masculinities all appear subordinated to the hegemonic imagination of an intact (German) masculinity.

Within the gender binary of male versus female, it is noteworthy that Sharon is in a minority of one as a Jew, and as an American. The only other woman present, the German writer Ria, is portrayed somewhat negatively too, but less aggressive, less mocking and ironic in her diction, and less threatening to the males than Sharon. While all three men seem fragile and timid to varying degrees, Hannes's weakness is pronounced only when he is confronted with Sharon's attacks. The damage to the male that we witness in Schlink's protagonist's physical injury, and that finds its expression in Schneider's hero's sexual failure is here reflected in Hannes's inability to stand up to Sharon, to counter her arguments and to engage with her rants about German guilt and the German past. Sharon rants, for example, "'These beautiful emotions in your beautiful Germany. Why, then, did you buy a Panama hat and take the next flight?'"[23] and Hannes merely thinks to himself, "Whatever is driving her, now it is only about the fact that I am a criminal"—but he does not say anything. Later in the same dialogue, Sharon continues, "'Your beautiful Memorial,' she says, 'this wall in the German self consciousness. Emotion contra Reason,'" and again, Hannes does not reply: "Cinderella is what I think, but I am not saying a word."[24] Hannes's silence is then explained in the narrative frame, where the narrator reflects on his visit to Berlin which took place after Sharon's death, as the reader learns halfway through the text.

While the other two texts inscribed damaged and subordinated German masculinities directly onto the body of the German male, or in the bodily function or absence thereof as reflected in the female partner, it is here represented in the dialogic expressions of the two main protagonists. Interestingly, this "dialogue" never functions to properly address or overcome any of the blatantly represented prejudice, either the anti-Jewish or the anti-American ones. Instead, Sharon comes across as unreasonable in her aggressive and anxiety-ridden rants, and Hannes seems oddly submissive, docile, and unable to defend his points of view. Because of his not knowing of Sharon's true identity, the partners never get to the point in their conversations where they could talk meaningfully about Germans and the Holocaust, about German guilt and shame, or even about the complicated nexus of Germans, Americans, and Jews. Importantly, it is Sharon's inability or refusal to disclose her past that leads to both the misunderstandings concerning German-American issues, and, ultimately, to the decline of their love relationship. The inability to love on display in this text is thus represented as almost entirely caused by the Jewish woman, just as the German male is merely a bystander and victim. His failure to understand Sharon is caused by her aggressive irrationality, or so it seems. This text thus performs a precarious twist via the image and imagination of a damaged, weak, subordinate German male: the account of Hannes's innocent gentleness, even endearing cluelessness, and his injured German masculinity aids to suggest a discourse where the—timid, gentle, and reasonable—German is blame-free when it comes to addressing Germany's past, whereas the—crazed, deranged, hyper-feminine[25] and hence dangerous—Jewish woman is a cunning con artist whose deception prevents the German's thoughtful and earnest engagement with the German past. The deus ex machina-like discovery of Sharon's German Jewish identity, once again evoking Mona Körte's *judaeus ex machina* structure discussed in chapter 2, thus prevents a true and meaningful engagement of German masculinity with a Jewish woman rather than enabling it, both for Hannes, the German male—and, likewise, for the German readership, who is left with the binary and anti-Semitic inscriptions as they are presented by this text. Due to the absence of such engagement, this text once more recalls Otto Weininger's fusion of anti-Semitism and misogyny. Weininger represents the "'eternal Jew' through the 'eternal feminine,'" and Sharon's presence remains, in this novel, eternal and perpetual to Hannes and to the reader, via her untimely death.[26] For the discourse of German masculinity this has the effect of presenting the "new" German male as the innocent victim who cannot properly engage with his past, not because of any flaws of his own, but because the female other prevents this. In addition to the notion of a damaged, weak, subordinate German masculinity, as in Schlink's short story, we thus also encounter an endearing, guilt-free, and sincere German male who is, by the female other, prevented from engaging his past.

In the texts of three distinct contemporary writers (Schlink, Schneider, and now also the younger Riedel) the innocent male is German, and the cunning, scheming female is American, just as the male is, in all cases, German and not Jewish and the female is Jewish. Related to the examples from chapter 2, the female is cast as psychotic, mocking (the male), ill, and mentally ill, whereas the male comes across as a bit awkward, self-conscious, but overall sane, rational, decent, and honest by comparison with the female. We might surmise that this is merely a coincidence, and relates back to the authors' identities (in that male German, non-Jewish writers are more likely to depict that very perspective positively), yet, with Riedel, we encounter a female, German, non-Jewish writer who presents the male German and non-Jewish perspective, again, vis-à-vis the Jewish, American female. Therefore, we must conclude that the imagination of a male German and non-Jewish identity against the backdrop of German male hegemonic identity is not necessarily a construction that is tied to that very author position, suggesting that the binary opposition installed here runs much deeper in the collective German psychosocial imagination than the merely superficial explanation of author perspective would merit. Accordingly, the imagination of a threatened German masculinity when faced with threatening Jewish femininity seems to conform to a pattern that is not specifically tied to any of the authors' gender identity, but rather seems to be ingrained in the power relationship between gender and history. The German conflation of Jewish equals American is furthermore disturbingly reminiscent of Nazi ideology, as Dan Diner and others have shown.[27] This intertextual, transnational German-American dimension renders the problem of the representation of gender identity in Schlink's and

Schneider's Jewish characters even more acute. Apparently, memories of German masculinity, seduced and threatened by Jewish and American epitomes of femininity, are still broadly evident in the post-unification discourse of Germany's second and third generations after the Shoah. When thinking about "the German-Jewish hyphen" in conjunction with German masculinity, we as readers, analysts, and interpreters must urgently resist the temptation of a monolithic approach that automatically equates Germanness with Nazism and hegemonic patriarchy. Such an interpretation, while of course inherently flawed, also relegates the Jews to a perpetual and antecedent victim status, as Harry Brod has so eloquently described.[28] Yet the German texts under discussion here end up performing just that: they all imagine Germanness along the lines of masculinity and patriarchy. Later generations appear damaged, emasculated, and broken—against the backdrop of their Nazi fathers' heroic masculinity, and in direct opposition to the Jewish females.

Contemporary German masculinities of course do not in all cases appear opposite Jewish femininity. The texts by Günter Grass and Martin Walser that we considered earlier provide examples of German masculinities constructed by writers of the first and second postwar generations whose characters envision an absence of guilt and shame, along with the noticeable absence of Jews in Germany, while women only play minor roles in these narratives. The psychopathological mechanism in those German males of the first generation apparently functions differently from that of the second- and third-generation writers' texts that are the focus in this chapter. The male protagonists in Grass's and Walser's novels imagine their German guilt and shame as the cause for their injured masculinities, and killing a male Jew helps liberate them from culpability, even if it is only imagined in fiction, aiding in the repair of their damaged German maleness. Their German identity is still largely tied to an imagination of what it means to be a heroic, intact, authoritarian, and patriarchal male. The extent of the injuries that war and Holocaust guilt might have imposed on their formerly hegemonic masculinities is thus appropriately remedied by crude acts of retaliation—against Jewish males. The psychopathological dimension of Martin Walser's particularly disturbing text, modeled on murder fantasies of a real, living person, thus gains renewed relevance in the context of German masculinities. For younger, or second-generation German males (as in Schlink's short story, Schneider's novel, and Riedel's novel), damaged masculinities are clearly on display, and they are turned into their affirmative opposites from the first-generation fathers. Acknowledging the damage, accepting the resulting flaw of the German male, but imagining the responsibility for that damage to rest with the Jewish woman lets Andi, Eduard, and Hannes fantasize themselves as guilt-free. The emasculation of these protagonists via the sexual power of the Jewish woman (Eduard), the religious practice of Judaism and female Jewish identity (Andi), or via the subordination to the Jewish woman (Hannes) might thus serve to enable these males' neglecting or silencing their German past. The trauma of the Holocaust appears, rather than acted out directly, as in the first generations' accounts, to be repressed twice over: once by the deliberate disavowal of a traditional, unbroken German masculinity in favor of a damaged, submissive, weakened masculinity, and again by projecting any lingering trans-generational guilt and shame onto the (Jewish) woman who is blamed for direct or indirect acts of emasculation and silencing. The displacement strategies at work in the texts under consideration here thus point to a novel way of relegating Holocaust trauma, but one that is apparently, considering the many claims of evidence of "normalization" in the Berlin Republic, successful at convincing many of the Germans' earnest plights.

These failures to address guilt and shame in current literary representations of second- and third-generation German males must be considered in a dynamic relationship with Germans today. Do isolated works of literature echo widespread fears and anxieties, especially since several texts enact the same strategies? Does the discourse of German masculinity, elsewhere suggesting that German males have, more recently, come to be represented as damaged, broken, and submissive, inadvertently aid in the repression of the German past? If the answer is yes, then the works discussed here taken together suggest an ongoing inability of second- and third-generation Germans today to productively engage the memories of the Holocaust on a personal, individual level. Collectively and publicly, we have built memorials, read Holocaust witnesses' accounts, and engaged in varied performances of Holocaust remembrance. What Stuart Taberner describes, in Henryk Broder's terms, as the Germans' attempts at "Germanisierung des Holocaust" (the Germanizing of the Holocaust), is clearly on display here via the appropriation of anti-Semitic and Judeophobic imagery, but more important still is the issue of individual Germans' ongoing troubled relationship with their history and memory.[29] Hence, the fictional representation of acted out trauma might reveal that, while it is possible for today's Germans to name some of the guilt, shame, and gender anxieties, these emotions cannot be overcome but are only reproduced throughout different generational perspectives and in different works of art. This is why the protagonist in "The Circumcision" considers the possibility of Germans and Jews living together a 'Utopian project."[30] Both texts by Schlink, as well as the debate on *The Reader*, then, are pertinent when it comes to thinking about masculinity because of the ways in which they illustrate how Germans today confront (or fail to confront) their traumatic history. Today's Germans have only just begun to address issues of guilt and shame, and, despite the many public faces of mourning, significant layers of not yet worked through anxiety and guilt are still preventing a meaningful confrontation with German history, and this in turn contributes to—perhaps involuntary—instances of secondary anti-Semitism. Thus, not only have today's Germans not "forgiven the Jews for Auschwitz," they have not yet been able to ask how they themselves may be forgiven or how, today, they might coexist with "the Jews"—male and female, past and present.

Disguised and Other Jewish Masculinities

Michael Kimmel describes in his moving "Afterword" to Roy Jerome's *Postwar German Masculinities* the Jewish perspective as it concerns the shame of the silenced: "What a revelation it was for me to finally find the stories of the Jews who did fight back," pointing to a vital aspect of Jewish identity and Jewish masculinity when thinking about Holocaust memory.[31] Kimmel underscores the need of later generations of Jewish males to not be shamed into a perpetual victim status. This need is arguably greater, and more important, than the need of German (males) to not be relegated to the state of permanent perpetrator. At the same time, however, Kimmel reminds us of the similarity of the struggles of today's German and Jewish men, "joined in the terrible knowledge that illegitimate power demands a false consensus based on the silencing of all dissent."[32] It will thus be especially important to consider if, and if so, to what extent German perceptions of Jews and Judaism recognize this similarity, at least in fictional portrayals of Jewish males, or whether the clichéd, victimized Jew is still the predominant mode of the German representational discourse in today's stories. While some physical sites of memory such as the Jewish Museum in Berlin make a concerted effort to render a multifaceted public representation of Jews that defies the singular categorization of Jews as victims of the Shoah, it will be important to consider here whether this also applies to German literary representations of Jews, and, hence, to more hidden and personal, private discourses in today's Germany.

In order to cross-examine German memory discourses from both male and female viewpoints, and to escape any binary categorization, both male and female author/narrator perspectives are sought to be taken into consideration here. Yet, when thinking about German, non-Jewish representations of the Jewish male, it soon becomes clear that in first and second generations' accounts by male German and non-Jewish writers, Jewish men are either absent or negatively stereotyped. Thinking back to chapter 1 and the fantasies of murder in Günter Grass's and Martin Walser's accounts most plainly illustrates this void. Furthermore, the absence of any male Jews in Schlink's, Thomas Hettche's, and Schneider's narratives is conspicuous. While there is, at least in outward appearance, a Jewish male present in Schneider's text in the character of Theo Warenberg, this particular Jew is not at all cast as a Jew: he has no relation either with his religion, with Jewish culture, with the Holocaust, or with any family ties that could link him with Judaism. Furthermore, his presumed Jewishness is mostly discussed in *Paarungen* (Couplings), Schneider's 1992 prequel to *Eduard's Homecoming*. It appears as if he is Jewish in the earlier novel merely to grant Eduard the philo-Semitic imagination of having a "Jewish friend." His appearance in *Eduard's Homecoming* is entirely tied to his position as an East German writer who is expected to perform that particular role for German and American post-unification audiences. The only reference to Theo's Jewishness is in passing, referencing anti-Semitism "'Kein Vopo würde deine Nase als meine durchgehen lassen!'—'Dann huste ich ihm was wegen Antisemitismus. Da steht er stramm!'" (*Eduard's Homecoming*, 60) This dialogue ensues when Eduard and Theo discuss the possibility of Eduard living in East Berlin, assuming Theo's identity. Such a fictional exchange assumes a decisive stance on the part of East German officials (Vopo) against anti-Semitism, which, as studies by Jeffrey Herf and others attest to, was decidedly not the case.[33] More importantly, Theo's past thus further obscures his Jewishness in the present. This suppression of Theo's Jewishness is especially unexpected when compared to the novel *Couplings*, where both Theo and Andre served the specific purpose of alleviating Eduard's trans-generational guilt. As Ernestine Schlant so appropriately observes for *Couplings*, a reading that uncovers Eduard's overt philo-Semitism is difficult to avoid: "Only now, sensitized by his own situation does he [Eduard] realize that Andre and Theo are not just friends of his, but Jews marked by a devastating history."[34] Hence, the peculiar containment and disguise of Theo's Jewishness in *Eduard's Homecoming* serves to underscore the notion of absence of any Jewish males in this text, and relegates the imagination of the male Jew to outward appearances only—much like the many physical sites of Holocaust remembrance in Germany today.[35]

This absence of a representation of a male Jew still holds true for the previously analyzed text by Susanne Riedel, who is younger than Schlink and Schneider, and female. The lone exception of a fictional text putting a male Jew clearly on display, is, once again, W. G. Sebald's *Austerlitz*, whose main protagonist Austerlitz is revealed to be clearly Jewish, clearly male, and whose depiction does not function along the lines of crude physical or psychological stereotyping, but rather, his persona is configured via an intricate setup of fictional frames to uncover lost memories of the Holocaust past (both of himself and of Germany). I have, for reasons that pertain to the aim of this study, bracketed Sebald and his works, and this particular exception confirms once more both the significance of the findings in more mainstream texts, as well as the decision to bracket Sebald's texts here. Therefore, the analysis of Jewish men in works of contemporary non-Jewish Germans must center on two novels by women of the third generation, Katharina Hacker and Julia Franck, whose major novels, perhaps not coincidentally, were also winners of the 2006 and 2007 German Book Prizes, respectively.

Katharina Hacker's *Die Habenichtse* (*The Have-Nots*; translated by Helen Atkins, 2008) follows the deteriorating love story between Jakob and Isabelle, both in their early thirties, educated, professional non-Jewish Germans, whose lives center on friendships and work relationships.[36] The aftermath of the terrorist attacks on the World Trade Center marks the starting point of the narrative, and the 9/11 death of Jakob's colleague leads the protagonists to London. Jakob, a lawyer specializing in restitution cases that result from German unification, is characterized as placid, fearful, and uninterested in confronting his more personal German past. Isabelle, the mundanely successful yet flamboyantly girlish and bored well-to-do female protagonist, finds herself caught up in her neighbor's parallel universe of drug addiction, child abuse, and poverty. In the course of the narrative, and during the couple's sojourn in London, Jakob is revealed to be attracted to Bentham, the homosexual and Jewish head at the law firm where he is employed. Jakob's homoerotic desires are thus oddly tangled up with his involvement in the German Jewish property restitution cases in Berlin that Bentham assigns him to. Soon Jakob and Isabelle find their relationship and the comfortable life they had imagined for themselves falling apart, mostly due to their own inability to empathize: Isabelle is a mere bystander to Sara, a little girl who is abused next door, and Jakob turns out to be both closet gay and unable to come to terms with his—Jewish—love object's Holocaust past. As a couple, they showcase both an inability to mourn their individual personal past, and an inability to love in the present. This is especially true of Jakob, the German male protagonist, who suffers from the trans-generational memory of Holocaust guilt that haunts him, and that seems in part responsible for his inability to "come out" in terms of his sexual identity. This is again linked with his inability to accept the responsibility of being a present-day German, much like the other German males already depicted by Schlink and Schneider. At the same time, the imagination of America serves as a crucial site here as in many of the other books, even though the plot of this particular story is set in London. Had it not been for the attacks of 9/11, which killed Jakob's senior colleague, he would not have left Berlin for the appointment in London that leads him to both his futile attraction to Bentham and to having to confront the Nazi retribution cases. America, as in Schlink's, Schneider's, Riedel's, and Hettche's narratives, functions as the cataclysmic backdrop for the plot of the novel.

Apart from the fragmented implausibility of the story line that this text presents, and the fact that it might indeed seem overwrought with contemporary issues, the style of this novel is, much like that of the previously discussed ones, neither experimental nor particularly artistic. The narrative stance is once again that of the omniscient third-person narrator, just as in the other texts analyzed thus far. As in Peter Schneider's and, as we will see, Thomas Hettche's novels, we moreover encounter a male German protagonist who is haunted by an elderly Jewish Holocaust survivor. Interestingly, both elderly Jews are not living in Germany, and especially Bentham's nomadic lifestyle furthermore alludes to the stereotype of the wandering Jew. Yet, as opposed to the other novels depicting Holocaust survivors, we finally encounter a key Jewish character—who is male. Gerstenberger's analysis is thus accurate when she points to a "marked contrast" between Schneider's and Hacker's novels, but the "generational difference" that she reads is located elsewhere than in the fact that in Schneider's novel the investigation of property is linked to family history, and in *The Have-Nots* it is situated "beyond the realm of blood relationships."[37] On the contrary, the uncanny remoteness of Jakob's individual or empathic involvement with the retribution cases merely underscores the extent to which he does not seem to wish to engage with the German memory of the Holocaust. The difference between the two texts—and perhaps the generations—can thus be located in the depiction of Jewish masculinity. Whereas there are virtually no Jewish males depicted in any of the texts by those second-generation German writers whose works tackle the memory of the Holocaust (Schneider, Schlink, Riedel), and Jewish identity is almost exclusively linked with femininity (and, in some cases, with American identity), this particular narrative depicts a German Jew, and a Holocaust survivor, and this representation is not consigned to the periphery of the narrative, since he also functions as the love object of the German male protagonist.

Bentham, the stereotypically "wandering" Jew whose parents emigrated to Great Britain but who never felt at home there, in spite of not being relegated to the margin regarding the narrative configuration in that he is at the center of Jakob's desire, functions as an "other"—towards Jakob the protagonist, and vis-à-vis the British society he currently inhabits. Monika Shafi's excellent piece on the interconnectedness of physical dwellings, bodies, and the prevailing absence of empathy underscores this assignment, when she concludes, regarding Bentham: "in the juxtaposition of those unburdened with the past and loss with exiles like Bentham, Hacker paints a nuanced picture of life after 9/11 that probes moral choices in a world unguarded by binding frameworks."[38] While Shafi's analysis, pinpointing Bentham as an exiled other, is less concerned with insider/outsider, gender, or Jewish issues, her findings relating to the absence of empathy or any moral benchmark in the text are crucial. Accordingly, the significance of Bentham's exile status or "otherness" is twofold. First and foremost, his otherness originates from his homosexuality, here depicted as a disturbing, unsettling quality that, in Jakob's detailed description of his nightly encounter with another man in a public park, alludes to homosexuality as an obscure, forbidden, abnormal, and promiscuous behavior, that is, it appears as altogether negatively stereotyped. "Two naked men on the Heath, and himself as a peeping Tom in the bushes, bushes reserved for women."[39] This characterization of Bentham's sexual orientation even more clearly stigmatizes him as a negative "other," and together with Jakob's inability to honestly confront his own confused sexuality calls into question Bentham's masculinity. For, according to George L. Mosse's pioneering work on masculinity and modernity in Germany, "the male stereotype remained intact in spite of the structural changes that modern society experienced; . . . masculinity was in fact dependent upon a certain moral imperative; upon certain normative standards of appearance."[40] Bentham's hands that stroke his partner are described as "rather small, too small for the strong white arms,"[41] in other words, the physical representation of the gay and Jewish male is depicted as deviating from the normative standards of appearance, just as the entire scene of Jakob witnessing the two lovers underscores the violation of moral norms. Most importantly, still, Bentham's and his lover's nakedness at night in a public park turn Jakob, the observer, into a peeping—woman. Not only are the homosexuals thus at the margins of society, and clearly "others," but the German male protagonist is—via his forbidden homoerotic gaze—in danger of violating his own gender norms of hegemonic masculinity as well, since he finds himself in a "Gebüsch fur Frauen" ("bushes reserved for women"). Once again, German masculinity is threatened by means of the sexually enticing Jew, although the Jew is now male and homosexual. This subordination of the Jewish male against the backdrop of the current society's hegemonic masculinity functions both via his homosexuality and via his Judaism. Such a constellation is oddly reminiscent of "Girl with Lizard," the short story by Schlink, where the male and German observer is also emasculated via his gaze, yet the gaze in Schlink's text is directed at the Jewish female. Thus, even though Jewishness in Hacker's novel is no longer primarily associated with femininity, as in the earlier texts, it still bears many of the previously encoded marks of Jewish otherness and of emasculation along with subordination, while the representation of the Jewish male who is homosexual serves to underscore the stereotypically binary relationships of insider versus outsider, male versus effeminate, normal versus deviant, in opposition to the—previously "straight"—German male. Bentham, the Jewish homosexual, is thus an "other" twice over, and his male body is marked, accordingly, in opposition to the German.

In keeping with the import of power structures that are negotiated via gender relations in society, Frantz Fanon defines race as socially inscribed onto the male body in two distinct ways: first, via the "disempowerment by the Western colonial rhetoric," and, secondly, via the fear of emasculation, as Sander Gilman also explicates in *The Jew's Body*.[42] At stake here seems to be, for Jakob and Bentham, both the "colonial rhetoric" of a society that still, in contemporary settings, cannot tolerate homosexuals, as well as, for Jakob, a fear of emasculation that he associates with Bentham's homosexuality and his own, illicit homoerotic desire. Curiously, Jakob seems similarly incapable of coming to terms with his homoerotic and homosocial desire as Gustav von Aschenbach circa one century earlier. In the context of German perceptions of Jewish masculinity, the image of the Jew's body has, with Fanon, long functioned as a "counter-image" to that of the German, and Jewish masculinity was defined by referencing German masculinity as the master narrative. According to Gilman, the caste standards that define and legitimize racial difference thus construct a biological other as the secular product of the originally religious differences between Jews and Christians, or, by extension, between Jews and Germans.[43] Hence, the Jewish body was, in the German imagination, socially devalued as an ethical rhetoric which contrasted the darkness of the Jewish physical features with the lightness (morality and purity) of Aryan and hegemonic features. This discourse of race then, via the fear of emasculation, is transferred onto the discourse of gender in the following way. Both the construction of the Jewish male body and the German male body come at the expense of the female body, or, in the case of Hacker's text, the male homosexual who is subordinate. Emasculation as a means of domination and subordination presupposes an inherently negative quality in femaleness, translating this discourse into a subordination of women to men. Thus, the emasculation of the Jewish man is accomplished via the feminization of the Jewish body (as reflected in discourses surrounding circumcision), just as the anxieties of the German are transferred to the "self-hating" Jew. Hence, Jewish self-hatred, when represented from the perspective of Germans, takes on an entirely new, essentially anti-Semitic meaning, in the sense of stereotyping the other, as the figure of Bentham in Hacker's text reveals. Femininity and the homosexual male therefore both inhabit a space that is also linked with Jewishness and subordination. As a consequence, homosexuality is, in Hacker's text, marked as illicit and dangerous (to the straight German male). According to Sander Gilman, the medical discourse of physical and biological difference in previous, eighteenth- and nineteenth-century times clearly served to legitimize the inscription of otherness, domination, and racial and gender discrimination. What purpose, then, does the representation of the Jewish male as an "other" twice over in a popular contemporary novel by a young female German writer serve? As per our premise for this chapter, there is nothing culturally innocent about such inscriptions. Therefore, we might conclude that this depiction of the Jewish male as self-hating and homosexual, inhabiting a space reserved for femininity and subordination, is the only form of Jewish masculinity that is bearable or tolerable—to straight males such as Jakob, as well as to contemporary Germans. This disturbing notion is underscored via the explicit self-hatred that the figure of Bentham displays, and which appears to stem from both his Jewish otherness as well as his homosexual otherness. The representation of a Jewish male character, when cast as a self-hating other, is thus structurally comparable to the emergence of the image and self-image of the "black" Jew as described by Sander Gilman.[44] The otherness is, in the case of Bentham, furthermore conflated with his status as a victim that is not immediately linked with his Judaism, but rather with the premature death of his former lover.[45]

However, Bentham, the love object of Jakob, is not the only male Jewish character in the novel. There is also Andras, a Hungarian Jewish friend who stayed behind in Berlin. Andras is heterosexual and a former love interest of Isabelle's. Interestingly, Andras is the one who directly reflects on the possibility of Jewish life in contemporary Germany, whereas for Bentham, whose parents immigrated to Great Britain, this is not an issue he considers. "And is there such a thing as German-Jewish coexistence?" Andras muses, "I'm not at all sure there is."[46] Bentham appears to be more interested in the abstract ethics of the German restitution cases than in the prospect of how Germans and Jews might coexist peacefully, pointing to the fact that, as the child of

Holocaust survivors in exile, such a question may not carry relevance for him. Andras, on the other hand, does not openly live, or even disclose his Judaism, and, at least in conversation with Jakob, it seems of little relevance to him: "Who actually knows that I'm Jewish?" he asks, and concludes that it is not important since he himself does not exactly know what it means, and that he is, first and foremost, an exiled Hungarian.[47] The figure of Andras can thus be read in two distinct ways: once as a representation of a Jewish male who, on the surface, has successfully worked through the German-Jewish past and the trauma associated with this past. Owing to his enlightened, secular, assimilated, and contemporary lifestyle in present-day Germany, religion no longer plays a significant role, and, accordingly, Judaism is only relevant as a cultural heritage that he considers less pertinent than his Hungarian legacy. He is no longer a victim of today's Germans, who are mostly two to three generations removed from the Holocaust. Secondly, and this is perhaps a reading that the novel's context suggests, Andras could also be read as yet another male Jew whose Jewishness is, to a large extent, disguised, denied, and repressed. Neither Peter nor Isabelle, two of his closest friends, realize that Andras is Jewish, and the conversation with Jakob mainly serves to allay Jakob's negative feelings concerning Bentham. In other words, the purpose of the dialogue between a German and a Jewish male is acted out on the stage of Jakob's, the German male's, anxieties over the German past. Jakob has doubts both regarding the ethics of his involvement in the restitution cases that he is assigned to, as well as about his decision to live in London. Andras's concerns only matter insofar as he helps Jakob solve his problems. "And the fact that Israel exists makes me feel more comfortable about living here," Andras says in the same conversation.[48] Yet, Jakob does not engage with how or why Andras lives more securely in Germany due to Israel's existence. This could be a question of importance, especially since Jakob is purportedly interested in the morality of the restitution claims. Nor does Jakob ask any questions pertaining to Andras's relationship with Judaism. Accordingly, when Andras is first introduced as a character, he is determined by his relationship with Isabelle, and by his situation as a Hungarian refugee living with his aunt and uncle, and his Judaism is not addressed at this point. Even though the issue of Germans and Jews living in contemporary Germany is mentioned in Andras's dialogue with Jakob, it is not significant to the plot of the novel, or to any of the characters' development. Likewise, Andras's masculinity is not figurative to the plot of the novel. He showed some interest in Isabelle, but settled for another woman, Magda, suggesting that his masculinity is weak and subordinate (to the German protagonist). Yet, mostly, Andras's obscured Judaism and Jewish identity serve to underscore and emphasize the absence of the heterosexual Jewish male in today's Germany. This absence, in turn, recalls the notion of the Jew as victim. The story's disengagement with Andras's Jewish heritage is especially glaring when compared with the stark presence of Bentham's Judaism, which, incidentally, is also not religious, but paramount to the development of the plot and the characters of Jakob and Isabelle. After all, their "inability to love" is partly a result of the homoerotic bond between Jakob and Bentham.

Absence, Again

Taken all together, "Hacker's intergenerational dialogues and German-Jewish connections" do indeed "participate in a 'globalization' of the Holocaust," as Katharina Gerstenberger suggests, yet the moral implication of such participation for today's German and Jewish relationships needs to be fleshed out in more detail.[49] While it is, on the level of the plot, correct that "Bentham and Andras are not cast as victims," it is less evident that they are, indeed, "better equipped to deal with the challenges of post-modern society." I also question Gerstenberger's assertion that, in this novel, "gender and sexual difference have no political implications."[50] Such a statement is diametrically opposed to Kaja Silvermann's premise, a premise that holds true even if authors' intentions or the outward appearances of texts do not immediately or overtly communicate political intent. The implications of how Germans deal with the Holocaust past and the presence of Jews in today's Germany remain vast, and, due to the negatively typecast homosexuality of the visible Jewish male, intrinsically political. They are, as such, inherently tied up with representations of gender and sexuality. It might be astonishing that this is the case even for a recent, successful novel by a young writer. The setting of London can, along with the Hungarian cultural identity of one of the male Jewish characters, indeed be read as an effort to "globalize" the Holocaust. Yet, "globalization" is not an innately positive quality, and especially not when it comes to the issue of politics in literature. In Hacker's text, the Jewish male appears either disguised in his Jewishness (Andras), or emasculated (Bentham), and a victimized other in the imagination of the German, non-Jewish male. This meticulous attempt at "globalization" and suppression of the Jewish male might therefore originate from a German desire to relocate the acting out of German Holocaust guilt—to a place outside of Germany. Similarly, poverty, physical abuse, and trauma are all displaced in the character of five-year-old Sara, the abused and neglected girl next door, while the actual trauma that is haunting the Jewish protagonists (Bentham's Holocaust past, Andras's uneasy life in contemporary Germany) remains invisible. Just as Isabelle is incapable of helping the abused girl, the readers are not able to empathize with the characters most affected by the German past. Hacker's novel, while introducing readers to a terrifying world of moral void, along with an absence of empathy, and the main protagonists' inability to love, concomitantly performs this very absence and void. Yet, this text's purposefully constructed emotional and ethical emptiness requires our careful and deliberate deconstruction of such "globalized" and dislocated settings, in order to invoke and restore the readers' abilities to recover, and to relocate this text's deep-seated ethics and morality. As opposed to many of the other texts considered here, the narrative posture of purposeful disengagement can, if read carefully, point to the inherent problems in German memory discourses, rather than just reproducing them.

In order to think further about the German imagination of disguised or victimized Jewish masculinities, we need to consider the other novel by a young female writer depicting Jews and Germans. In the previous chapter, we determined Julia Franck's *Die Mittagsfrau* of 2007 (*The Blind Side of the Heart*) an important contributor to the discourse of Jewish femininity, particularly as it helps us reflect on representations of the "Jewish mother." In addition, and importantly for this chapter, Selma's mental illness is, insofar as the plot of the novel is concerned, rooted in yet another absence of the Jewish male. Selma's traumatic stillbirths and miscarriages of her four male offspring cause her obsessive compulsive hoarding disorder, her inability to love her daughters, and, ultimately, with Helene's trans-generational acting out, the abandonment of Peter, the second-generation German (Jewish) male. While the absence of the Jewish male in the first generation, that is, the stillbirths of the Jewish males, could still be rooted in the veracity of the overly dominant discourse of the hegemonic German male that functions to virtually erase and overshadow all "others," similar to the absences described in Walser's and Grass's texts as discussed in chapter 1, this particular absence appears to be coded differently for Peter and, hence, for the second-generation German Jew. For, the multiply overdetermined absence of any Jewish male in the first generation, in Franck's text, helps to precipitate the suppression of Peter's, the second generation's, Jewish identity. According to Halakha, Peter is clearly Jewish, since his mother is Jewish, even though his father is German and gentile. Likewise, Selma's children are Jewish, even though her husband is not. Finally, Helene is clearly Jewish, while Wilhelm is not only gentile but a German Nazi. Yet, Peter's affiliation with Judaism appears completely purged from the plot of the novel, as it is never mentioned, and does not seem to figure at all, especially when compared with the pronounced and visible Judaism of the females in the story. In the final portion of the narrative frame, when Peter looks inside the hollow of the fish, once his mother's remnant symbol for Judaism, he does not recognize its meaning. "Peter had looked at the fish for a long time, every evening he had opened it and looked inside, but there was nothing there, just a hollow space."[51] Just as the hollow inside of the fish, or shofar[52] (Katharina Gerstenberger suggests that the fish is a representation of a shofar although the text does not specifically indicate this) does not reveal any meaning for Peter, no matter how long he stares at it, his Judaism has vanished—in fact, it was never present in the first place. Because there was present, at one point, inside the hollow of the fish, a document indicating the last will of Selma's uncle Herbert, as well as a necklace. Neither one of these objects signifies Judaism.

Thus, while, as Gerstenberger observes, "the novel's main characters are female and Jewish,"[53] some of the male characters are also Jewish—yet, their Judaism is entirely disguised, or eradicated from the plot of the novel. What does this suppression of Peter's Judaism and Jewish heritage, then, mean for the discourse of the German memory vis-à-vis the Jewish male? It is especially interesting to consider this question since, presumably, the need to disguise Peter's Jewish heritage is no longer pertinent with the fall of National Socialism. In the absence of Peter's Judaism, or visible Jewish identity, we find the metaphysical representation of the historical loss of Jewish experience and identity in Germany. In other words, Peter's character embodies what most Germans experienced in their perception of Jews in Germany. After 1945, Jews were absent. With this particular staging of the figure of Peter, this absence does not get represented as a loss, even though, both in the case of Germany over the generations, and for Peter as Helene's son, the reference should rather be to the *loss* of Jews in Germany, and of Judaism for Peter. While "loss" signifies something that was once there, "absence" means it never existed in the first place. In Dominick LaCapra's evaluation of trauma, absence, and loss, we are reminded that an inadvertent *conflation* of absence and loss can have considerable and, at times, devastating consequences. While, according to LaCapra, the distinction of absence and loss cannot be construed as a binary, just as the difference of structural trauma and historical trauma evades such categorization, its conflation "involves the tendency to avoid addressing historical problems, including losses, in sufficiently specific terms or to enshroud, perhaps even to etherealize, them in a generalized discourse of absence."[54] And this is exactly what this text performs: by framing Peter's vanished Judaism as an absence rather than a loss (with the hollow of the fish as its stark, almost overdrawn, visual representation), the historical problem of the deportation and genocidal murder of the Jews by the Nazis is also eclipsed. At issue here is not that there is no representation of a real, living male Jewish character, as in Grass's text, where the "Jew" David Frankfurter appears only in his and Konny's digital and virtual imagination. In Franck's novel, it is instead the Judaism of the Jew that is disguised and eradicated, while Peter, the male character, is not only present in the narrative, but also functions as its focal point and textual frame reference. The fact that he survived, he is still there in post-1945 Germany, but his Judaism is absent, once more indicates the conflation of absence and loss, and of structural and historical trauma, while concurrently referencing the German perception of the absence of Jews in Germany after 1945. At the same time, the fact that Peter, still a child for most of the frame narrative, is not represented in his masculinity, serves to underscore this particular absence. Not only is he no longer Jewish, he is also not yet male.

This particular and renewed conflation of absence and loss in the more recent discourse on Germans and Jews is therefore even more significant than the mere absence of the Jewish male—as represented in the deaths of Selma's sons, or in Grass's and Walser's texts, or even the void in Dückers's novel. Hence, while the historical trauma of eliminating Jews from Germany might still have been at the root of the imagination of the absence of Jews of the first generation, and of generating the philo-Semitic/anti-Semitic representations of David Frankfurter and Andre Ehrl-König, respectively, with Peter, the issue has now shifted to signify the structural trauma of a fundamental and irrevocable loss of Judaism for today's Germany. The fact that this representation of structural trauma is mediated, in this text, via a Jewish male (albeit a child)—as opposed to the female—is furthermore significant in tracing male domination in both Judaism, where Orthodox and Conservative observances still favor men, and German masculinity cults, where, up to the second generation after the war, the predominant mode was that of uncontested male hegemony. This nexus, in turn, reflects the extent to which both Judaism and German nationality are still tied to images and imaginings of hegemonic masculinity. While second- and third-generation females are currently, after 1945, imagined as clearly Jewish, even if they are physically removed from Germany (Schneider's Jenny, Riedel's Sharon, Schlink's Sarah), the imagination of Jewish masculinity is called into question for second- and third-generation Germans.

Yet, Jewish males are not entirely absent or invisible in this story. *The Blind Side of the Heart* furthermore presents, with Carl Wertheimer, a male German and Jewish character. Carl is central to the plot in that he is the only true love of Helene, the protagonist. Since the account involving Carl Wertheimer centers on the time before Nazism and World War II, rendering him a contemporary of Helene, and a first-generation Jewish male, his Jewishness is not disguised, although the need to cover up any Jewish identity is a theme later on in the plot, due to Helene's half-Jewish heritage. Neither Carl nor his family appear to be observant, however, and as a student of philosophy, Carl is cast as a modern, enlightened, secularized, emancipated, and fully assimilated Jewish male who enjoys professional and financial independence. The liberalism of the Weimar Republic seems to afford Carl a carefree life. He is also described as ethically well grounded—in stark opposition to the Jewish females in this text, who are either promiscuous, or drug addicts, or lesbian, or a combination thereof. Yet, traits that also distinguish Carl are his effeminate physical features and personality. Both in bodily appearance and in temperament, we get to know Carl as soft, sensitive, and he does not at all emanate masculinity. Unlike Bentham, who, in spite of his homosexuality, is clearly cast as masculine in his diction and behavior (he drinks whiskey and talks little), Carl appears both boyish (childlike) and feminine in his life habits and physical presence. "Leontine . . . made him seem like a small child . . . his eyes were level with hers; his physique was that of a small boy," is how Helene describes Carl when they first meet.[55] In addition, he recites poetry by Else Lasker-Schüler,[56] invokes both his affinity for the suffering of Lenz by Georg Büchner[57] as well as his atheism,[58] and Helene enjoys the smell, smoothness, and softness of the fur collar of his coat, which immediately reminds her of Carl's Jewishness via her sister Martha: "how soft it was, how nice it smelled; a fur collar in the summer. Martha works at the Jewish Hospital."[59] Carl Wertheimer, Helene's true love, thus appears inconsistent in his masculinity, and where his effeminate traits are emphasized, they are immediately linked with his Jewishness, just as Daniel Boyarin describes: "In the antisemitic imaginary of Christian Europe (and perhaps Muslim Africa and Asia as well), male Jews have been represented traditionally as female."[60] Carl's boyish features that are indicative of his resisting masculinity rather than exhibiting specific feminine traits chime well with Boyarin's further observations that "the identification with women is epiphenomen of resisting manliness" (*Unheroic Conduct*, 11). Especially when compared with the hyper-masculinity of Wilhelm, the binary between the hegemonic German and the subordinate Jewish man is almost painful in its overdrawn generalization. This combined with the fact that there is no Jewish male that appears as a traditional, heterosexual man—in this text or any of the others under consideration here—functions to further emphasize Carl's childlike and effeminate qualities. If a Jewish man is represented as heterosexual, it seems, he needs to be coded as "other" in ways that undermine, suppress, and deny his masculinity.

Yet, putting the depiction of Carl as effeminate and subordinating hegemonic masculinity aside, his character might presumably still allow us to witness a firsthand story of Nazi persecution and deportation of a Jewish male. For with Carl, we finally do encounter the German memory of a Jewish male, one close to the center of the narrative on the eve of 1933. However, Carl dies mysteriously in 1932 in a bicycle accident. The accident is sudden, seems random, and, on the level of the plot, leaves Helene devastated. This calamity has the added effect of leaving the reader perplexed, since it appears as much of a surprise as the emergence of Edita Marwitz in Peter Schneider's *Eduard's Homecoming*. The *judaeus ex machina* function of Edita, as Mona Körte had originally conceived it for Feuchtwanger's eternal Jew, is comparable not so much to Carl as a figure, but to Carl's unexpected and, as it turns out, expedient, demise. For the bicycle accident, not a likely cause of death for a healthy young man at a time when motorists are not yet overpopulating streets, even in Berlin, here works to avoid the depiction of Carl's future fate as a Jewish male. Had Carl continued to live in Berlin after 1933, and especially after 1938, the narrative would have needed to broach different and more difficult issues pertaining to Jewish masculinity: the deportation and/or exile of a young German Jewish male, perhaps even of a young couple, on the eve of the Shoah.

My aim here is not to implicitly criticize the author for choosing a mode of character development that is flawed in some way, or that does not sufficiently dramatize or popularize the Holocaust. It would be wrong to expect a novel that is not meant or received to be a Holocaust memoir to become one in order to live up to some unsustainable claim for authenticity. By the same token, I am also not suggesting that the male Jewish characters in Hacker's novel should be portrayed differently. Rather, I am trying to uncover and bring to the fore an underlying discourse as it concerns the German engagement—or, as in the case of this text, sudden disengagement—with Jewish masculinity. The depiction of the Jewish males is, in the few cases that are on display, similarly broken—yet, not necessarily merely by depicting broken Jewish males. On the contrary, all male Jews appear as attractive and desirable men, well mannered, well spoken, and likable. Instead, the break lies in the modes of representation or in the positions they inhabit in their respective narratives: they all appear marginalized, "othered," feminized, or emasculated. In the case of Carl, we additionally encounter a sudden disappearance of the Jewish male, exactly coinciding with the beginning of the more severe persecution of Jews in Germany. This, combined with the fact that we do not come across any of the Jewish characters, male or female, being deported or living in a camp, creates the illusion that Jews suddenly vanished, were no longer visible, with the exception of Helene, who has to have her identity forged, but is otherwise not immediately or physically suffering Nazi persecution. This notion of the vanishing of visible male Jews might be close to the lived experience of many Germans at the time, as Jews living in Germany and not (yet) deported had to hide their Jewishness soon after 1932. Yet, since this is a text primarily concerned with the current German *memory* of Jews and Germans, this void does leave a bitter side taste—albeit not immediately to the reader, as the reader is not made to empathize with any male Jewish character. The lone exception to this peculiar absence of male Jews in the wake of the Holocaust can be found towards the end of the narrative, when Helene and Peter look for mushrooms, and the stench and sounds of the trains, presumably full of deportees, causes an eerie and disturbing sensation in both Peter and the reader. Helene imagines Martha among the deportees, and the trauma of this vision leads her to nearly abandon Peter for the first time: "Helene saw Martha in the cattle truck, she saw Martha's bare feet slipping on the excrement, trying to find somewhere firm to stand, she heard the groaning of the people crammed into the trucks . . . ," and later "Helene was not to be deterred. She just went on."[61] It is therefore, once again, Helene's trauma over the Holocaust that ultimately leads her to abandon her son.

German masculinity and Jewish masculinity in contemporary texts referencing the memory and trauma of the German Holocaust past range from the foil of German hyper-masculinity, serving as the backdrop for previous, hegemonic Nazi masculinity, to images and imaginings of damaged, weakened, effeminate, homosexual, or absent masculinities. Within second- to third-generation representations, the injuries to German masculinities are caused either by more remotely mediated Holocaust guilt (as depicted in Grass's Paul Prokiefke), or more directly by Jewish women (as in the cases of the German male protagonists in Schlink, Schneider, and Riedel), their repetition exposing anxieties over anti-Semitism and gender that point to a sustained and deep structural trauma that has not yet been worked through. Surprisingly, this pattern is still to be found in more recent accounts of German men (Hacker, Franck). Contrary to expectations, constructions of Jewish males, when represented in recent texts by younger writers, are not portrayed altogether negatively, do not appear overly stereotyped, and are occasionally cast more sympathetically than their German counterparts (Franck, Hacker), signaling a change from the depiction of Jewish masculinity in Walser's text, where the male Jew was portrayed unambiguously negatively and laden with anti-Semitic stereotypes. Yet, the position of Jews in more recent narratives is usually that of the marginalized "other" vis-à-vis the German gentile protagonists. This notion is especially pronounced in the character Bentham in Hacker's story, but also in Julia Franck's construction of the characters Carl and Andras. In Franck's text, Jewish characters or their Jewish traits disappear entirely, shielding the reader from fully engaging the memories of Jewish masculinities past and present. All Jewish males are furthermore portrayed as more or less tragic figures who are unable to love or to be loved. Bentham's former lover had died catastrophically, Andras settles for Magda even though he really loves Isabelle, Carl dies before he can announce his engagement to Helene, and Peter, who is in any case not depicted as Jewish, is presumably damaged for life by the cruelty of his Jewish mother. Thus, to return to the premise for this chapter, taking the cultural expressions of such psychopathologies of German and Jewish masculinities seriously suggests a current and ongoing need in German contexts to repress, marginalize, and pathologize Jewish males—especially in their relationships with gentile partners (regardless of whether they are male homosexuals or females). At the same time, the image and imagination of German masculinity vis-à-vis Jewish identity and especially Jewish femininity is not culturally innocent. Damaged German males function to elicit sympathy, and their inability to love—the Jewish "other" as in all of the texts considered here—is systemic and telling of a deep cultural anti-Semitism that is particularly insidious because it is not immediately visible in the characters themselves.

Chapter 4

✦

Jews and Germans in America

"The black guy had a muscular neck with a pronounced Adam's apple. Kalf's thumbs found purchase there and he pressed it hard to the sound of a shrill scream."[1] This particular scene, reminiscent of a film shot, where a young African American male is portrayed in the most stereotypically racist terms as a thuglike criminal, would be disturbing in any context. The African American male is here assaulted for conspiring against and ultimately killing a white man and ally of the German, gentile protagonist Niklas Kalf. In a work of literature, such a rendering might be palatable if it is clearly set apart via irony, or any other rhetorical device, as a textual element to be critically examined. Yet in Thomas Hettche's 2006 novel *Woraus wir gemacht sind* (*What We Are Made of*, 2008), the entire nexus of German guilt over the Holocaust is set in a phantasmagoric and cinematic display of post-9/11 America that does not exhibit literary devices that could evoke critical distance. The text as a whole thus raises a host of questions pertaining to the representation of Germans vis-à-vis Jews and African Americans as they are displaced to America. Parallel with the Bush administration's plans announcing the invasion of Iraq, the plot's unabashedly positivistic and cheerful image of America conversely retraces the trajectory of European disenchantment over the American war path, and is turned into its frightening and nightmarish opposite. When the pregnant German girlfriend of the German protagonist Kalf is kidnapped in America, he is blackmailed to release secret materials on a Jewish scientist who, before 1933, went into exile to escape the Nazis. Although working on a biography about this scientist, Kalf is not in possession of the materials, so he embarks on a voyage through the United States reminiscent of that of Peter Handtke's protagonist in *Der kurze Brief zum langen Abschied* (*Short Letter, Long Farewell*).[2] Handtke's introspective narrative of 1972 offers dreamlike sequences that trace and retrace the protagonist's search for his ex-partner Judith and his escape from her violent threats. Incidentally, in spite of the name "Judith," the narrative does not indicate whether or not she is Jewish. The physical space of America and the protagonist's introverted observations of that space finally enable the couple's successful separation. The extent to which the threats by Judith and Handtke's protagonist's encounters with her are real even on the level of the plot, or whether they belong mostly to the realm of dreams and imagination is purposely ambiguous, as is the image and imagination of America as a physical location. Hence, in spite of the dated narrative techniques (the device of "new subjectivity" seems as overdrawn as the self-indulgent portrayal of the protagonist's "crisis of masculinity" is excessively put on display), Handtke's text provides an exceptional account of successful "working through" of past trauma, rather than acting out, here especially as it concerns the protagonist's unsettled past with his ex-lover. America, in 1972, served as an ambivalent foil that enables the protagonist's geographically and emotionally erratic, yet ultimately productive, quest for resolution. However, in contrast to the introspective travelogue in Handke's narrative, roughly three and a half decades later, Hettche's text maps out instances of—presumably involuntary—racism (the kidnappers appear to be exclusively African American) and anti-Semitism (the Jewish widow of the scientist is a key player in the conspiracy responsible for the kidnapping). After German unification, America turns into a negative utopian, or dystopian site against which long-repressed German sentiments appear to be, in Dominick LaCapra's terms, "acted out," rather than "worked through." Furthermore, the stark visual and cinematographic imagery of a German white male who finds himself threatened and physically attacked by African Americans seems to evoke the notion of the (African) American male as an evil, threatening "other," particularly since the plot of the novel is set after 9/11 and on the eve of the Bush administration's invasion of Iraq. This stunningly racist and negative representation in Hettche's novel moves German-Jewish relations and the issues surrounding the German representation of Jews and of Holocaust guilt into the contested space of German-American relations. German Jewish writers Maxim Biller and Edgar Hilsenrath already pointed to the import of the question of the role and function of America within contemporary German memory culture when they wrote their satirical novels *Fuck America!* (re-released 2003; original *Bronsky's Geständnis*, 1980) and *Harlem Holocaust* (1998), thus showcasing the space of refuge that America provided to Jews dealing with postwar German memory culture.[3]

Of course, not all recent German texts invoking America articulate instances of anti-Semitism or racism. As is well documented, America in the German imagination has long served as the physical and imaginary location to act out both utopian and dystopian fantasies.[4] The more positive and emphatic forms of such acting out (most prominently in film and literature) concerned societal, political, and psychological aspirations of German (national) identity formation that proved impossible to materialize within the geographic, cultural, and political boundaries that defined "Germany." Likewise, German images and imaginings of the New World have included somberly negative projections of distaste and anxiety. As Dan Diner convincingly summarizes, "'America' mirrors negatively one's own anxieties of death, positively hopes for the future are nourished. In their effects those images persist; they reach from premodern times far into the 20th century."[5] Nineteenth-century literature in particular produced a plethora of opposing and divergent German love-hate representations of America. Because America has repeatedly functioned as a long-standing site for images and imaginings of political love and admiration on the one hand, as well as of hate and repulsion (of American barbarism, American capitalism, etc.) on the other, much of the scholarship on German-American relations, already during the 1990s, yields detailed and rich stories of this binary projection that, for the postwar period, peaked during the 1960s and 1970s.[6] West German and East German writers such as Rolf Dieter Brinkmann or Günter Kunert offer ambivalent and emotional accounts during the Cold War period, where America serves as a contested space for images and imaginings of adoration and disgust—and as a space that is imagined as a fixed "other," visible, for example, in the title of his *Der andere Planet* (1974, *The Other Planet*), a travelogue by Günter Kunert.[7] Interestingly, these binary projections, of which the previously mentioned narrative by Peter Handtke is a more sober example, continue well beyond the years of German unification, and are not always neatly aligned with writers' textual or political aspirations. Rather, divergent fantasies and projections are frequently found within the utterances of one single author, pointing to the ambivalence (rather than binary) that pertains to the attitudes of several different writers regardless of generational, political, or gender affiliations. These conflicting emotions persist throughout different times in history, that is, they are not merely reflections of postwar insecurities or Cold War alignments. Hans Magnus Enzensberger, German intellectual wunderkind par excellence, can serve as a prominent example for such an ambivalent projection that often sets up a false dichotomy between American politics and the American people. While Enzensberger adored the American poet William Carlos Williams and other American writers, as well as "the American people," he was highly critical of the Vietnam War and American government in general. In 1962, Enzensberger wrote of Williams and contemporary American poets that they will turn American English into a poetic language that can be understood throughout the world, a poetic "world language,"[8] and only six years later he resigned from a fellowship at Wesleyan University, publicizing a statement where he considered the ruling class in America as dangerous to the population.[9] Given this assessment, it seems especially incongruous that this same Enzensberger made headlines in 2003 as one of the few German leftist defenders of the American invasion in Iraq, adding yet another twist to the binary love-hate projections.[10] The case of Enzensberger might be one that is extreme, but it showcases the persistent ambivalence of many intellectuals' engagements with America, and indicates how the roots of such ambivalence are usually tangled up with conflicting emotions concerning German identity and the German past. Notwithstanding contradictory assessments on the parts of German intellectuals, scholarly and essayistic contributions on the subject of America might additionally have helped to sustain this particular discourse unknowingly, by reiterating the tempting but ultimately reductive binary of love versus hate projections.

One of the most acute and most vastly popularized examples of the more affirmative collective German fantasies of America, yet one that contains deep ambivalence as well, can be found in the adventure novels of the illustrious and enormously successful German writer Karl May (1842–1912).[11] In his particularly well-known fictional travelogues, German colonial fantasies of the nineteenth century find their expression in the notoriously heroic, Protestant, and chauvinistic domination of the German (white) male over the Native American (or Muslim, occasionally Asian) savage "other." May wrote twenty-five of his adventure novels between 1892 and 1899 alone, mostly while in jail in Saxony for petty criminal offenses. Considering the subject of German anti-Jewish sentiment, the most decisive point of reference with May's texts is not, as might be expected, the fact that Karl May was one of Hitler's favorite German authors, even though this is a remarkable confluence. It is also not to be found predominantly in the immense and sustained popular success of Karl May's writings, bringing his novels in some proximity to today's winners of the German Book Prize (Hettche's novel was a close finalist in 2006), where popular success is also a major consideration. Of course Karl May's accomplishment is culturally significantly more relevant since his publishing success was sustained over many decades, and not initiated by a jury or other body or normative panel of judges, as is the case with the German Book Prize. Rather, the key point of comparison for this analysis concerns the theme of "the German" attempting to sustain a moral victory over a racial "other" in the face of previously uncharted "wild" territory (America), as it is on display in so many of May's fictional texts. Katrin Sieg's 2002 study *Ethnic Drag* compellingly reveals the import of Karl May and the Winnetou myth, particularly for West German discourses of nationality, race, and gender.[12] May's writings, while overtly pursuing a pacifist, moral, and empathetic practice of encountering—and colonizing—Native Americans, and painting Winnetou, the noble savage, in condescendingly positive terms, actually reveal deeply rooted xenophobic and anti-Semitic sentiments that can be traced back to an anti-Enlightenment message that is part of the package of Karl May's novels as well as long-standing German colonial fantasies. Hartmut Lutz's essay on "German Indianthusiasm" explicates this phenomenon, particularly for the most popular series of Karl May's novels, that is, the ones set in America.[13] The German colonial fantasy of creating, with "Old Shatterhand," a German male character who could defy the realities of the Berlin conference of 1884, where Germany received only a small portion of its "place in the sun" when Africa was distributed among the Western colonial powers, provided the reading public with a German hero they could identify with, and one that allowed an escape from the harsh realities of contemporary German politics. According to Lutz, the imperialist imaginings of a benevolent, steadfast, strong, and heroic leader afforded Germans, via Old

Shatterhand, a role model that led German ethnocentrism "from the Kaiserreich via Nazi times to today." Lutz's important argument concludes that this proto-German, Siegfried-like figure and his Native American counterpart Winnetou—who, as the noble savage par excellence, of course admires and happily adopts those beautiful German and Christian values—indicates the Indianthusiasm that created ethnicity as a blood-based, anti-Enlightenment ideology that served the construction of self-aggrandizing German nation-building via the exclusionary racism against a religious and ethnic "other." The close ties with anti-Semitism as they appear embedded in this particular ideology are obvious: "The *Indianer* as the external other, who, from a safe distance, loves the self, would compensate and cover up for the internal other whom the self could then hate and annihilate."[14] Particularly interesting for our analysis, continuing along the lines of Lutz's arguments, is the fact that it is precisely the notion of loss and inferiority compared with other (nations) and resulting xenophobic anxieties that first provoked the colonial fantasies as they are articulated in May's texts, ultimately resulting in an ideology of exclusion and self-aggrandizement that is based almost entirely on imaginings and fantasies of German hyper-masculinity (depicted in the character Old Shatterhand). At the same time, America functions as *the* primary utopian location where those fantasies are acted out—particularly as it concerns putting the positive and heroic external other on vivid display. This is crucial when we think about mechanisms of anti-Semitism in contemporary Germany, where, albeit in different historical and cultural contexts, a positive external "other" is often used to cover up internal anxieties resulting from German guilt and shame. This link becomes especially pertinent considering that already Max Horkheimer astutely observed the conflation of anti-Americanism and anti-Semitism during the Weimar Republic: "everywhere where there is anti-Americanism, anti-Semitism spreads."[15]

Hence, while the more obviously negative images and imaginings of America seem to point more directly to German trauma and anxiety over political and cultural developments at home, even the outwardly positive representations of America and Americans—as they were so prominently put on display already over a century ago by the fashionable novels of Karl May, novels that continue to be popular well into the latter part of the post-World War II period—reveal deep-seated German anxieties. My investigation in this chapter considers both the positive and the negative stereotyping of American culture, politics, and physical, geographic landscape by contemporary Germans, to study the Germans' more recent widespread conflation of America with Jewishness. I read this conflation in the context of the geographic space of "America" as the physical and imaginary site to locate an ethnic "other." My critical examination does not merely follow the binary construction of love versus hate images, or retrace notions of images of the self versus images of the other, but rather explore positive and negative representations with the assumption that both result from underlying ambivalences that, ultimately, refer back to German concerns with German identity. Thus, my analysis yields insights into the reasons for the merging of two separate long-standing cultural tropes, that of the images and imaginings of Jewishness, and that of the ambivalent images and imaginings of America in order to ultimately determine whether, and if so, how today's Jews are still considered ethnic or racial "others," and what their displacement to America means for the notion of Jews in Germany today. This question is especially fraught since the displacement of Jews to America is an anti-Semitic projection referring back to common tropes of stigmatization prevalent during Weimar Germany, as Dan Diner and others have shown. Taking into consideration the nineteenth-century construction of the Other as Jewish *and* black, or, in Sander Gilman's terms, as "white negroes,"[16] on display in Hettche's novel, adds another disturbing dimension to this particular setting. For the first part of this chapter, some of the texts analyzed in previous chapters will serve as examples of how America functions as a site to project external philo-Semitic images and imaginings that point to German anxieties over anti-Semitism, as well as guilt rejection reflexes and political disillusionment. In the second part of the chapter, then, the dystopian elements concerning America and German imaginings of Jews, as they are on display in Hettche's text, but also visible in Katharina Hacker's *The Have-Nots*, and in a short story by Gregor Hens, will be considered. While, at first glance, America as a dystopia might provide a more obvious and conventional analytical model, the texts and contexts in which these dystopian fantasies appear are all but predictable.

Utopian Space, or The Philo-Semitic Imaginary

The fact that philo-Semitism is no less problematic than its presumed opposite, anti-Semitism, and merely reveals poorly concealed anti-Semitism is by now well established within anti-Semitism research. As a stereotype, its suggestion of an unambiguously positive stance makes it potentially insidious, particularly as the philo-Semitic imagination predictably does not represent an individual's experience of the reality of contemporary Jewish life. Adam Sutcliffe summarizes this relationship compellingly: "Alongside anti-Semitism, it is a form of 'allosemitism': the view that Jews are, in some sense, radically different or exceptional."[17] In some of the prominent German narratives analyzed here, philo-Semitism furthermore seems intrinsically linked to images and imaginings of America (with imaginary projections filling in for real lived experience), and this association is vividly exhibited in texts that imagine German Jews living in happy prosperity—in America. Another philo-Semitic fantasy concerns the "love" relationship between a male German protagonist and an American and Jewish woman who is in various stages of displacement.

Beyond exposing German male fantasies, and psychopathologies concerning the conflations of Germans and their anxieties vis-à-vis a Jewish other as considered in the previous chapters, Schlink's "The Circumcision" establishes a curious tie between Jewishness, femininity, and America as a geographic location. This text is therefore exemplary not only regarding gender assignments, but also as it concerns representations of space and place. New York City is the physical space where the "love" story in "The Circumcision" is acted out, and Sarah is American. This setting might be coincidental and, essentially, be rooted in the historical fact that comparatively few Jews reside in today's Germany, and therefore American Jews, as they appear in German public and cultural life, are more visible, even to Germans, than German Jews might be. While this relatively benign circumstance is worth taking into consideration, it is also called into question by Jeffrey Peck's study of 2006,[18] where the exterior visibility of Jews in Berlin is widespread and a source of newfound multicultural pride. More importantly, the gender paradigm where a German, gentile male is cast opposite a Jewish American female is common in other recent literary texts depicting German-American and German-Jewish relations. As chapters 2 and 3 indicate, the novels by Peter Schneider and Susanne Riedel as well as Schlink's *The Reader* provide similar articulations. Therefore, this spatial dislocation can, indeed, be read as paradigmatic to a German cultural imagination in the context of German-Jewish relations, rather than merely reflecting the perception of an absence of Jews in Germany today. Furthermore, exploring the link between space and memory in these texts will add an important dimension to current considerations of the relationship of space and memory in the Berlin Republic.

The detailed analysis of Schlink's short story in chapter 3 disclosed a central and intricate relationship between German masculinities and gendered anti-Semitism, exposing the persistence of Judeophobia, homophobia, and misogyny in contemporary Germany. Yet, the function of America as a corporeal space for the development of the plot in "The Circumcision" (vis-à-vis Germany) and, with Sarah, as a gendered space where the female Jew resides, has thus far been eclipsed, also from this analysis. It appears that America, in this text by Schlink, clearly functions as the space where (female) Jews reside, and, increasingly throughout the course of the narrative, with the distinct purpose of reminding Germans of their repressed guilt and shame. In *The Reader*, this spatial relationship appears even more conspicuously on display, even though it is merely Hanna's victims' daughter, a German Jew, who resides in New York City at the end of the plot. It is she who is to provide absolution for Hanna—and thus for Michael Berg. "The daughter lived in New York on a street near Central Park."[19] After a brief conversation between Michael Berg and the daughter (where the daughter, a Holocaust survivor, is described as elegant and "ageless," but never referred to by name, as Ernestine Schlant already noted), the daughter decides to donate the money that Hanna Schmitz left to the American-based Jewish League Against Illiteracy.[20] But whether the conversation between Michael Berg and the daughter does, indeed, amount to a representation of Dan Diner's "negative symbiosis," as

Schlant's thoughtful analysis suggests, or whether the much more extensive portrayal and naming (!) of the daughter in Stephen Daldry's Hollywood rendition of this scene functions to certify Berg's victimhood, as William C. Donahue's brilliant reading shows,[21] in both instances "America" is decidedly the location where the Jewish woman resides, and where she has the power to grant—or refuse—absolution to the German male concerning his transgenerational Holocaust guilt.

Sarah, the female Jewish protagonist in "The Circumcision," repeatedly and directly performs a similar role when she accesses and unleashes Andi's obscured memories of family guilt and shame, and it seems that this is, in fact, the only task that she completes for Andi, the German male protagonist. As such, the presence of a female Jew in America (a site apart from Germany, yet intimately and ambivalently intertwined with it) could yield promising and desirable results for the German character in the form of Sarah's actions as those of a therapeutic interventionist who might allow Andi to articulate some of his mixed feelings concerning the German past. The promise of the location of America as a utopian "other," a space unburdened with the immediacy of German-Jewish history, could thus present an unambiguously positive and important site for the German and gentile protagonist. And indeed, the beginning of the short story seems to yield this possibility. Andi finds himself at the end of a bar mitzvah, and reflects upon the events of the celebration. Yet, when "Uncle Aaron" addresses him by telling the story of his family's legacy, and asks about his father's whereabouts during the war, Andi begins to retreat. The full extent of Andi's hurt feelings is visible when he later talks to Sarah about the presumed reasons why Uncle Aaron had shared his family's history. Andi's presumption is that they, Sarah's Jewish relatives, sought to make Andi feel guilty about being German.

> [Sarah:] "He told you our family history so you'd know who you're dealing with." After a while he asked, "Why didn't he want to know who you're dealing with?" . . . [Sarah]: "What's wrong? . . . Why should they pester you to tell your story? They know you're German."[22]

This dialogue foreshadows the main frontiers of their arguments, in that it establishes and at the same time solidifies the opposition of German versus Jewish and American. This binary inscription is repeated several times throughout the narrative, when Andi encounters Sarah's American friends, when Sarah encounters Andi's uncle (the symmetry of the two uncles, not fathers, performing the roles of chauvinistic interrogators on both Andi's and Sarah's side is inadvertently comical), and, finally, when Andi feels that he has to leave Sarah due to their unbridgeable differences. In all cases, American identity is merged with Jewish identity in order to oppose Andi's non-Jewish German identity. Yet, absent from this binary opposition is any attempt on either Sarah's or Andi's part to turn this binary into a productive quest for resolution, much less utilize it to facilitate any progressive interventions or dialogues. On the contrary, the text performs the antagonism of German versus Jewish American relentlessly in the delineation of increasingly heated arguments between Andi and Sarah, culminating when Andi asks the Americans in his office whether an adult male wishing to convert to Judaism had to be circumcised.[23] It is then that Andi decides to get circumcised—but not to convert, or to seek to understand Judaism. Andi's act of leaving Sarah to go home, literally and metaphorically, albeit with a mutilated penis and damaged masculine identity, therefore comes as no surprise also in this context. America is cast as the unambiguous space where female Jews reside to pass judgment over German males. The philo-Semitic imagination of America as a contested, perhaps utopian site to work through German guilt and shame of the past is therefore merely a lure, and a trap, that utilizes its attractive surface, an anti-American discourse brilliantly exposed in Jean Baudrillard's *America* of 1986, to entice the German male.[24] Once the honest, purportedly repentant German seeks to attach himself to America and/or the Jewish woman, she reveals her actual disposition, displaying a promiscuity and femininity that cruelly permeates and at the same time impedes the German's quest for resolution. These conflations of female, Jewish, and American characteristics work as a triple bind to reinforce stereotypical imagery espoused by long-standing tropes of cultural labeling in each of the three categories. At the same time, this nexus taps into anti-Semitic and sexist stereotypes such as that of the Jewish American Princess, which might not be too familiar to the average German reader, but which loom large in the American popular culture discourse.[25] Nevertheless, the oppositions of Jewish, American, and female versus gentile, German, and male seem much less coincidental, or even circumstantial, if we consider the cultural settings within which those tropes function. For this outwardly philo-Semitic yet intrinsically anti-Semitic cultural labeling to be of import, we need to discern if and how the binary, and ultimately, anti-Semitic, opposition of the Jewish American female versus the gentile German male holds true for contemporary German narratives beyond those by Bernhard Schlink. As is expected from previous analyses, the binary inscriptions show similar patterns in both Peter Schneider's *Eduard's Homecoming* as well as in Susanne Riedel's *Eine Frau aus Amerika* (*A Woman from America*). Since both texts have been analyzed extensively in chapters 2 and 3, I here merely touch upon the relevant points of comparison with the paradigmatic short story by Schlink.

Eduard Hoffmann's German masculinity is again cast in opposition to Jewish American female identity. This time it is the representation of both Jenny, his American wife, and of Edita Marwitz, who is German and Jewish in origin but now resides in Florida. While most of the novel is set in Berlin, the site of America thus functions as a foil, or a physical "other" that is meant to juxtapose the German site. Especially with the appearance of Edita Marwitz, America visibly serves as the physical location where the German past can, ostensibly, be recovered and resolved. In contrast to Bernhard Schlink's or even Peter Handtke's texts, Schneider's novel therefore appears outright unambiguously utopian and positivist when it comes to representing America. On the other hand, Jenny, the Jewish American woman, is characterized by her emancipated yet aloof and mocking behavior, and by her beauty (compare *la belle Juive*). This more ambiguous portrayal mainly serves to typecast her as a female Jew. She is furthermore depicted as American when she despises "typical German" expressions such as "Halt!" "Stehenbleiben!" "Achtung!" and "Schnell, schnell!" all of which Eduard dutifully bans from his vocabulary. It is interesting that Jenny does not appear as American in any way that does not reference Germany and its Nazi past. She is frequently described as American, and remains in America for much of the narrative, even though her early childhood was spent near Rome, as she is the daughter of an Italian father and a German-Jewish (!) mother. Hence, her American identity seems altogether tied up with her position vis-à-vis the German male, much like that of Schlink's Sarah. Both "America" and American identity in this text seem to function merely as a spatial placeholder for the "other," particularly as it concerns the location and identity of Jenny. While Schlink's Sarah resides in New York, and is surrounded by her American friends and family, Jenny is depicted as culturally and spatially isolated from her American surroundings (we only meet her when she is with Eduard in Berlin), adding to the impression of her American identity as remote, even while it is persistently verbally invoked. This particular construction of the "stereotypical American," a representation that is actually void of any immediate or distinct features that render her American, underscores the notion of "America" as an imaginary location, a utopian space where Jewish-German relations can, ostensibly, be addressed. However, as the earlier analysis indicates, the relevant issues between Eduard and Jenny are not attended to in the course of this narrative, and the stereotypical invocation of Jenny's Jewishness alongside her femininity merely serves to whitewash Eduard's past. Thus, in this setting, the construction of American identity without American characteristics is reminiscent of what Henryk Broder, in 2003, termed, for Germany, the appearance of anti-Semitism without Jews, and thus anti-Semitism without anti-Semites.[26] His contention is that contemporary Germans, not aware of any contemporary German Jews—since they are largely not discernible—obscure their latent anti-Semitic feelings, and are consequently also not visibly anti-Semitic. Broder's argument is that the anti-Semitism without anti-Semites ultimately produces more and more severe anti-Semitic acting out, since concealed resentment is more difficult to grasp and address than any sentiments that are explicitly and publicly voiced. Likewise, Jenny's American identity that is repeatedly declared but not enacted by her character becomes more visible through this absence, especially in light of the concurrent invocation of her prominent "Jewish characteristics." The meaning of America as a utopian space, by means of its very negation, therefore inadvertently aids in displaying German philo-Semitism, in this text conveyed via the "American" exterior of Jenny, the Jewish female, who is desirable and beautiful. The German protagonist's inability to love, a core theme of the entire novel, manifests itself when he is faced with an attractive "other" that appears to provide resolve, but consistently negates and rejects this possibility on several levels. She, too, entices via her exterior beauty, but does not provide resolution.

This emphasis on America as an imaginary, utopian space apart, a space where German guilt and shame are negotiated and ultimately eradicated, is accentuated when Edita Marwitz, the *German* Jewish Holocaust survivor, enters the plot as a *judaeus ex machina* (compare Mona Körte, chapter 2). It is interesting that Marwitz, clearly cast as German, voluntarily speaking German with Eduard when he visits, is residing in Florida, however, she is not coded as American.[27] Her function in *Eduard's Homecoming* is eerily similar to Schlink's Jewish Holocaust survivor in New York, to provide absolution to the German protagonist. Yet, presumably, Edita's American identity should be equally pertinent as that of Jenny, since she has lived in Florida for decades, just as Jenny had lived in California since "the early 1960s."[28] This particular depiction therefore confirms how America as a utopian space is used deliberately and vicariously as a means to devise a guilt-free German past. It seems, in this context, that the deus ex machina–like appearance of Edita is made possible via the philo-Semitic imagination of the forgiving Jew, imported directly from America. Adding to these layers of iconoclastic hyperbole in the imagination of America as the site of German guilt obliteration is the novel's suggestion that not only was Eduard's grandfather not culpable with respect to his involvement in Nazi property confiscations, but he was also in love with Edita, the Jewish woman. Eduard's inability to love Jenny properly and satisfy her sexually is thus magically revoked after his visit to America. Now that the Jewish woman, located in the utopian space of America, away from the burdened space of Germany, has revoked his guilt, he, too, can properly love Jenny, the American Jew. The philo-Semitic imagination of the Germans' resolved past has, via America, come full circle. America serves as the space for forgetting and erasing the painful German past, and the woman in/from America is there merely to aid the German protagonist in this mission.

Predictably, Susanne Riedel's *A Woman from America* seems to follow a similar pattern. This text takes the imagination of America as the site of wishful philo-Semitic projections even one step further: Hannes, the German protagonist, is lured into believing that Sharon, his life partner of thirty years (!), is an American Jew, when, as it turns out, she is actually German and Jewish. In contrast to Schneider's Jenny, much of the plot in *A Woman from America* revolves around Sharon's specifically "American" characteristics, and German-American differences are the focal theme in this text. While Jenny is revealed to be German early on in Schneider's story, but labeled American, Sharon is both labeled and presumed American, and the disclosure of her German identity—after her death and at the very end of the narrative—indicates a significant shift in the reader's perception—of her and of the representation of America. While in the previously discussed novels, the depiction of America is more consistently positive regarding its location of a utopian site to redress German Holocaust guilt, the Germans' disillusionment regarding America's status as a political and economic superpower after the attacks of September 11, 2001 in this novel introduces a new element of instability. This instability concerns both the identity of Sharon, the "American" Jew who suddenly dies, and America as a positively coded space. German disillusionment and American vulnerability could therefore, in this narrative, help create a new level of reflection where the previous binary relationship enters a more dynamic, open, and productive stage, one where "working through" reductive binaries and the German past might finally be possible. Indeed, the explicit revelation of Sharon as a German Jew could aid in this reading, since it points to the very constructedness of the image of the figure Sharon, and with that of the image of the Jewish American woman, and of America writ large. In Schneider's text, Jenny's German origins are largely hidden, and only a careful reader will notice them, whereas Hannes's discovery of Sharon's Germanness takes center stage: "She is one of the German children who no longer have parents because their parents were turned into soap," is what Hannes ponders when he discovers her true identity, and then continues, "the awful thing is that it changes everything."[29] The representation of America as a utopian space where German males can find absolution from Holocaust guilt, and the disturbing philo-Semitic imagination that this representation engenders, seem to have been called into question. For, if America is now turned into a more fluid, contested space, and the unambiguous American Jew's identity is no longer truly "American," the parameters are, indeed, changed. Instead of constructing an "American" without American characteristics, as Jenny in Schneider's narrative, this novel imagines exaggerated American characteristics—without actually being American. America is, once again, represented as an invented space, and one where identities of Jewish women are both staged and questioned—by German males.

Yet, while the death of Sharon as an American, rather than just the death of Sharon, could open up this text, allowing for such a more productive reading, the story's twist revealing Sharon to be German yields yet another interpretation. Not only Sharon, the American, dies at the pinnacle of the arguments concerning German-American differences, but in retrospect also Sharon, the German Jew. The German disillusionment with and questioning of America thus seems to invoke notions of latent anti-Semitism that are, at this point, no longer masked as philo-Semitism set in the utopian space of America. While Hannes and the other Germans present at Sharon's death might have assumed that their rants contributed to the demise of an American Jewish woman, it was, first and foremost, a German Holocaust survivor who perished. Hence, the question that Hannes and the text leave unanswered, is, what exactly changes so radically with Hannes's discovery of

Sharon's German origins? The reader can merely speculate that it is Hannes's feelings of guilt and shame that change. Might the demise of an American and Jewish woman have been less troubling than the decease of a German Jewish woman? If so, then America merely functions as a transient placeholder to disguise the fact that, in spite of the repeated and pertinent invocation of America, American identity, and American characteristics in this text, this story is, ultimately, again merely concerned with German identity and German guilt and shame. After his discovery of Sharon's identity, Hannes muses, "Until I left America, I did not realize that the motionlessness of the images is not mercy, but a sin."[30]

Hence, America functions as a spatial venue to stage the conclusion that, for Hannes, overcoming German guilt and shame is not possible. The construction of America as an open, contested space where Jewish women's identity is fluid, changeable, and transient aids in the construction of this particular German imagination. While in the case of Schneider's novel, the positively coded space of America produced forgetting of the German past, the more ambivalently coded incantation of "America" in Riedel's text obliterates the German Jewish past by removing the Jewish woman, while allowing the German male protagonist to return home. Hannes's failure to work through German guilt and shame is here put on display in self-pitying helplessness when he is faced with images and imaginings of the falling Twin Towers. The text thus utilizes the media spectacle that dominated the American and Western cultural space after 9/11 to emphasize that the Germans' obligation to address the memory of German history is now obsolete. Since the previous moral and cultural superiority of America is called into question after the events of 9/11, it seems, Germans no longer need to concern themselves with working through the memory of the Holocaust past.

Taken together, the ostensibly utopian and philo-Semitic articulations in Riedel's, Schneider's, and Schlink's fictional texts are indicators of a memory discourse that shifts its focus from the apparent celebratory memorial culture of the Berlin Republic (see Anne Fuchs et al.) to representations of an internal, invisible forgetting, repressing, and obliterating of the German past.[31] Even though the narrative perspective in the three (or four) stories differs slightly (Schlink and Schneider employ omniscient third-person narrators, while Riedel uses a more limited and limiting first-person narrative), the fictional accounts all engage tropes of memory and space invoking America, placing the emphasis on the external or surface structures (the women's beauty, America's landscape, dichotomies between East and West). The instances where German guilt and shame are visibly displaced to America, or to the image and imagination of America, accordingly result in stereotypical articulations of anti-Americanism and Judeophobia. The Germans' inability to love the Jewish American female furthermore reveals tropes of an anti-Semitism that is part of today's "German memory contests": a memory culture where the desire to recover an untainted German past results, via its dislocation to the cultural and geographic space of a transient America, in the revelation of a memory discourse that falls short on this promise of recovery. This discourse is, instead of recovering memories, contributing to a new anti-Semitism where German guilt and shame are—still—repressed. Because of its displacement to the explicit yet imaginary location of America, this nexus refers back to discourses of German colonial fantasies that were prominent before World War II, and, perhaps more significantly, even before World War I. Specifically, the representations of Hannes, Eduard, Andi, and to a lesser extent Michael Berg recall key traits of Karl May's Old Shatterhand, the German hero, whose encounters with the racial other(s) in America puts his heroic external other on display. Just as the xenophobia that resulted from the German defeat in the contest for colonial supremacy are covered up via the displacement of the German hero and his victory over the racial other in May's novels, so are the memories of German guilt and shame hidden within today's memory contests that are acted out in the imagination of the American, female, and Jewish other. In view of the eerily persistent representation of the American as female in all four contemporary texts, they all recall May's casting of "Winnetou," the noble Apache chief who functions as the good savage, and features a strikingly feminine appearance (long, black hair, beautiful eyes, etc.). At the pinnacle of the relationship between Old Shatterhand and Winnetou, he dies, much like Riedel's Sharon. Beyond the more obvious May reading of a homoerotic desire that is clearly also at play between the German hero and his "primeval" counterpart, Winnetou's physical and relational resemblance to the inscriptions of the recent novels' Jewish American women is salient, underscoring the close connection between those current articulations of anti-Semitism and a more culturally and historically extensive xenophobia linked with specifically German nineteenth-century fantasies of domination and conquest. The contemporary texts' philo-Semitic imagination, mapped onto a utopian representation of America and the Jewish American woman, thus ultimately propagates a fortuitous dislocation of German memory culture.

Dystopia and Cross-Cultural Transference

Rather than dislocating and repressing memories buried in ostensibly pro-American articulations, Thomas Hettche's 2006 narrative *What We Are Made of*, alongside its problematic stance towards racial "others," appears to more explicitly voice concerns with America and the German cultural imagination thereof. It will thus be important to observe if the dystopian, rather negative projections of America and Americans allow for a more successful "working through" of issues of German guilt and shame, or if the nostalgia for an unattainable German past combined with the absence of any visible empathy for the "other" are, still in light of a more negative rendering of America, predominant emotions. Considering that Thomas Hettche's *What We Are Made of* is a successful German novel, more alarming than the unabashed racism against African Americans is perhaps the anti-Semitism that finds its peak towards the end of the plot. Elsa Meerkaz, the Jewish widow of the Jewish scientist Eugen Meerkaz, is exposed as the operator behind the schemes against Niklas Kalf, the German protagonist. She is responsible for the abduction of Kalf's girlfriend, for the murder of one of her opponents' associates, as well as for attempting to have Kalf himself murdered. All this she presumably undertakes merely to avoid tarnishing her late husband's legacy. We again encounter the figure of an American female Jew, but this time it is one who does not assist the German protagonist to resolve or redress his tainted past. The anti-Americanism that is here so plainly conflated with anti-Semitism is, once again, reminiscent of the Weimar Republic's paranoid ideology of a worldwide "plutocracy" where an invisible capitalist conspiracy, lead by Woodrow Wilson, is responsible for the Germans' downfall in World War I, a conspiracy theory that enjoyed high prominence throughout the twentieth century, particularly on the Left.[32]

The questions that this text, too, raises concern German ways of addressing the memory of the Shoah in the context of German-American relations, more specifically, how this trans-generational memory is, roughly one and a half decades after German unification, framed in the contexts of East versus West. We already saw how Anne Fuchs, Stuart Taberner, Mary Cosgrove, and others have thought about German memory discourses in the nexus of post-unification and the "normalization" of the Berlin Republic. As Andrea Bachner, along similar lines, observed in her essay "Thomas Hettche's Wound Ethics," Hettche's second novel *Nox*, published in 1995, is the text that "invokes German reunification as the basis for a reflection on connection," and, as Bachner's arguments proceed, the figure of the cut is, in Hettche, employed in order to underscore its exact opposites: empathy and connection instead of separation and pain.[33] We may agree or disagree with Bachner's interpretations, but if we read *What We Are Made of* in a similar vein, we might arrive at an analysis where the anti-Semitic and racist articulations in the text are meant to evoke their opposites in the readers also. Yet, in order to determine whether or how such a reading might be viable, the text's narrative strategies will need to provide some insight.

In contrast to the earlier novels by Hettche, *What We Are Made of* does not work with narrative approaches mirroring the body and corporeality, even though (injured) bodies are still scattered throughout the text. The cuts, scrapes, dissections, and bodily fluids that shocked and perhaps disturbed the reader in previous Hettche novels are gone. Instead, the emphasis is now placed on the motif of the journey, the theme of (romanticized) homelessness, exhibiting elements of the crime story, both recalling and deviating from the aforementioned travelogue by Handtke. The reader's suspense of "whodunit" is a key element to Hettche's work, and might account for its success when this text was short-listed for the German Book Prize in 2006, on top of being included in the "Bestenliste" of the critically acclaimed TV and radio station SWR (Südwestrundfunk). When compared with Hettche's former novels, and also with Handtke's first-person narration *Short Letter, Long Farewell*, *What We Are Made of* appears conventional and less experimental in both narrative stance and technique. Hettche's text traces the plight of the omniscient third-person narrator and protagonist chronologically, and we are to empathize particularly with his multiple losses: the loss of his home, his girlfriend, and, at times, his safety. Even though ostensibly still in love with his girlfriend, we are to easily forgive the protagonist's numerous erotic encounters with a young, stunning beauty—incidentally, also marked as a racial "other" (she is Mexican). Most strikingly, this text's narrative facade resembles that of a film, and operates with vivid imagery that is to draw us in medias res. Yet, none of these techniques particularly invite a critical stance or perspective on that which the text articulates. This might explain why, widely reviewed as it was especially after its nomination to the short list of the Book Prize, none of the reviews take note of the racism, misogyny, and anti-Semitism so obviously scattered throughout. The stereotyping of America is what several reviewers mention—both positively and negatively—but the anti-Semitic, sexist, and racist articulations remain disregarded, and hence seem subject to a widespread amnesia in German memories of East and West, and of the Shoah.[34] In this respect, Hettche's novel does summon up the narratives by Schneider, Schlink, and Riedel, in spite of the more dystopian and negative imagination of America.

Keeping with the familiar theme of amnesia and nostalgia regarding the German past that this text also projects within the contested space of America, this novel's most essential moment occurs when the protagonist recalls his visit to Auschwitz coinciding with his initial meeting of Elsa Meerkaz: "What was he made of? He stared at Elsa Meerkaz until he suddenly thought of an encounter he had forgotten a long time ago. 'In the early nineties, shortly after the opening of the borders, I went to Auschwitz for the first time.' "[35] The fact that Kalf remembers and recounts his trip to Auschwitz when he for the first time meets and stares at Elsa Meerkaz, and that this memory is constitutive in some ways of "what he is made of," underscores and exhibits Niklas Kalf's complicated and unresolved link with his German and Nazi past. We are, via *this* German's imagination of the Jewish woman in America, reminded once more of Riedel's Hannes, of Schneider's Eduard, and of Schlink's Andi. While this novel does not primarily rely on the depiction of a sexually enticing American Jewish woman to establish the German male's racist and anti-Semitic acting out, the decisive moment in the text operates along similar lines. Elsa Meerkaz is elderly, Jewish, and German, resides in America, is evil, and she is clearly marked as "other." When she turns out to be the perpetrator, Niklas Kalf takes an uncanny pleasure in his perpetual imagined victim status. The memory of the "German as victim," familiar from Schlink's and other inversions of perpetrators and victims, is here performed in a basic and improbable twist of the story line. The protagonist's racist imaginings are furthermore acted out against a Mexican woman and against African American males. Hence, what this novel depicts, and again without any obvious textual markers of critical reserve or questioning, is a crude and apparent case of a chauvinistic German anti-Semitism, ostensibly made more palatable by its cultural and geographical displacement to America. The novel's later turn in the final showdown, where Jack Jackson, a film producer gone mad scientist, is discovered to have plotted against both Elsa Meerkaz and Kalf, does not counteract the obtrusive anti-Semitic and anti-American, not to mention misogynist references in the text. Accordingly, even though the—rather forced and entirely improbable—happy ending does reunite Kalf with his girlfriend and their newborn baby, the issue of how we, as readers, are to come to terms with the racism and anti-Semitism embedded in the text is not addressed or resolved. America as a dystopia thus functions as an expedient setting to act out German guilt and shame, just as America as a utopia did for the texts by Schlink, Schneider, and Riedel. The philo-Semitic imagination that accompanied the more positive images and imaginings of America is now replaced with crude and unveiled instances of German anti-Semitic, anti-American, sexist and racist performances and images.

To obliterate any suspicion that such a reading of this novel is not sufficiently differentiated, instead of reiterating the model of the displacement of German cultural issues to America, we might take the analytical stance of a transnational, cross-influential model of a German-American setting where subnational, informal, and semiofficial transferences of cultures and attitudes help to shape this text's semiotics. Reading Hettche's novel in this way, we may discern new grounds for the textual occurrences of anti-Semitism and racism in the context of this American dystopia. The main question for this part of the analysis is why racism and anti-Semitism appear so blatantly and uncritically evoked in this text, and in the context of contemporary German-American relations. Uta Poiger and especially Heide Fehrenbach's work on "race" in post-World War II Germany finds that, due to Nazi ideology, public invocations of race became essentially taboo in Germany soon after the war, while the "problem" of the Black "Besatzungskinder" was exaggerated.[36] Their findings suggest for the context of Hettche's novel a form of delayed "acting out" of racism in a now reunified, "normalized" post-9/11 Germany, where negative and racially prejudiced conceptions of African Americans might still be perceived as a predicament, but one that has been mostly repressed, and that seems, from the German perspective, less obscene or at least sublimated when acted out in an American setting, where America can take the cultural blame. At the same time, racist clichés might also have been uncritically adopted from the well-known everyday racism common to American film and literature. Either way, the imagery of a German white male who finds himself threatened and physically attacked by African American males alongside a Mexican woman seducing him to be unfaithful to his pregnant partner here functions to reinforce the long-standing notion of America as the site of a threatening "other." Furthermore, with German-German unification, and, even more significantly, in the aftermath of September 11, Germans felt increasingly removed from their parents' Nazi past.[37] While outspoken racism against African Americans is typically unacceptable in today's public arena in America, visible anti-Semitism is largely taboo in the contemporary German-speaking world. In the German-American encounter as Kalf experiences it, however, both instances of xenophobia—though for entirely different cultural, historical, and political reasons—suddenly appear, and are presented as acceptable. Kalf as a German does not feel responsible for American racism against African Americans or against Hispanics, and hence does not seem to feel the need to frame this as a problem. As for Kalf's anti-Semitism, it seems to be the physical space of America that provides him with relief from confronting Jews and the German past, similar to the German male protagonists of Schlink's, Schneider's, and Riedel's narratives. Yet, when he is finally faced with a German-American Jew, she turns out to be evil, thus allowing him the fantasy of moral superiority over her, helping him offset the painful memory of his German guilt and shame. America, for the German protagonist, here functions as the cross-cultural and transnational catalyst for the uninhibited articulation of anti-Semitic and racist emotions that would not be acceptable in either a predominantly American or a largely German setting.

Yet, notwithstanding these articulations, we may feel that this novel, since it is so clearly marked as fiction, and the imagery it evokes is comparable to the neo-romantic, magical realist film settings of David Lynch's works, is purposely toying with utterances of racism and anti-Semitism, and expects the reader to deconstruct those very instances as problematic. In such a reading, fiction itself becomes a marker of the critical distance alerting the reader to take a cautious stance towards those speech acts. However, none of the published criticism—either in praise or in rejection of the text—has remarked on those scenes and utterances as problematic, or in need of deconstructing, and we must therefore conclude that if the author intended such a decoding of fiction as a distancing strategy, it seems to have failed.

To illustrate the extent of such cross-national and sub-cultural transferences facilitating instances of xenophobic acting out, I would like to draw a comparison with another novel from 2006, and this one was not only shortlisted for the German Book Prize, as Hettche's novel, but actually won it. I am of course referring to Katharina Hacker's aforementioned *Die Habenichtse* (*The Have-Nots*). In Hacker's novel, we again come across a curious conflation of German, American, and Jewish themes and protagonists, but this time the actual spatial setting is post-9/11 London. Yet had it not been for the attacks of 9/11, attacks on the physical site of America, killing Jakob's senior colleague, Jakob would not have left Berlin to work in London, leading him to both his failed attraction to Bentham and to having to confront the Nazi restitution cases. In spite of the location of London as the predominant material place, America, once again, functions as the cataclysmic backdrop for the plot of the novel. Apart from the improbability of the story line that this text presents, and the fact that it does seem overwrought with contemporary issues, *The Have-Nots*'s narrative technique is, again, neither experimental nor particularly inventive. The narrative stance is that of the omniscient third-person narrator, just as in Hettche's text, and even though Hacker's is not following the pattern of the crime novel as clearly as Hettche's, crime (child abuse) and violence (of the drug dealers) are vividly present in both. Accordingly, in both novels, we encounter a male German protagonist who is haunted by an elderly Holocaust survivor. While in Hettche's novel, Elsa Meerkaz is also an evil co-conspirator against the protagonist, Bentham in Hacker is merely "guilty" of rejecting Jakob's absurdly feeble advances. However, the unrequited love becomes Jakob's obsession, and Bentham's Jewishness an important source of Jakob's overall feelings of inadequacy. Interestingly, both elderly Jews are not living in Germany, and especially Bentham's nomadic lifestyle corresponds to the stereotype of the wandering Jew.

While in Hettche, the Jewish widow deliberately seeks to inflict a physical wound onto the German protagonist, the psychological injury that Bentham imposes—unintentionally—onto Jakob appears even more painful and detrimental to the protagonist's emotional stability. Therefore, while at first glance, both novels appear to not have that much in common, except for the publication year of 2006 and their relative prominence among German critics and audiences, a closer reading reveals that in their accounts of the themes of German Holocaust guilt, racism, and post-9/11 America, as well as in their narrative stances and literary techniques, both work along similar lines of stereotyping of Jews, gender, race, and this time also class. They imagine a German male who is not "at home," and who experiences substantial alienation, distress, anxiety, and deep emotional insecurity when confronted with Jews, homosexuals, African Americans, Hispanics, or people of lower class.

The recurring setting of cross-cultural, transnational, and transgenerational spaces thus explicitly functions to cover up the problematic racist stereotyping. As a result of the naive narrative structures, rather than exposing it, acting out anti-Semitism and racism goes largely unnoticed in these novels, contributing to the vast and unacknowledged, subconscious and growing accumulation of anti-Semitism that Europe, and Germany especially, has seen in recent years. If we compare the narrative stance and perspectives of the two German texts with recent Holocaust literature from America, we must conclude that the German texts under discussion here do not utilize literary techniques that might detach the reader from the material at hand to evoke a critical distance, or questioning, of the stereotyping speech that the texts present. Jonathan Safran Foer or Nicole Krauss's novels, just to mention two contemporary examples that engage the memory of the Holocaust, work with multiple story lines, purposely distorted narrative perspectives, humor, irony (especially Foer), and numerous other clever, innovative literary devices. They can thus alert the reader to the multiple layers of meaning that trauma literature—as any Holocaust memoir or text dealing with Holocaust memory by definition is—can expose to render a meaningful and rich textual fabric that does not lend itself to one-sided stereotypical articulations. This taken together with Hacker's case, in which, again, there is no mention on the part of the numerous reviews of the anti-Semitic or racist stereotyping, leads to the conclusion that Hacker's text does not seek to evoke a subversive stance on the part of the reader towards this troublesome acting out of anti-Semitic fantasies.

America and Textual Self-Reflexivity

Yet, even in the German context Hacker's and Hettche's novels are not the only recent texts invoking a cross-cultural, transnational setting where matters of race, gender, and Jewish identities are negotiated in a German-American setting. Thomas Meinecke's 2001 novel *Hellblau* (*Pale Blue*, 2012) could be read as a counterpoint to Hettche's text, as well as to many of the other novels considered in this chapter.[38] In Meinecke's decidedly post-colonial, anti-authoritarian, non-hierarchical ethnographic narrative we encounter five protagonists whose perspectives are frequently interchanged. Tillmann, the main protagonist, is German, and renting a cottage at North Carolina's Outer Banks. His research on German wartime submarines is interspersed with thoughts and conversations with his Jewish American girlfriend, Vermilion. Also involved in the dialogue with Tillmann is Yolanda, an African American army brat residing in Chicago, and who is engaged in a large, nonspecific writing project with Vermilion. The German Cordula, a professional diver, exploring the war submarines that are the subject of Tillmann's research, is Tillmann's former girlfriend, and studying in Berlin at the Humboldt University together with Heinrich, her current boyfriend. Heinrich is originally from Bitburg, referencing the contested 1985 visit of U. S. President Ronald Reagan to the site of the Bitburg cemetery. The five protagonists' conversations and thoughts, some referring to widely known as well as more remote icons of popular culture and academia, center on issues of cultural hybridity, multiculturalism, anti-Semitism, Jewish identity, racism, and gender. The protagonists' multiple and interchangeable perspectives add to the negotiations of identities that are deliberately fluid, and that evade any fixed categorization concerning space or ethnic or national identity. Some, but not much of the characters' identities is revealed in their written communication to one another. Boundaries of male/female are questioned, and the protagonists' exchanges are interspersed with pertinent scholarly literature on anti-Semitism, gender, and race (in addition to performances of extensive dialogues on music, art, and popular culture in general). The popular music star Mariah Carey serves as a key reference, invoking especially her mixed race background. At the same time, London-based intellectual celebrity Paul Gilroy's works on race and culture are cited intermittently. The performativity of any previously set categories in German contemporary cultural discourse (such as national identity, German, Jewish, American, male, female, etc.) is, via multiply coded citations and references, purposely staged as ambiguous. The boundaries of identities are permanently and continually put into question alongside the boundaries of the characters' narratives themselves (we persistently need to decipher who is speaking at any given moment so as to remain engaged). Direct quotations and excerpts from everyday materials and scholarly sources undermine the notion of any narrative authority, just as there is no single narrative perspective, and help the text point to the fictionality and inauthenticity of fiction itself. In short, this novel is the perfect enactment of all that might have been amiss in the previously mentioned texts, or, of what academic discourse would like to imagine in an ideal contemporary novel that is sensitive to all aspects of gender, identity, and race. In Meinecke's novel, scholars like Sander Gilman and Daniel Boyarin, whose works are critically important to this study, are not only mentioned, but actually quoted, so as to yield a comprehensive view of all that current academic thought has to offer in perspectives on Jews and gender in Germany. The following passage is typical for its free associations, evoking several concurrent discourses, while erasing any hierarchy between "authentic" or "original" material:

> Mir fällt wieder ein, dass ich den Namen Kafka auf dem Etikett einer Red Planter Maxi gelesen habe. Ich rufe Wendy an und lasse sie Sander L. Gilman's 1995er Aufsatz Damaged Men heraussuchen; wenig später werden mir die gewünschten Seiten zugefaxt. Masculinity is a complex and even contradictory construction, and no Jewish writer of the early twentieth century is more implicated in the confusion and difficulties associated with being a feminized male Jew than Franz Kafka.[39]

Florence Feiereisen and others have described this technique of Meinecke's "Politics of Pop," a theory of writing that attempts to depict surface materials in order to reproduce his own writing process.[40] Embedded throughout the entire novel are quotations of cultural material that is never identified with quotation marks, eliminating any hierarchies, and moving away from any concept of authorial subjectivity: "My working hypothesis, for now, is: the autonomous subject no longer exists."[41] Thus, Sander Gilman is quoted, but the quotation marks indicating his original text are removed, even if they are still referred to, in order to signify this absence of subjectivity, authority, or individual control in any cultural context, even in academic writing, blurring the boundaries between readers and writers. The origins of the material, and with that, any subjectivity, no longer matter, as, for Meinecke, all notions of originality and identity have been deconstructed in the writing process itself. This move has the added function to negate the proposition that ideas are the personal intellectual property of any one thinker. Referring to Judith Butler's theory of gender performativity, drag becomes the mode of textual authenticity, and thus reveals the constructedness of gender, of any (national) identity—and of texts.

This narrative technique adds a decidedly new and important layer to the cross-cultural German American setting. Yet, Vermilion, the American Jewish woman who is the love interest and current girlfriend of the German protagonist Tillmann, is represented in ways that are reminiscent of the previous, formulaic, and clichéd inscriptions of the Jewish and American woman: when Tillmann and the reader first meet her, a waitress in a restaurant, she is seen collecting her tips, and with a golden Star of David as a necklace.[42] When Tillmann discovers an injury on his thigh after they take a fun bath in the ocean, Tillmann divulges the following: "Vermilion asks carefully, if she might have caused me the scratch on my thigh, perhaps with her fingernails. She seemed to like that thought. American women usually grow their nails longer than European women."[43] Vermilion, the Jewish and American student who is working at a seafood restaurant and writing a Ph.D. dissertation about Hasidic Jews in Crown Heights, Williamsburg, and Borough Park, is here characterized as a seductress, interested in money (since money is the very first reference to her appearance), and a clichéd shallow American (wearing long fingernails). She is furthermore, even if only playfully, excited at the idea of injuring the German protagonist, confirming the all-too stereotypical notion of the threatening and seductive *belle Juive* found in the texts by Schlink, Schneider, and others. Yolanda, to further promote the imagination of Jews as "others" populating a non-Jewish German world, then relates her impressions upon stumbling upon a Hasidic community in New York City, which leave her feeling estranged and surprised at their appearance and language.[44] However, while these kinds of representations of Jews and Jewishness in any other text might, indeed, have come across as unreflective, naive, and offensive in their predictable typecast, this particular representation does not. Reading Eldrige Cleaver out loud, Vermilion, the *belle Juive*, observes towards Tillmann: "with the Nazi Germans the hyper masculine slave reigned; clearly with the Nazis the body dominated the mind."[45] This and other similar invocations contradict and subversively undermine the previous stereotypical depiction of Vermilion, the association of her persona with an ultra-feminine Jewish seductress. The use of the subjunctive, as well as the questioning mode that characterize Vermilion's act of reading from Tillmann's text all contribute to the subversive position that she takes towards any preset impression of Jews, Germans, Americans, or of women. This narrative thereby explicitly challenges any anti-Semitic or sexist representations that the reader might have unknowingly assigned to her, or to any other character. And this is how Meinecke's text works to subvert stereotypical representations of Jews, of femininity, of masculinity, of Germans, and of Americans. The main reason for this "novel" working so successfully against a multitude of predetermined clichés is because the "offending" material is represented in ways that force the reader to question and analyze the content, rather than allowing him or her to identify and empathize with the German protagonist. Meinecke's literary style, the permanent change in narrative perspectives, and the techniques of arranging cut-up and borrowed cultural materials side by side work together to produce critical distance and questioning as the primary receptive modes in the readers. The *belle Juive* in America, as she is evoked and constructed in the persona of Vermilion, is therefore at the same time deconstructed in the reader's imagination.

Ultimately, cutting up and rearranging diverse cultural materials side by side, as it is so skillfully carried out in *Pale Blue*, points to the crisis of representation while denying historicity or authenticity to any of the material, its context, or even its—fictional—creator. This technique is not entirely new, since much of Meinecke's poetic practice is borrowed from Rolf Dieter Brinkmann's poetic invocation of American popular culture in the late 1960s and early 1970s, as I have shown elsewhere.[46] Accordingly, the politics of subversion are, for Meinecke, emerging from a total removal of subjectivity and the installation of textual performativity. As a result, Thomas Meinecke's novel *Pale Blue* seems to be the paradigmatic text that, in borrowing from the U.S. discourse of politics as pop (as in Leslie Fielder's pop manifesto), provides the much-needed resistance to the apparently more outdated narrative techniques and discourses put forth in the novels by Hettche, Hacker, Schneider, Riedel, and Schlink. Furthermore, Meinecke's fiction seems to consciously enact and perform the cross-cultural, subnational, and transnational setting that the aforementioned texts merely seem to propagate. In other words, Meinecke's text *performs* America and American culture, while novels like that of Hettche utilize the (utopian or dystopian) space of America in order to act out concealed German sentiment. According to Meinecke's novel, then, the situation in contemporary Germany with respect to the memory of Jews and Germans might not be as dire as previous readings suggests. And indeed, Jeffrey Peck seems to reach similarly optimistic conclusions in his 2006 scholarly study *Being Jewish in the New Germany*. Whereas Peck's study, a social history taking stock of a current trend, might be accused of naively overestimating both the Germans' wish to address their Holocaust memory,[47] as well as the possibility for the largely Russian and Polish-based Jewish communities to successfully integrate, Meinecke's text works with fiction. The fantasies and projections that his novel performs might therefore, indeed, point towards a productive and progressive potential to address past German trauma. As Cecile Zorach asserts in her excellent analysis of Meinecke's representation of America, *Pale Blue*, in contrast to Meinecke's 1996 novel *The*

Church of John F. Kennedy, underscores the connections between America and Germany, rather than exploring the differences or assuming the familiar pose of critiquing American capitalism and hegemony.[48] Zorach sees one of these links between Germany and the United States in *Pale Blue* in the texts' multiple references to the legacy of anti-Semitism that the two nations share (in American culture referenced by the import of Henry Ford and Louis Farrakhan), as well as racism (the Crown Heights and Chicago riots), as well as popular music (Detroit and German techno). Zorach furthermore points out that Meinecke's America purposely excludes any appraisal for mainstream or "Leitkultur" America, thereby emphasizing the subversive potential that marks American popular culture.

Meinecke's apparent desire to explore and exploit American popular culture to, above all else, infuse a sense of diversity into German national identity, can be explained by his observation that the Americans, as opposed to Germany, have always already had to contend with their ethnic, racial, and cultural hybridities, making themselves the perfect subjects to be studied and deconstructed. Even though this particular assessment of "America" as a reverse colonizing and hybrid cultural space seems a bit optimistic from the vantage point of roughly a decade later, and after September 11, 2001, his basic argument that America is more ethnically hybrid and varied than Germany, and has historically been so, is still valid, even if the metaphor of a melting pot or even a mosaic of diverse cultural identities living together in harmony does not hold true. At the same time, Meinecke's sanguine assessment of America as the "better" cultural space might also point the way to a more recent and more widely expressed sentiment in the German media post-1989. When Barack Obama was elected as the first African American president, the desire on the part of many progressive, liberal Germans, that a Turkish German might one day be elected chancellor, referred to a similar optimistic and naive assessment of the United States, and presumes a similarity between Germany and the United States regarding cultural and ethnic diversity that is historically and culturally inaccurate. Not unlike Meinecke's optimism, such a fantasy once again expresses in literal terms how the location of "America," still, after 9/11, the wars in Iraq and Afghanistan, the catastrophe of the Bush administration's response to Hurricane Katrina in 2004, and the financial crisis that began in 2008, serves as a site for a utopian space where the shortcomings of Germany, in particular pertaining to Germans dealing with their guilt-ridden past, can be overcome. Therefore, Meinecke's positivistic and hopeful appraisal of the utopian potential of German-American cross-cultural transference via subversive popular culture and the academic elites is as commendable as it might be deceptive and, in this context, predictable.

In sum, Thomas Meinecke's novel *Pale Blue* implicitly and explicitly performs Roland Barthes's contention of the death of the author, where a text is merely a "tissue of quotations drawn from innumerable centres of culture."[49]

One could thus argue that Meinecke's aesthetics are intrinsically postmodern. His narrative samples of American literary and cultural theories (Judith Butler, Sander Gilman, Daniel Boyarin, etc.) appear to be aimed at working through issues of Germany's past, and specifically German guilt and shame over the Holocaust, along with issues of gender and national identity. Interestingly, the timing of Meinecke's writings coincides with the German claim for a "neue Lesbarkeit" (new readability), which precipitated an array of German narratives that were highly popular, and that sought to incorporate contemporary culture and a fairly traditional narrative style that would attract large reading audiences.[50] The implicit and often even explicit aim of the new German readability movement was to revive the German book market by selling more novels made in Germany. Yet, Meinecke rejects such profit-driven poetics in favor of a postmodern, self-conscious and self-critical performative practice that undermines dominant discourses rather than buying into them. By explicitly making Jews, the Holocaust, gender, sexuality, ethnicity, and race relations subjects of study, Meinecke's texts attempt to more vigorously reject the hierarchical structures that National Socialist "realism" promoted, and to break the silence numerous German postwar narratives continue to display when it comes to addressing the Germans' dealing with the past. Meinecke does so by turning his back on the mass audience in favor of a limited academic readership. Yet Meinecke's narrative style, in spite of the numerous references to American music artists, American writers, and citations from U.S.-based popular culture, is also deeply German in its extensive self-reflexivity. Many critics lament that his novel is therefore, as a novel, "failed," and, essentially unreadable.[51] Undeniably, the marked self-reflexivity of the text and the text's engagement of fiction unmistakably distinguish *Pale Blue* from the more conventional narratives by Bernhard Schlink, Peter Schneider, Susanne Riedel, or Thomas Hettche. The absence of any critical markers in those more "readable" texts is disturbing because it engenders the uncritical and unconscious adoption and absorption of stereotypical speech. On the other hand, because of the deliberate removal of *any* textual authority, and the perpetual invocation of intellectual elites that even educated readers might not be familiar with, the remoteness and inaccessibility of Meinecke's text also poses a quandary, particularly when dealing with questions of empathy or ethical responsibility (as texts wishing to engage the memory of the Shoah are intrinsically obliged to do). If moral arguments, even implied, or the mere possibility for readers to consider moral issues are impeded to the point where the text, due to its own self-reflexivity, no longer presents any viable or meaningful options for moral engagement, then this text has successfully deconstructed itself. It has also, by means of this very process, left readers with a total void of ethical responsibility. Because of this construct of self-reflexivity, Meinecke's subjects are aware of their own complicity in the workings of power discourses. His narratives therefore performatively enact that which they seek to deconstruct: there is no outside of power, of ideology, of politics. Germans, according to Meinecke's poetics, must, then, clearly be complicit in the crimes of National Socialism, as the reference to Tillmann's grandfather also indicates,[52] but we can't say that this matters any more. Since subjectivity, historicity, authentic experience, space, place, and, with that, any categories for moral judgment have been deconstructed, all that remain are texts and performances of identities. Obviously, the resulting absence of any possibility for moral judgment is, in spite of the good intentions that this narrative propagates, just as much of a problem in today's Germany.

To conclude, these different textual engagements of a transnational, cross-cultural, German-American space seek to come to terms with Holocaust guilt, but they do so in divergent and sometimes conflicting ways, while all of them invoke fantasies of America as a space apart where German guilt and shame can be forgotten, erased, buried in racism against African Americans, or, as in Meinecke's text, deconstructed. If we, moreover, apply Dominick LaCapra's terms of post-traumatic memory to this nexus of the displacement of German issues to the untainted space of America, these divergent fantasies of America can be read as a delayed acting out of anti-Semitic fantasies in the wake of trauma. The original trauma of the German aftermath of World War II with the gradual realization of the massive German guilt over the Holocaust that had been repressed for a long time, appears, in Hettche and Riedel's novels, additionally compounded by the trauma of 9/11. In all texts considered in this chapter, the German-American setting helps to displace the site of traumatic memories to a fictional space that is not tainted or stigmatized by National Socialism. If we consider those dislocations a result of (repressed) trauma, the Mitscherlichs' approach to trauma and mourning is here, again, relevant due to the delayed *and displaced* acting out that is evident in all of these texts. Once again, thinking about *The Inability to Mourn* can help explain that German silence and the rejection of mourning, resulting in prolonged melancholia after World War II, are still crucial to the ways in which transferred trauma affects contemporary Germans, despite ongoing public Holocaust memorial culture. The Germans' over-identification with Adolf Hitler and their enthusiastic support of National Socialism had, after the fall of the Third Reich, resulted in an intense defense against guilt, shame, and anxiety, which in turn led to a pronounced absence of mourning, inciting prolonged melancholia after World War II and during much of the time of divided Germany. The absence so hauntingly visible in the works of older, first-generation writers such as Günter Grass and Martin Walser is now, in the works of second- and third-generation writers, characterized by displacement to a purportedly different physical site.

Considering the multi-generational repercussions of such profoundly repressed or displaced trauma, including trauma resulting from guilt, Vamik Volkan's important work contends that traumatic memories are not simply handed down intergenerationally. What is instead transmitted—or "deposited"—to the next generation are "the scarred self-images of the parents who have been unable to mourn the damage done to their individual and group selves." Consequently, in today's German memories, we deal with "children's reactions to parents,"[53] or, in the cases of Niklas Kalf's, Jakob's, Andi's, or Tillmann's generation, with grandchildren's reactions to their grandparents. This also means that each generation, while still affected by the silence and melancholia that the original trauma had evoked, develops strategies to repress, erase, or dislocate those painful, embarrassing, and still traumatizing memories. Volkan's adaptation of the Mitscherlichs' thesis is further developed by A. Dirk Moses (2007), who emphasizes that children's reactions to their parents can vary. Hence, according to Moses, there are two separate groups of German identities: the non-German Germans who deny (and repress) their unbearable past, and the German Germans who use displacement strategies to make their national past bearable and affirmable. The latter seem to correspond especially well to the texts inscribing past Holocaust guilt, in the form of anti-Semitic, racist, and sexist acting out, onto the physical site of America. More recently, Moses contends, the previously binary relationship of Jewish–German has become triangular, because of the existence of the State of Israel.[54] Taking this suggestion one step further, not only has this previously binary relationship regarding space and location become multilayered, because of America and Israel, and also because, as Moses acknowledges, of the addition of Turkish identities, but German German versus non-German German identities have, in view of the diverse ways in which the texts here engage America as a space of displacement of German guilt and shame, themselves become multifaceted.

Indeed, rather than trying to fit the third-generation protagonists Niklas Kalf, Jakob, Tillmann, or even Schlink's Andi into either one of those two categories, the above readings suggest that the texts' anti-Semitic and racist utterances represent both expressions of non-German German as well as German German identities, and the many spaces in-between, especially as they concern the intersection of German identity and masculinity. As non-German Germans, Niklas Kalf and Jakob, but also Andi and Tillman, suppress not only their German past but also their German heritage, in that they escape from Germany, and fantasize themselves immersed into American (or, for Jakob, British) society. All clearly feel both fascinated, attracted, and threatened by the racial "other" in "America," and by the lower-class "others" in London. At the same time, all of these male protagonists are German Germans who use displacement strategies when confronted with the stigma of their heritage: as soon as Niklas Kalf meets Elsa Meerkaz, he remembers his trip to Auschwitz. But rather than leading him to revise his earlier articulations, his—apparently largely unconscious—acting out becomes even more intense. When Jakob feels rejected by Bentham, a homosexual Jew, his unrequited love turns into a narcissistic obsession. Andi's realization of the meaning of Sarah's Judaism for his German identity leads him to self-mutilate, and to end their relationship. Tillmann, on the other hand, does seem to raise important questions as his reading of other critical narratives, questions that encourage a productive engagement on the part of the German German and non-German German reader. In other words, the interactions of subjects in Meinecke's narrative that is perhaps inaccessible to larger audiences does yield the potential for the reader's critical engagement with stereotypes. The relevance of Meinecke's text, therefore, is that it depicts identities that are not only situated in-between German and Jewish, male and female, or German and American characteristics, but, likewise, spatially located in-between cultures of minorities and German "Leitkultur," Germany and Israel, Germany and Turkey. As such, Meinecke's "novel" references the complexities of German-Jewish, German-Turkish, and other minorities' inclusion. Accordingly, Jeffrey Peck was, although for different reasons than the ones he cites, perhaps not too far off in his optimism, at least as it concerns the mindset of the academic elites. Yet, at the same time, such confidence, whether it concerns issues of minority inclusion or gender equality, is still to be bestowed with caution. For a narrative that offers, via its likeable protagonists, reader identification and empathy with the self rather than the other is prone to be significantly more effective than a text requiring and engendering critical distance with both its subject matters and abstract and remote figures. The relative success of Hettche's, Hacker's, and Schneider's novels, all of which are also available in English translations, as compared to *Pale Blue*, which is no longer in print in the original German, speaks volumes, and should make us, at the very least, suspicious. We may finally discern that, even two decades after German unification, past memory discourses concerning German guilt and shame over the Holocaust have not at all been resolved, and may have resulted in more intense acting out of previously repressed fantasies of racism and anti-Semitism. In the present cases of young, third-generation German males, the displacement of the anti-Semitic and racist performances to an American setting seems all the more disturbing, particularly since the fantasies articulated in these narratives implicitly refer back to a discourse of anti-Semitism and anti-Americanism that was prevalent before and during Nazism and on the eve of World War II. In many of these texts, sexism is equally widespread, when women only appear in the periphery and are depicted as passive, sexual prey, or evil conspirators, while homosexuality appears, again, stigmatized. Most of these images and imaginings, particularly where they are not deconstructed by the texts that engender them, represent, still and again, problematic identity positions that are never problematized. Even though they are created by younger writers, depicting third-generation Germans, the images they portray most closely emulate the ones found in texts by much older, more established writers such as Günter Grass and Martin Walser.

Epilogue

My readings suggest that current German representations of Jews and Germans continue to be dominated by underlying emotions of guilt, silence, and obscured anti-Semitism. The anti-Semitism resulting from guilt rejection that was prominent in works by older German writers such as Günter Grass and Martin Walser, under discussion in chapter 1, unexpectedly resurfaces in third-generation writers' fiction, such as that of Tanja Dückers, even when geographically displaced to America, as in Thomas Hettche's novel. More recently published novels that were either short-listed or winners of the German Book Prize in particular indicate the extent to which xenophobia is, still, intrinsically linked with German national identity. The Mitscherlichs' "Inability to Mourn" is, in many contemporary German texts, acted out as an inability to love, indicating that the "Negative Symbiosis" between Jews and Germans has not been overcome.[1] The novels' frequent recourses to Weimar Republic conflations of images and imaginings of America, capitalism, and Judaism exhibit ingrained racism and anti-Semitism alongside the colonial fantasies that can be traced back to Karl May's notorious successes. The ways in which gender is imagined in the context of German-Jewish relations indicate both an overwhelming desire to show how Germany is free of anti-Semitism and xenophobia, and the surprising degree to which gender and race relations in contemporary German society are still silenced and repressed. It appears that an extensive yearning for normalization in the Berlin Republic helps to trigger oppressive and discriminating gender and race sentiments. Those emotions are, in many popular second- and third-generation texts, acted out against women as gendered anti-Semitism, or in the typecasting of male Jews as "weak" compared with German males. As is evident especially from the discussions in chapters 2 and 4, the wish for "normalization" then turns out to yield its desired opposite. While, on the surface, many popular texts seek to depict a "normalized" Germany, the images and imaginings that are less visible easily work their way into the collective unconscious, perpetuating myths and stereotypes that we imagine ourselves to have left behind long ago. The inability to love that so many characters from first-, second-, and third-generation fiction after the war exhibit, most prominently Jakob and Isabelle in *The Have-Nots*, haunts Germans to this day, even though none of the writers "intended" this. My readings thus also showcase how we should never accuse writers for exposing, even if merely implicitly, what ails society writ large. Daniel Goldhagen's mistake was, among others, to pronounce a blanket indictment for all Germans. The lessons learned from the Goldhagen debate are not only that such an indictment is false, but that it is also, and more importantly, wrong.[2] Blaming writers would be even more wrong, for their texts merely reflect the present condition of contemporary discourse.

Yet, not all is as bleak as this conclusion might indicate. There are two recent German novels that give hope to the project of counteracting these by now familiar narratives of trauma. The first is by one author from the set of writers that this study purposefully excluded.[3] He is a German Jewish writer, and one who unambiguously self-identifies as Jewish. Benjamin Stein, born in 1970 in East Berlin, is a new phenomenon in the literary and cultural landscape of Germany, because he does not attempt to disguise, deny, or excuse his Jewish identity, as many public figures of previous generations did, and several details of his biography point to a newly emancipated stance towards German history and memory.[4] More importantly here, his 2010 novel *Die Leinwand* (2010; *The Canvas*, 2012) a significant critical success, candidly speaks to many of the issues that this study exposed.[5] Two separate first-person narratives can be read from either end of the book, either parallel, or in succession. No text is thus privileged over the other, both coexist. The story of psychoanalyst Amnon Zichroni, who grew up Orthodox Jewish in Israel, and who encourages the Swiss Holocaust survivor Minsky to record his traumatic memories, intersects with that of Jan Wechsler, an East German reformed Jewish journalist seeking to uncover Minsky's memories as the lies of a Holocaust-remembrance poseur. The core narrative of course references the scandal around Binyamin Wilkomirski's memoir, yet most significantly it performs, via its intricate narrative structure, the unreliability of memory, identity, and history.[6] The allegorical play that enacts the canvas[7] as the site of projection in the end reveals Zichroni and Wechsler to be one and the same character, further unsettling our perception of what is real, what is imagined, and how memory is mediated. The brilliance of this particular text lies in the ways in which it engages reader expectations, while at the same time educating readers about Judaism. The physical middle of the book, where both narratives meet, is a glossary explicating terms that typically, German, non-Jewish readers might not be familiar with (such as "kashrut," "Haredim," "Gemara"). This basic and crucial elucidation of religious terms and customs of Judaism by way of playfully referencing the memory of Holocaust trauma does not quite indicate that we have now overcome the problems of contemporary German anti-Semitism, or that the many issues pertaining to the silenced or repressed history and memory of the Holocaust have vanished. It also does not mean that Germans no longer suffer from trans-generational guilt and shame when they find themselves confronted with Jews in contemporary Germany. But Benjamin Stein's novel, as it seems to gain popularity, can provide an important step in the direction of addressing those very issues.

Uncovering and bringing to the fore more of the rich and important contemporary German Jewish literature by Jewish writers, especially in texts that seek to address the history and memory of the Holocaust, is therefore an important next step that this particular project could not yet take. Analyzing the works of writers such as Esther Dischereit, Barbara Honigmann, Maxim Biller, Viola Roggenkamp, and Rafael Seligmann as well as the public discourse created by the artist Anna Adam can teach us much about how to address past trauma without perpetuating the victim-perpetrator binary.[8] Accordingly, Benjamin Stein's text, as thoughtful, enriching, positive, and thought-provoking as *The Canvas* turns out to be for the project of addressing contemporary German Jewish issues, does fall outside of the boundaries of the investigation this study seeks to undertake. Other Jewish writers and artists might be similarly well placed to engage this nexus productively. Yet the questions raised here remain directed towards the German, non-Jewish memory of the past, and its concurrent perception of the present.

Remarkably, there is another recent literary and fictional text that deserves consideration, and this one is by a German, non-Jewish writer. Markus Flohr's *Wo samstags immer Sonntag ist* (2011; Where Saturday Is Always Sunday; not translated) is an entertaining, lighthearted, and humorous report about a twenty-something German student who spends time in Israel.[9] The ways in which stereotypes are referenced in this particular narrative by a young writer and journalist (Flohr was born in 1980, and can almost be considered a representative of the fourth generation after the Second World War), are appealing and playful, but they never invoke anti-Semitic clichés so that they could be silently accepted or condoned by the reader. In contrast to the texts by Peter Schneider, for example, Flohr's first-person narrative exhibits and openly subverts any such disarticulations by utilizing humor in the main narrative, rather than ascribing it as an oddity to one of the characters. When the German and non-Jewish protagonist arrives at his new apartment in Jerusalem that he is to share with three fellow students, two of whom are American Jews, a conversation ensues where the Jewish roommates think he, too, is Jewish because of his nose.[10] Preceding this dialogue is an extensive conversation between the protagonist and Friedrich, another young German in Israel, about Jews, Germans, and Auschwitz. This comical conversation directly references Henryk Broder's quote of the Israeli psychoanalyst Zvi Rex when he remarked that the Germans could never forgive the Jews for Auschwitz.[11] In weaving humor and the protagonist's self-reflection into a narrative fabric that directly and immediately references the German Holocaust past, this text invites us to reflect upon anti-Semitic as well as anti-German clichés, by demonstrating how irrational and incongruous they—along with their continued invocation—really are. The difference between Schneider's and Schlink's writing and that of Flohr lies in the direct and unambiguous way in which issues are confronted, and then illuminated by means of the German in Israel who is cast as the other (rather than the Jew, or the woman, representing the other). Unlike any of the texts by the older German writers, religious, cultural, and political issues are here presented as everyday themes, all of them subjects of discussion between the multifaceted characters who display different levels of very specific engagements with Judaism (from Orthodox to Reform Jewish to not religious at all). Whenever any cultural stereotypes are invoked in Flohr's text, they are represented in characters that are aware of them, thus making us, the readers, aware, too. Flohr's entertaining, pleasurable piece is, not coincidentally, furthermore telling the love story between a German Protestant and Noa, a Sephardic Jew from Jerusalem. Instead of displaying a mysteriously erotic and dangerous *belle Juive*, Noa is cast as an emphatic, lovable, loving, and impulsive character whose manners and political opinions are as contemporary as they are emancipated. This love story, while not unproblematic due to Noa's family, who insist that she marry a Jew, and preferably a Sephardic one (a theme that is familiar from Schlink's "The Circumcision"), exhibits two young people who are partners, in love, and who communicate about their differences while celebrating what they have in common. Yet, in stark opposition to the relationship between Sarah and Andi, or Jakob and Bentham, or even Peter and his mother, they specifically address their differences and the memories of their past when Noa explains why and how the relationship between them is fraught:

> The issue is not that with every kiss I was worried that you too have a little Nazi sitting inside a tiny millimeter of your head. I also did not think of the Holocaust when we were together. But it is, of course, always there. . . . In every person who is born, the history of his family, his relatives, somehow all of humanity, is entrenched. I am now certain that there is no mini-Nazi inside your head ready to jump out. But I don't want to find out one day that there are things that I can't deal with.[12]

No such exchange occurs in any of the other texts, and this is how this particular narrative is different, noteworthy, and new. Love is clearly on display. Also on display is the protagonist's moving visit to Yad Vashem, and many edifying exchanges concerning kashrut, as well as the Jewish high holidays. Even though the relationship between the German protagonist and Noa, the Sephardic Jew in Israel, does not take all the expected turns, we come away feeling that there is dialogue, empathy, trust, and truthfulness. It seems that with Markus Flohr's lively narrative, the German inability to love has just been turned into its delightful opposite.

NOTES

Introduction

The epigraph for the introduction is from Milan Kundera, *The Book of Laughter and Forgetting*, trans. Michael Henry Heim (New York: Penguin, 1981), 22.

1. Günter Grass, "Was gesagt werden muss." http://www.sueddeutsche.de/kultur/gedicht-zum-konflikt-zwischen-israel-und-iran-was-gesagt-werden-muss-1.1325809.

2. Translation by Michael Kiefer and Nica Mintz. http://pulsemedia.org/2012/04/07/what-must-be-said.

3. On the spelling of "anti-Semitism" vs. "antisemitism," see Richard S. Levy, "Forget Webster," *German Studies Review* 24, no. 1 (February 2006): 145–46. While I agree with Levy's sentiment, I decided to follow the common practice of the conventional spelling. The fact that the term implies, and indeed enacts some of its own troubled and troubling history, seems important. If we erase this history by instituting a new spelling, we also erase the important reminders that the conventional spelling provides.

4. One of the more interesting and recently invoked misrepresentations of Adorno's dictum is the one by Paul Celan, where he precisely zones in on the question of aesthetics: "Kein Gedicht nach Auschwitz (Adorno): was wird hier als Vorstellung von Gedicht unterstellt?" In referencing this quote, Aleida Assmann interestingly makes the same mistake as Celan, in that she refers to Adorno's dictum as a "prohibition," indicating the extent to which Adorno's verdict had, indeed, become a prohibition in the general public imagination. However, Adorno said that writing poetry after Auschwitz (and not just poetry about Auschwitz!) is barbaric. He did not say that it is prohibited, nor did he say that one should not write poetry after Auschwitz, although this might easily be concluded. See Aleida Assmann, "History from a Bird's Eye View: Reimagining the Past in Marcel Beyer's *Kaltenburg*," in *Debating German Cultural Identity Since 1989*, ed. Anne Fuchs et al. (Rochester, N.Y.: Camden House, 2011), 205–20, 212. The wider context of Adorno's quote (*Kulturkritik und Gesellschaft* [Frankfurt: Suhrkamp, 2003], 30), needs to include the fact that he later retracted it ("das perennierende Leiden hat soviel Recht auf Ausdruck wie der Gemarterte zu brüllen; darum mag falsch gewesen sein, nach Auschwitz liesse kein Gedicht mehr sich schreiben"; Theodor W. Adorno, *Negative Dialektik* [Frankfurt: Suhrkamp, 1994], 355). In some ways similar to the "poem" by Grass, Adorno's dictum is more relevant due to its (often misunderstood) reception rather than due to its original context or intent.

5. Matthias Lorenz published an important piece on Schlink and "political correctness" in *Literarischer Antisemitismus nach Auschwitz*, ed. V. Klaus-Michael Bogdal, Klaus Holz, and Matthias N. Lorenz (Stuttgart: Metzler, 2007).

6. The publications on recent German memory contests are numerous and important. For now, the most relevant ones are Jeffrey Herf's *Divided Memory: The Nazi Past in the Two Germanys* (Cambridge, Mass.: Harvard University Press, 1997); Anne Fuchs, Mry Cosgrove, and Georg Grote, eds., *German Memory Contests: The Quest for Identity in Literature, Film, and Discourse Since 1990* (Rochester, N.Y.: Camden House, 2006); Lauren Cohen-Pfister and Susanne Vees-Gulani, eds., *Generational Shifts in Contemporary German Culture* (Rochester, N.Y.: Camden House, 2010); and Anne Fuchs, Kathleen James-Chakraborty, and Linda Shortt, eds., *Debating German Cultural Identity Since 1989* (Rochester, N.Y.: Camden House, 2011). Also noteworthy are Stuart Taberner and Karina Berger, eds., *Germans as Victims in the Literary Fiction of the Berlin Republic* (Rochester, N.Y.: Camden House, 2009); Stuart Taberner and Frank Finlay, eds., *Recasting German Identity: Culture, Politics, and Literature in the Berlin Republic* (Rochester, N.Y.: Camden House, 2002); and Stuart Taberner, ed., *Contemporary German Fiction: Writing in the Berlin Republic* (Cambridge, Eng.: Cambridge University Press, 2007).

7. By "non-Jewish writers," I am referring to those who do not self-identify as Jewish *or* who are not perceived as Jewish by the reading public. My aim is to focus on the public perception of the writers as it pertains to their identities. Julia Franck might serve as a borderline case here since she does have Jewish heritage, but she is not perceived as a "Jewish writer" by most. She discusses her Jewish heritage in terms of her grandmother and her great-grandmothers' Jewishness, but mostly denies or negates her own, pointing to her and her family's atheism, while admitting that according to Jewish law, she "would be" Jewish: "Narben sind häufig taub," interview with Julia Franck, *Die Welt*, August 29, 2003, http://www.welt.de/print-welt/article256146/Narben-sind-haeufig-taub.html; and Bettina Spoerri, "Bitte keine jüdische Folklore: Eine Begegnung mit der Buchpreisgewinnerin Julia Franck," *Jüdische Allgemeine*, October 18, 2007, http://www.juedische-allgemeine.de/article/view/id/4497. Interestingly, *Die Mittagsfrau* utilizes the lived history of her father's mother, who was not Jewish (and the scandalous abandonment of the seven-year-old boy at the train station was hence committed by a German, non-Jewish woman). Yet, in the novel Franck imagines her maternal grandmother's Jewishness, merging the German non-Jewish grandmother with the Jewish one. In "On the Track of Family History," Franck herself describes how discovering her uncle's diaries earlier might have changed *Die Mittagsfrau* (see *Jewish Quarterly*, July 23, 2010, http://jewishquarterly.org/2010/07/on-the-track-of-family-history/#more-840).

8. For a recent study on the "new" anti-Semitism in Germany, see Philipp Gessler, *Der neue Antisemitismus: Hinter den Kulissen der Normalität* (Freiburg im Breisgau: Herder, 2004). While I am not sure that the phenomenon that Gessler describes is all that new, the working definition for anti-Semitism that he proposes is useful here: "a recurring and latent structure of hostile beliefs held against Jews as a collective, that manifests in individuals as an attitude, in culture as myth, folklore, ideology, or in imaginings and acts of social or legal discrimination or political activism against Jews resulting in or leading to eliminate, destroy, or remove Jews as Jews." Original: "eine anhaltende latente Struktur feindseliger Überzeugungen gegenüber Juden als Kollektiv, die sich bei Individuen als Haltung, in der Kultur als Mythos, Ideologie, Folklore sowie Einbildung und in

Handlungen manifestieren—soziale oder rechtliche Diskriminierung, politische Mobilisierung gegen Juden und kollektive oder staatliche Gewalt—die dazu führen und/oder darauf abzielen, Juden als Juden zu entfernen, zu verdrängen oder zu zerstören" (9). Also see Wolfgang Benz's *Was ist Antisemitismus?* (Munich: Beck, 2004), admittedly more from a historian's point of view, but essential in its treatment of "secondary" (rather than "new") anti-Semitism.

9. That is, *agape* and *philos* as well as *eros*.

10. In addition to the more recent works by Erin McGlothlin and Caroline Schaumann, Friederike Eigler's *Gedächtnis und Geschichte in Generationenromanen seit der Wende* (Berlin: Erich Schmidt, 2005) are serving as important points of reference for this study.

11. Sigrid Weigel, "'Generation' as a Symbolic Form: On the Genealogical Discourse of Memory Since 1945," *Germanic Review* 77, no. 4 (2002): 264–77.

12. Eric Santner, "History beyond the Pleasure Principle," in *Probing the Limits of Representation: Nazism and the Final Solution*, ed. Saul Friedlander (Cambridge, Mass.: Harvard University Press, 1992), 143–54.

13. Matthias Politycki's efforts in establishing a "new" generation of the 1978ers that were to reform German fiction in response to the 1968ers is a prominent example.

14. One recent example of how Jewish issues are now negotiated differently in the German public arena is Wibke Bruhns's memoir, where her father's position in the resistance against Hitler seems to serve as a safeguard against anti-Jewish articulations when she ruminates about a "Jewish psyche": "Aber was wusste ich von jüdischer Psyche, von deren Beziehung zum göttlichen Geist, der in diesem geschichtsträchtigen Land in jeder Ecke wohnt?" (Wibke Bruhns, *Nachrichtenzeit, Meine unfertigen Erinnerungen* [Munich: Droemer, 2012], 109).

15. Jeffrey Peck's *Being Jewish in the New Germany* (Rochester, N.Y.: Rutgers University Press, 2006) indicates some of the extent to which today's German Jewish relations are complicated. His study is, however, an overview and thus does not provide much detail on anti-Semitism today, glossing over some of the more troubling recent trends.

16. Interestingly, most writers whose texts engage the Holocaust past are writers who were born in West Germany, and grew up in West Germany. Exceptions are Julia Franck, who spent the first eight years of her life in East Germany, and Tanja Dückers, who grew up in West Berlin, but engages the German memory of Polish victims, typically more an "Eastern" rather than a "Western" story. All others are more or less unambiguously West German.

17. "Analyse ist nicht Verbot. Sie benennt und kritisiert, was so und nicht anders geschrieben wurde." Klaus-Michael Bogdal, "Literarischer Antisemitismus nach Auschwitz. Perspektiven der Forschung," in Bogdal, Holz, and Lorenz, *Literarischer Antisemitismus nach Auschwitz*, 1–12, here p. 7.

18. Linda Hutcheon, "Historiographic Metafiction: Parody and the Intertextuality of History," in *Intertextuality and Contemporary American Fiction*, ed. Patrick O'Donnell and Robert Con Davis (Baltimore, Md.: Johns Hopkins University Press, 1989), 3–32; and Linda Hutcheon, "The Postmodern Problematizing of History," *English Studies in Canada* 14, no. 4 (December 1988): 365–82.

19. Marianne Hirsch, *Family Frames: Photography, Narrative, and Postmemory* (Cambridge, Mass.: Harvard University Press, 1997).

20. See Stephen Brockmann's excellent essay that names some of the reasons why there is, as of 2006 at least, only a mere wish for normalization, "'Normalization?' Has Helmut Kohl's Vision Been Realized?" in *German Culture, Politics, and Literature into the Twenty-First Century: Beyond Normalization*, ed. Paul Cooke and Stuart Taberner (Rochester, N.Y.: Camden House, 2006), 17–30. Also, William Collins Donahue's recent books about Bernhard Schlink's fiction illustrates these points with admirable acuity. Donahue's study is methodologically more firmly grounded in historical analysis whereas mine seeks to uncover the archeology of emotions. See William Collins Donahue, *Holocaust Lite: Bernhard Schlinks "NS-Romane" und ihre Verfilmungen* (Bielefeld: Aisthesis, 2011); and William Collins Donahue, *Holocaust as Fiction: Bernhard Schlink's "Nazi" Novels and Their Films* (New York: Palgrave, 2010).

21. A. Dirk Moses, "The Non-German German and the German German: Dilemmas of Identity after the Holocaust," *New German Critique* 101 (34.2; Summer 2007): 45–94; and A. Dirk Moses, *German Intellectuals and the Nazi Past* (New York: Cambridge University Press, 2007).

22. Leslie Adelson, "Opposing Oppositions: Turkish-German Questions in Contemporary German Studies," *German Studies Review* 17, no. 2 (May 1994): 305–30; and Leslie Adelson, *The Turkish Turn in Contemporary German Literature: Toward a New Critical Grammar of Migration* (New York: Palgrave, 2005).

23. See Sander Gilman, "Salome, Syphilis, Sarah Bernhardt, and the 'Modern Jewess,'" *German Quarterly* 66 (1993): 195–211; and Ann Pelligrini, "Interarticulations: Gender, Race, and the Jewish Women Question," in *Judaism Since Gender*, ed. Miriam Peskowitz and Laura Levitt (New York: Routledge, 1997), 49–55. Nadia Valman summarizes the qualities of *la belle Juive* best for the European imagination: "Often conflated with the stereotype of the Oriental woman, she could be recognized by her stylized sensual beauty: her large dark eyes, abundant hair and languid expression. Scholarly studies of the figure of the *bellejuive* in French and German Romantic literature have interpreted images of her exotic allure and stories of her tragic self-sacrifice as an allegory justifying the political subjugation or social exclusion of Jews. In other words, the image of the Jewish woman in European Romantic writing can be seen as an aspect of what Edward Said described as the culture of Orientalism—a symbolic system that served to sustain a conceptual dichotomy and power differential between West and East." Nadia Valman, "La Belle Juive," *Jewish Quarterly* 205 (Spring 2007), http://www.jewishquarterly.org/issuearchive/articlee2fe.html?articleid=263.

Chapter 1

1. Richard T. Gray, "Fabulation and Metahistory: W. G. Sebald and Contemporary German Holocaust Fiction," in *Literarische Experimente: Medien, Kunst, Texte seit 1950*, ed. Christoph Zeller (Heidelberg: Winter, 2012), 271–303.

2. Primo Levi, "The Memory of the Offense," in *The Drowned and the Saved*, by Primo Levi, trans. Raymond Rosenthal (New York: Summit, 1988), 23–35.

3. W. G. Sebald, *Austerlitz* (Munich: Hanser, 2001); translated by Anthea Bell as *Austerlitz* (New York: Random House, 2002). Sebald's works are important and crucial for the topic under discussion here. However, his texts are not the main focus, since he does fall outside of the boundaries of my studies. Because he has, for the most part of his life, lived in England, he is not a "contemporary

German writer." More importantly, his works are mainly read by scholars of literature, and not by the reading public in Germany (as evidenced by the relatively sparse reviews in Germany). Hence, Sebald's work serves as an important point of reference here, but is not the main subject of study.

4. Bogdal, "Literarischer Antisemitismus nach Auschwitz," 7.

5. Mona Körte, "'*Judaeus ex machina*' und 'jüdisches *perpetuum mobile*': Technik oder Demontage eines Literarischen Antisemitismus?" in Bogdal, Holz, and Lorenz, *Literarischer Antisemitismus nach Auschwitz*, 59–74..

6. Günter Grass, *Im Krebsgang: Eine Novelle* (Göttingen: Steidel, 2002); translated by Krishna Winston as *Crabwalk* (Orlando: Harcourt, 2002). Martin Walser, *Tod eines Kritikers* (Frankfurt: Suhrkamp, 2002), not translated (all translations are my own).

7. Moses, *German Intellectuals and the Nazi Past;* Tanja Dückers, *Himmelskörper* (Berlin: Aufbau, 2003).

8. For an in-depth discussion of the full media impact of Grass's 2006 "confession," and the import of the epistemological difference between autobiography and fiction, see Anne Fuchs, "'Ehrlich, du lügst wie gedruckt': Günter Grass's Autobiographical Confession and the Changing Territory of Germany's Memory Culture," *German Life and Letters* 60, no. 2 (April 2007): 261–75, especially 263–64. I disagree with Fuchs's thesis that Grass "needed" to write an autobiography in order to "deal with" the question of personal responsibility, ultimately arguing that the autobiography somehow makes up for the "deficit" of literature—rather, I think, Grass's "confession" came at a time when he knew it would be both publically acceptable and helpful to the sales of his autobiography. Instead of admitting guilt, his gesture was one of guilt rejection because of his young age and naivety and his insistence that he was merely "verführt" (seduced) into participation (Günter Grass, *Beim Häuten der Zwiebel* [Göttingen: Steidel, 2006], 44). Additionally, writers' public statements are often staged or fictionalized, so we need to remain skeptical of ascribing more referentiality to autobiography than to fiction, as Fuchs is suggesting. Nevertheless, Fuchs's account of the media debate and its meaning within and impact on contemporary German society is highly useful.

9. Ernestine Schlant, *The Language of Silence: West German Literature and the Holocaust* (New York: Routledge 1999), 71.

10. Ruth Kluger in Schlant, *The Language of Silence*, 70. Schlant cited Sander Gilman, "Jewish Writers in Contemporary Germany: The Dead Author Speaks," *Studies in Twentieth Century Literature* 13, no. 2 (1989): 218–19.

11. Günter Grass, *The Tin Drum*, trans. Brean Mitchell (New York: Harcourt, 2009), 395. German: Günter Grass, "Paradiesische Zeiten," in *Die Blechtrommel: Roman* (Neuwied: Luchterhand, 1959), 510.

12. Grass, *The Tin Drum*, 380. German: "schlug er die Hände auf ähnliche Art ausdrucksvoll über dem Kopf zusammen, wie Oskar es vor Jahren bei seinem Spielzeughändler Sigismund Markus beobachtet hatte." Grass, *Die Blechtrommel*, 490.

13. For a comprehensive account of the debate, see Elizabeth Dye, "'Weil die Geschichte nicht aufhört': Günter Grass's *Im Krebsgang*," *German Life and Letters* 57, no. 4 (October 2004): 472–87; and on normalization, Stephen Brockmann, "'Normalization': Has Helmut Kohl's Vision Been Realized?" in Taberner and Cooke, *Beyond Normalization*, 17–29.

14. See Aleida Assman's excellent "On the (In)Compatibility of Guilt and Suffering in German Memory," *German Life and Letters* 59, no. 2 (April 2006): 187–200.

15. Gilad Margalit, "Grass und das jüdische Alter Ego," in Bogdal, Holz, and Lorenz, *Literarischer Antisemitismus nach Auschwitz*, 159–69.

16. Rebecca Braun, "Cultural Impact and the Power of Myth in Popular Public Constructions of Authorship," in *Cultural Impact in the German Context: Studies in Transmission, Reception, and Influence*, ed. Rebecca Braun and Lyn Marven (Rochester, N.Y.: Camden House, 2012), 78–96.

17. Grass, *Crabwalk*, 42; Grass, *Im Krebsgang*, 43: "Denn nicht nur Gabi, auch Mutter hat in mir den typischen Versager gesehen."

18. Grass, *Crabwalk*, 41; Grass, *Im Krebsgang*, 42: "Als dann Gabi klammheimlich die Pille abgesetzt hatte, eindeutig von mir schwanger war und mich vors Standesamt geschleppt hatte, wurde mir, kaum war der Schreihals da und die zukünftige Pädagogin wieder im Studium, sonnenklar: Ab jetzt geht nichts mehr. Von jetzt an kannst du dich nur noch als Hausmann beim Windelwechseln und Staubsaugen bewähren."

19. On "political correctness" as a symptom of the 1968ers' generation, see Matthias N. Lorenz in Bogdal, Holz, and Lorenz, *Literarischer Antisemitismus*, "'Political Correctness' als Phantasma," 219–42. It is furthermore Walser's repeated rant against "political correctness" that seems to legitimize his stance vis-à-vis "Vergangenheitsbewältigung." In this context, he coined the phrase of Auschwitz as a "Moralkeule" already in 1998.

20. On the generational succession of victims and perpetrators after the Holocaust, see Erin McGlothlin, *Second-Generation Holocaust Literature: Legacies of Survival and Perpetration* (Rochester, N.Y.: Camden House, 2006).

21. Grass, *Crabwalk*, 207–8; Grass, *Im Krebsgang*, 210: "Was tun wenn der Sohn des Vaters verbotene, seit Jahren unter Hausarrest leidende Gedanken liest, auf einen Schlag in Besitz nimmt und sogar in die Tat umsetzt? Immer bin ich bemührt gewesen, zumindest politisch richtig zu liegen, nur nichts Falsches zu sagen, nach aussen hin korrekt zu erscheinen. . . . So hielt ich Mittelmass . . . naja, das mag wohl mit den Umständen meiner Geburt zu tun gehabt haben; damit liess sich fast alles erklären."

22. Gary L. Baker, "The Middle Voice in Günter Grass's *Im Krebsgang*," *German Quarterly* 83, no. 2 (Spring 2010): 230–44, 231.

23. The most complete assessment of Walser's anti-Semitism is undoubtedly Matthias N. Lorenz's *Auschwitz drängt uns auf einen Fleck: Judendarstellung und Auschwitzdiskurs bei Martin Walser* (Stuttgart: Metzler, 2005), where he shows in painstaking detail how anti-Semitism was already prominent in Martin Walser's works well before the publication of *Tod eines Kritikers*. For a brief summary of the actual debate in the summer of 2002, see Wolfram Schütte, "Der Sommer der Ressentimentalisten," *Newsletter zur Geschichte und Wirkung des Holocaust: Informationen des Fritz-Bauer-Instituts* 23 (Fall 2002): 10–14.

24. Martin Walser, *Ein springender Brunnen* (Frankfurt: Suhrkamp, 1998). (*A Gushing Fountain*, not translated.) Also relevant here is the confession of his infamous speech in 1998: Martin Walser, *Erfahrungen Beim Verfassen Einer Sonntagsrede: Friedenspreis des Deutschen Buchhandels 1998* (Frankfurt: Suhrkamp, 1998).

25. Kathrin Schödel, "Martin Walser's *Ein springender Brunnen* (*A Gushing Fountain*)," in *The Novel in German Since 1990*, ed. Stuart Taberner (Cambridge, Eng.: Cambridge University Press, 2011), 108–22.

26. Walser, *Tod eines Kritikers*, 69. English is my own translation. German original: "Hans Lach ist der gequälte Christ, der sich helfen kann zuerst nur mit Delirium, dann mit der Tat. Ehrl-König war die Operettenversion des jüdisch-christlichen Abendlandes, das Antisaturnische schlechthin.'

27. Walser, *Tod eines Kritikers*, 45. German original: "Wenn Ehrl-König ermordet worden wäre, weil er Jude gewesen sei, hätten die anderen Recht. Aber es sei ja noch nicht einmal sicher, ob Ehrl-König Jude gewesen sei. Er, Leder, wisse an Ehrl-König nichts so sehr zu schätzen wie dessen Zurückhaltung in der Herkunftsfrage. Dass die Presse daraus immer wieder Tatsachen gemacht habe, sei nicht Ehrl-Königs Schuld, sondern zeige den Geisteszustand der deutschen Gesinnungspresse."

28. Marcel Reich-Ranicki, *Mein Leben* (Stuttgart: Deutsche Verlagsanstalt, 1999); Marcel Reich-Ranicki, *The Author of Himself: The Life of Marcel Reich-Ranicki*, intro. Jack Zipes (Princeton, N.J.: Princeton University Press, 2001).

29. See Holger Gehle, "Jüdischer Gott und deutscher Hiob: Über Martin Walser's Roman 'Tod eines Kritikers,'" in *Gerüchte über die Juden. Antisemitismus, Philosemitismus und aktuelle Verschwörungstheorien*, ed. Hanno Loewy (Essen: Klartext, 2005), 301–26, here 306.

30. See Binjamin Wilkomirski, *Fragments: Memories of a Wartime Childhood*, trans. Carol Brown Janeway (New York: Schocken Books, 1996). And, more easily spotted as invented, Herman Rosenblat, *Angel at the Fence: The True Story of a Love That Survived* (Berkeley, Calif.: Berkeley Publishing, 2008).

31. Christina Prüver, "Interview mit Martin Walser am 16. 07. 2003," in Matthias N. Lorenz, *Auschwitz drängt uns auf einen Fleck*, 495–503.

32. Mona Körte, "Erlkönigs Kinder. Überlegungen zu Martin Walsers 'Tod eines Kritikers,'" in *Jahrbuch für Antisemitismusforschung*, vol. 11 (Berlin: Metropol, 2002), 295–310.

33. Erin McGlothlin. *Second-Generation Holocaust Literature: Legacies of Survival and Perpetration* (Rochester, N.Y.: Camden House, 2006), 229.

34. William C. Donahue, "Revising '68: Bernhard Schlink's *Der Vorleser*, Peter Schneider's "Vati," and the Question of History," *Seminar* 40, no. 3 (September 2004): 293–311, here 299–301.

35. Bernhard Schlink, "Das Mädchen mit der Eidechse," in *Liebesfluchten: Erzählungen* (Zurich: Diogenes, 2000); translated by John E. Woods as "Girl with Lizard," in *Flights of Love: Stories* (New York, Vintage, 2002), 3–51.

36. Schlink, "Girl With Lizard," 47. German: "Hat Vater dich, als du mich empfangen hast, vergewaltigt? War es, als er in Strassburg war und gemeine Sachen machte und was mit der Jüdin hatte?" . . . Dann sah er, dass sie weinte (Schlink, "Mädchen," 50).

37. Donahue, "Revising '68," 301.

38. Schlink, "Girl with Lizard," 45. German: "Du glaubst doch nicht, dass Vater mich gefragt hat" (Schlink, "Das Mädchen," 48).

39. Klaus Theweleit, *Männerfantasien*, 2 vols. (Munich: Piper, 2000); Klaus Theweleit, *Male Fantasies*, 2 vols. (Minneapolis: University of Minnesota Press, 1987).

40. Dominick LaCapra, *Writing History, Writing Trauma* (Baltimore: Johns Hopkins University Press, 2001), 20.

41. La Capra, *Writing History*, 186–87.

42. LaCapra, *Writing History*, 188.

43. LaCapra, *Writing History*, 203.

44. Martin Swales, "Sex, Shame and Guilt: Reflections on Bernhard Schlink's *Der Vorleser* (*The Reader*) and J. M. Coetzee's *Disgrace*," *Journal of European Studies* 33 (March 2003): 7–22, 10.

45. Swales, "Sex, Shame and Guilt."

46. Hartmut Steinecke, "Die Shoah in der Literatur der 'zweiten Generation,' " in *Shoah in der deutschsprachigen Literatur*, ed. Norbert Otto Eke and Hartmut Steinecke (Berlin: Erich Schmidt, 2006), 135–53.

47. Gila Lustiger, *So sind wir* (Berlin: Berlin Verlag, 2005), 68. Not translated.

48. Lustiger, *So sind wir*, "Thus we are not, I cried out inside" (my translation) 250.

49. Lustiger, *So sind wir*, 251, my own translation. German original: "Als wären wir immer nur das: prädistiniert zu leiden. Aber dann habe ich das Foto gesehen und begriffen, dass Fakten nichts sind und historisches Wissen nichts. Dass Daten nichts sind und Tatsachen ein Blendwerk, weil man der Geschichte meiner Familie nicht beikommen kann, wenn man sich nicht dem Zufall ausliefert."

50. Bill Niven, "Bernhard Schlink's *Der Vorleser* and the Problem of Shame," *Modern Language Review* 28 (2003): 381–96, 395.

51. The idea that Enlightenment thought is actually what is needed to address German feelings of guilt and shame, though applied to a text where I would not fully agree that the idea actually figures that prominently, is formulated by Stephen Brockman in reference to Schlink's *The Reader*. See also Stephen Brockman, "Virgin Father and Prodigal Son," *Philosophy and Literature* 27 (2003): 341–62.

52. Friederike Eigler, "Beyond the Victim's Debate: Flight and Expulsion in Recent Novels by Authors from the Second and Third Generation (Christoph Hein, Reinhard Jirgl, Kathrin Schmidt, and Tanja Dückers)," in Cohen-Pfister and Vees-Gulani, *Generational Shifts in Contemporary German Culture*, 77–94.

53. Marcel Beyers's critically acclaimed *Flughunde* is one example that is frequently invoked when referring to texts that discuss German guilt and shame, and highly popular films such as Oliver Hirschbiegel's 2004 *Der Untergang* (*Downfall*) provide additional examples for invocations of German guilt and shame while Jews and the Holocaust are virtually absent.

54. Tanja Dückers, *Himmelskörper* (Berlin: Aufbau, 2003).

55. Tobias Haberl, "Tanja Dückers—eine sinnliche Geschichtsschreiberin: Tanja Dückers im Porträt," *Titel—Kulturmagazin*, February 20, 2004, http://www.titel-magazin.de/artikel/19/466.html.

56. Rebecca Partouche, "Der nüchterne Blick der Enkel: Wie begegnen junge Autoren der Kriegsgeneration? Ein Gespräch mit Tanja Dückers," *Die Zeit* 19 (April 30, 2003): 42.

57. Harald Welzer, Sabine Moeller, and Karolina Tschuggnall, *"Opa war kein Nazi": Nationalsozialismus und Holocaust im Familiengedächtnis* (Frankfurt: Fischer, 2002).

58. Dückers, *Himmelskörper*, 28.

59. Valerie Heffernan, "Matria History and the Matrilineal Narrative: Julia Franck's *Die Mittagsfrau*," in *Emerging German-Language Novelists of the Twenty-First Century*, ed. Lyn Marven and Stuart Taberner (Rochester, N.Y.: Camden House, 2011), 148–61.

60. See Caroline Schaumann, *Memory Matters: Generational Responses to Germany's Nazi Past in Recent Women's Literature* (Berlin: Walter de Gruyter, 2008), especially part 3, "In Search of Grandparents," which details Dückers's accomplishment as a woman to reflect on her Nazi grandparents' past. Schaumann's valuable study does not, however, sufficiently probe Dückers's or Wibke Bruhns's work in their lacking treatment of Jews and Judaism (which is also not Schaumann's aim).

61. Eigler, "Beyond the Victim's Debate," 91.

62. Dückers, *Himmelskörper*, 139. German original: 'Es sollte hinreissend eingerichtet sein, bezaubernde Säle und Salons haben, ein Kino, ein Schwimmbad, eine mustergültige Krankenstation und sogar eine Geburtsklinik, einfach alles, was man sich nur wünschen konnte. (. . .) Die hatten natürlich auch viel Zeit um zu phantasieren, die armen Leute, die da vorm Kreisleiterbüro standen und auf ihren Fahrausweis warteten."

63. Dückers, *Himmelskörper*, 187. German original: "So etwas gibt es eben nicht nur beim Menschen: diese Heimatlosigkeit, dieses Nomadentum. Für mich sind die Kuckucksbienen die Juden im Bienenvolk. Sie bereichern sich an den Grundlagen, die andere Völker geschaffen haben. Nutzniesserisch. Berechnend. Aber eine starke Bienenkönigin—immerhin hat sie ein Heer von bis zu 60 000 Arbeiterinnen an ihrer Seite (. . .)—lässt die Kuckucksbienen natürlich verjagen."

64. Dückers, *Himmelskörper*, 262–5.

65. Leslie Adelson, *The Turkish Turn in Contemporary German Literature: Toward a New Critical Grammar of Migration* (New York: Palgrave, 2005), 82.

66. Zafer Şenocak, *Gefährliche Verwandtschaft* (Munich: Babel, 1998), 90; translated by Tom Cheesman as *Perilous Kinship* (Swansea: Hafan Books, 2009).

67. Adelson, *The Turkish Turn*, 121.

Chapter 2

1. Most relevant to this study is her anthology. Hilene Flanzbaum, ed., *The Americanization of the Holocaust* (Baltimore: Johns Hopkins University Press, 1999).

2. Bernhard Schlink, *Der Vorleser* (Zurich: Diogenes, 1995); translated by Carol Brown as *The Reader* (New York: Pantheon, 1997). Ever since Oprah Winfrey's inclusion of the text into her notorious *Book Club*, the text became an international bestseller and since then gathered widespread attention also in Germany.

3. Donahue, *Holocaust as Fiction;* and, slightly expanded in German translation, Donahue, *Holocaust Lite.* While Donahue's studies are concerned with "Holocaust literature" as a problematic genre, where he analyzes with impeccable acuity the implications especially when played out in popular literature, and my readings are not centered on "the Holocaust," the themes of his study and this book are closely intertwined, and not only because he is concerned with Schlink's oeuvre. Donahue's concern with moral ambiguity and its relationship to higher-level moral inquiry is a main point in my work also, and thus my discussion touches on his frequently.

4. Klaus-Michael Bogdal, "Literarischer Antisemitismus nach Auschwitz," in Bogdal, Holz, and Lorenz, *Literarischer Antisemitismus nach Auschwitz*, 6.

5. Bernhard Schlink, "Das Mädchen mit der Eidechse"; Schlink, "Girl with Lizard."

6. See also Sander Gilman, "Male Sexuality and Contemporary Jewish Literature in German: The Damaged Body as the Image of the Damaged Soul," *Genders* 16 (Spring 1993): 113–40; and Sander Gilman, "Salome, Syphilis, Sarah Bernhardt, and the 'Modern Jewess,'" *German Quarterly* 66 (1993): 195–211.

7. Schlink, "The Circumcision," in *Flights of Love*, 197–255.

8. Schlink, "The Circumcision," 228. Original: "man erträgt nur seinesgleichen" (Schlink, "Die Beschneidung," 229).

9. See *Die Zeit* for a coherent summary of the final verdict in Berlin and the main arguments in the debate: http://www.zeit.de/gesellschaft/zeitgeschehen/2012–08/gesetz-beschneidung-religionsfreiheit and http://www.zeit.de/gesellschaft/zeitgeschehen/2012–09/beschneidungen-religion-berlin-straffrei.

10. Roy Jerome, "Introduction" to *Conceptions of Postwar German Masculinity*, ed. Roy Jerome (Albany: SUNY Press, 2001), 3–12, here 7.

11. Schlink, "Girl with Lizard," 4. Original: "Der Schatten, den das Haar auf Wange und Schläfe warf, war ein Geheimnis, und das Dunkel des bauschenden Ärmels, in dem der nackte Oberarm verschwand, eine Versuchung" (Schlink, "Mädchen," 8).

12. Schlink, "Girl with Lizard," 31. Original: "und auf dem Fels sonnte sich nicht eine Eidechse, sondern ein winziges Mädchen, allerliebst mit dunklen Locken und blassem Gesicht, hellem Mieder und dunklem Rock. Es lag auf der Seite, . . . halb verspieltes Kind und halb verführerisches Weib" (Schlink, "Das Mädchen," 34).

13. Schlink, "The Circumcision," 253. Original: "Sarah hatte Blumen gekauft . . . Sie erwartete ihn in einem kurzärmeligen Männerhemd, das knapp über den Po reichte. Sie sah verführerisch aus und verführte ihn" (Schlink, "Die Beschneidung," 253).

14. Schlink, "The Circumcision," 236. Original: "Er blieb. Sarah warb zu sehr, als dass er hätte gehen können. Aber er beschloss, nicht mehr über seine Arbeit zu sprechen" (Schlink, "Die Beschneidung," 237).

15. Gilman, "Salome," 204. Also see Pelligrini, "Interarticulations," 50–51.

16. Schlink, "The Circumcision," 254. Original: "Sie sah ihn an, und er wusste, was sie dachte. Aber, er merkte, dass es ihm gleichgültig geworden war. Er suchte in sich nach der alten Empörung und dem alten Bedürfnis, zu widersprechen und richtigzustellen, und fand nichts" (Schlink, "Die Beschneidung," 254).

17. Gilman, "Salome," 204.

18. Gilman, "Salome," 196.

19. Judith Butler, "Reflections on Germany," in *Queer Theory and the Jewish Question*, ed. Daniel Boyarin, Daniel Itzkovitz, and Ann Pellegrini (New York: Columbia University Press, 2003), 395–407, 405. Judith Butler has in the meantime become a newly contested target for issues surrounding Israel and anti-Semitism. Especially following her acceptance of the Adorno Prize in September 2012, Butler's persona is again much debated in German public intellectual venues.

20. Peter Schneider, *Eduards Heimkehr* (Berlin: Rowohlt, 1999); translated by John Brownjohn as *Eduard's Homecoming* (New York: Farrar, 2000).

21. Schneider, *Eduard's Homecoming*, 309. German original: "Alle im Roman vorkommenden Personen sind frei erfunden" (Schneider, *Eduards Heimkehr*, 409).

22. Peter Schneider, *Paarungen* (Berlin: Rowohlt, 1992), not translated.

23. Colin Riordan, "German-Jewish Relations in the Works of Peter Schneider," in *Jews in German Literature Since 1945: German-Jewish Literature*, ed. Pól O'Dochartaigh (Amsterdam: Rodopi, 2000), 625–36.

24. LaCapra, *Writing History*, 38.

25. LaCapra, *Writing History*, especially chapters 2 and 3.

26. Bogdal, Holz, and Lorenz, *Literarischer Antisemitismus*, 10–11.

27. Mona Körte, "'*Judaeus ex machina*' und 'jüdisches *perpetuum mobile*': Technik oder Demontage eines Literarischen Antisemitismus?" in Bogdal, Holz, and Lorenz, *Literarischer Antisemitismus nach Auschwitz*, 59–74, here 68.

28. Ulrich Baer, "The Hubris of Humility: Günter Grass, Peter Schneider, and German Guilt after 1989," *Germanic Review* 80 (Winter 2005): 50–73.

29. Susanne Rinner, "From Student Movement to the Generation of 1968: Generational Conflicts in German Novels from the 1970s and the 1990s," in *Generational Shifts in Contemporary German Culture*, 139–60, here 152.

30. Schneider, *Eduards Heimkehr*, 26; Schneider, *Eduard's Homecoming*, 16.

31. Schneider, *Eduards Heimkehr*, 53; Schneider, *Eduard's Homecoming*, 42.

32. Schneider, *Eduards Heimkehr*, 77–78; Schneider, *Eduard's Homecoming*, 68.

33. Schneider, *Eduards Heimkehr*, 77. These do not need translation.

34. Schneider, *Eduard's Homecoming*, 61. Original German: "Ihre Haut, die einen Hauch dunkler war, als er sie aus deutschen Breitengraden kannte, wirkte auf der ihm zugewandten Schattenseite des Gesichts noch dunkler, fremder und sprach vom Licht und den Windungen eines anderen Erdteils" (Schneider, *Eduards Heimkehr*, 87).

35. Schneider, *Eduard's Homecoming*, 62; German: "unschuldig plus intelligent plus pervers" (Schneider, *Eduards Heimkehr*, 88).

36. Schneider, *Eduard's Homecoming*, 77; German original: "Sich seiner Lust zu überlassen hieß, klein beigeben, das Spiel verlieren" (Schneider, *Eduards Heimkehr*, 109).

37. Compare for both the quotation and the description of Jenny *Eduard's Homecoming*, 172, and *Eduards Heimkehr*, 235.

38. Schneider, *Eduard's Homecoming*, 307; German: "Als du so plötzlich vor meinen Augen über die Dächer verschwunden bist, da ist irgend etwas bei mir gerissen" (Schneider, *Eduards Heimkehr*, 407).

39. Schneider, *Eduard's Homecoming*, 189; German: "Was für ein Glück es war, einer Frau nichts schuldig zu bleiben . . . Sich nicht mehr mit der lächerlichsten aller Männerfragen beschäftigen zu müssen" (Schneider, *Eduards Heimkehr*, 257).

40. Schneider, *Eduard's Homecoming*, 247; German original: "die Adresse für neudeutsche Parzivals, das Camelot für die Beschwörer eines besseren, heilen Deutschlands" and "ein Kurort für sein gekränktes Mannestum" (Schneider, *Eduards Heimkehr*, 327).

41. Schneider, *Eduard's Homecoming*, 38; German: "die schreibenden Frauen des anderen Deutschland" (Schneider, *Eduards Heimkehr*, 57).

42. Schneider, *Eduard's Homecoming* 38; German: "Wo im patriarchalischen Westdeutschland gab es Vergleichbares?" (Schneider, *Eduards Heimkehr*, 57).

43. Considering the last name Schlandt, one cannot help but be reminded of Ernestine Schlant's seminal works on German "Vergangenheitsbewältigung," although *The Language of Silence* was only published in 1999, the same year as *Eduards Heimkehr.*

44. During the conversation, there are four separate instances where Marwitz is described as "spöttisch" or "ironisch" in her diction. Schneider, *Eduards Heimkehr*, 356, 358, 365, 367.

45. Mona Körte, "*Judaeus ex machina*," 60. In the German original: "der Jude verkörpert den 'Ausweg aus der Klemme,' wodurch sein Auf- und Abtritt letztlich von den Anderen bestimmt erscheint; als mechanisch eingelassenes missing link bündelt und strafft, schraubt und klebt er in personam die lückenreiche Rede der Antisemiten und steht somit am eigenen Leib für Verfahren der Stereotypenbildung ein."

46. Peter Schneider, *"Und wenn wir nur eine Stunde gewinnen . . ." Wie ein jüdischer Musiker die Nazi-Jahre überlebte* (Berlin: Rowohlt, 2001).

47. Daniel Jonah Goldhagen, *Hitler's Willing Executioners: Ordinary Germans and the Holocaust* (New York: Knopf, 1996).

48. Schneider, in the German original: "Einem Verfolgten und Geächteten ein Stück Brot zuzustecken, ihn bei sich übernachten lassen, ihm eine nächste Unterkunft besorgen, dazu brauchte es Anstand, List und Courage, aber nicht gleich Todesbereitschaft" ("*Und wenn wir nur eine Stunde gewinnen . . .*," 14).

49. Levi, "The Memory of the Offense," 24.

50. Rafael Seligmann, *Der Musterjude: Roman* (Hildesheim: Claasen, 1997), not translated; Rafael Seligmann, *Die jiddische Mamme* (Frankfurt: Eichborn, 1990).

51. Martha A. Ravits, "Comedy and Controversy in American Popular Culture," *MELUS* 25, no. 1 (Spring 2000): 3–31, here 5.

52. Julia Franck, *Die Mittagsfrau* (Frankfurt: Fischer, 2007); translated by Anthea Bell as *The Blind Side of the Heart* (London: Vintage, 2009).

53. Claus Setzer, "Julia Franck Is Awarded the German Book Prize 2007 for Her Novel *Die Mittagsfrau*," press release of the Deutscher Börsenverein, October 5, 2007, http://www.boersenverein.de/de/13503.

54. Franck, *The Blind Side*, 101; German original: "Frau Selma Würsich stand dort im Nachthemd, dessen Ausschnitt mehr von ihren Brüsten sehen liess, als ihr recht sein konnte. . . . Das offene Haar aber wirbelte durch die Luft und ringelte sich auf ihren nackten Schultern, als lebe es. Die silbernen Fäden glänzten. Blindschleichen wanden sich auf ihren Brüsten."

55. Franck, *The Blind Side*, 30–31; German original: "Die Bewohner der Tuchmacherstrasse sprachen von der Fremden, . . . Ein Gerücht besagte, sie sei gottlos" (Franck, *Die Mittagsfrau*, 36–37).

56. Franck, *The Blind Side*, 44; German original: "Meinst du, es hat ihn interessiert, dass sie Jüdin ist?" (Franck, *Die Mittagsfrau*, 50).

57. Franck, *The Blind Side*, 44; Franck, *Die Mittagsfrau*, 50.

58. Gertrud Kolmar, *Die jüdische Mutter: Mit einem Nachwort von Esther Dischereit* (Frankfurt: Suhrkamp, 2003; also published as Gertrud Kolmar, *Eine Mutter* (Munich: Kösel, 1965). I would like to thank Esther Dischereit for

pointing me to this text. There is another, earlier re-edition of the same text, based on the same 1965 edition, with the editor Thedel von Wallmoden's comments (Göttingen: Wallstein, 1999).

59. Peter Fritzsche, "What Exactly Is *Vergangenheitsbewältigung*? Narrative and Its Insufficiency in Postwar Germany," in *German Memory Contests: The Quest for Identity in Literature, Film, and Discourse since 1990*, ed. Anne Fuchs, Mary Cosgrove, and Georg Grote (Rochester, N.Y.: Camden House, 2006), 25–40.

60. Anne Fuchs and Mary Cosgrove deliver a timely critique to Caruth's and Hirsch's attempts to understand any historical experience as traumatic. Anne Fuchs and Mary Cosgrove, "Introduction" to *German Memory Contests*, 1–21, esp. 11.

61. Jessica Prinz, "Jewish Mothers: Types, Stereotypes, and Countertypes," in *Mommy Angst: Motherhood in American Popular Culture*, ed. Ann C. Hall and Mardia J. Bishop (Santa Barbara: ABC Clio, 2009), 197–226, here 212.

62. Katharina Gerstenberger, "Fictionalizations: Holocaust Memory and the Generational Construct in the Works of Contemporary Women Writers," in Cohen-Pfister and Vees-Gulani, *Generational Shifts in Contemporary German Culture*, 95–114, here 104.

63. Otto Weininger, *Sex and Character: An Investigation of Fundamental Principles*, trans. Ladislaus Löb, ed. Daniel Steuer and Laura Marcus (Bloomington: Indiana University Press, 2005), especially 276ff.

64. Susanne Rinner, "From Student Movement to the Generation of 1968: Generational Conflicts in German Novels from the 1970s and the 1990s," in Cohen-Pfister and Vees-Gulani, *Generational Shifts in Contemporary German Culture*, 139–60, here 149.

65. Schneider, *Eduard's Homecoming*, 25.

66. Sebald, *Austerlitz.*

67. Thomas Steinfeld, "Und ewig singen die Sehnen: Ein Fall von Gefühlspolitik: Peter Schneider bleibt gern daheim," *Frankfurter Allgemeine Zeitung*, July 2, 1999, 45.

68. Thomas Wirtz, "Immer nur lebenslänglich: Bernhard Schlink verhängt Liebesstrafen," *Frankfurter Allgemeine Zeitung* 36, February 2, 2000, 5.

69. Verena Aufferman, "Der wunde Punkt: Neue Erzählungen des 'Vorlesers' Bernhard Schlink," *Süddeutsche Zeitung* 35, January 29, 2000, 21.

70. Edo Reents, "Das kalte Herz: Julia Franck's Roman *Die Mittagsfrau* rührt an eine Schicksalsfrage unserer Gesellschaft," *Frankfurter Allgemeine Zeitung* 235, October 10, 2007, L1.

71. Kristina Maidt-Zinke, "Ein Macho wie die Axt im Walde: Julia Franck hat sich mit ihrem Roman *Die Mittagsfrau* ganz dem historischen Genre verschrieben. Nur warum?" *Süddeutsche Zeitung* 223, September 27, 2007, 22.

Chapter 3

The epigraph for this chapter is from Susan Bordo, "Anorexia Nervosa: Psychopathology as the Crystallization of Culture," in *Feminism and Foucault: Reflections on Resistance*, ed. Irene Diamond and Renee Quinby (Boston: Northeastern University Press, 1988), 89.

1. Kaja Silverman, *Male Subjectivity at the Margins* (New York: Routledge, 1992).

2. Robert (Raewyn) Connell, *Masculinities* (Cambridge, Eng.: Polity, 1995), 37 and 77.

3. Robert Connell, *Gender and Power: Society, the Person, and Sexual Politics* (Palo Alto: Stanford University Press, 1987), 183.

4. Anne Fuchs, "The Tinderbox of Memory: Generation and Masculinity in *Väterliteratur* by Christoph Meckel, Uwe Timm, Ulla Hahn, and Dagmar Leupold," in Fuchs, Cosgrove, and Grote, *German Memory Contests*, 41–65. The terms "Väterliteratur" and "second-generation literature" are frequently used without sufficiently discussing and problematizing the relationship between the narrative perspective and that of the authors. This might in part be due to the fact that many Holocaust survivor texts are first and foremost autobiographical texts, even if they appear fictionalized. See Erin McGlothlin, *Second-Generation Holocaust Literature: Legacies of Survival and Perpetration* (Rochester, N.Y.: Camden House, 2006) as a recent example. Her study is exemplary in many ways, but lacks clear distinction between the author's generational affiliations and the texts' perspective.

5. See Sander Gilman, "Male Sexuality and Contemporary Jewish Literature in German: The Damaged Body as the Image of the Damaged Soul," *Genders* 16 (Spring 1993): 113–40, 126.

6. Schlink, "The Circumcision," 248; German original: "Du willst für Sarah ein Jude werden, aber um das, was es braucht, ein Jude zu werden, willst du dich drum herum mogeln. Das ist dir peinlich, das könnte dir weher tun als nötig, das willst du nicht" (Schlink, "Die Beschneidung," 248).

7. Schlink, "The Circumcision," 236; German original: "Über die Familie zu reden war heikel, über Deutschland, über Israel, über die Deutschen und die Juden" (Schlink, "Die Beschneidung," 237).

8. Michael Kimmel, "The Kindest Un-Cut: Feminism, Judaism, and My Son's Foreskin," in *The Gender of Desire: Essays on Male Sexuality*, by Michael S. Kimmel (Albany: SUNY Press, 2005), 175–84.

9. Schlink, "The Circumcision," 239–40; German original: "Wie würdest du dich fühlen, wenn ich dir sagen würde, dass ich dich liebe obwohl du Jüdin bist? Dass meine Freunde nach dem Jüdischen in dir suchen?" (Schlink, "Die Beschneidung," 240), and later, "Ich weiss nicht, ob ich damit zurechtkomme, gemocht oder geliebt zu werden, obwohl ich Deutscher bin" (Schlink, "Die Beschneidung," 241).

10. Kimmel, "The Kindest Un-Cut," 176.

11. Marc Shell, "The Holy Foreskin; or, Money, Relics, and Judeo-Christianity," in *Jews and Other Differences: The New Jewish Cultural Studies*, ed. Jonathan Boyarin and Daniel Boyarin (Minneapolis: University of Minnesota Press, 1997), 345–59.

12. See American Academy of Pediatrics: "Evaluation of current evidence indicates that the health benefits of newborn male circumcision outweigh the risks and that the procedure's benefits justify access to this procedure for families who choose it. Specific benefits identified included prevention of urinary tract infections, penile cancer, and transmission of some sexually transmitted infections, including HIV." First published August 27, 2012, http://pediatrics.aappublications.org/content/early/2012/08/22/peds.2012–1989.

13. For the latest recommendation, see http://www.zeit.de/gesellschaft/2012–08/beschneidung-betaeubung-ethikrat. Also see the references in chapter 2.

14. See Philip Eppelsheim's insightful chronicle in the *Frankfurter Allgemeine Zeitung:* http://www.faz.net/aktuell/politik/inland/beschneidungen-das-urteil-11820431.html.

15. The many different publications that recently dealt with the issue of "normalization" (mostly by Stuart Taberner and his colleagues) deliver an important indicator of the extent to which third-generation Germans perceive themselves—and are often perceived by scholars—as "normalized."

16. Barbara Kosta, "*Väterliteratur*, Masculinity, and History: The Melancholic Texts of the 1980s," in Jerome, *Conceptions of Postwar German Masculinity*, 219–224.

17. Susanne Riedel, *Eine Frau aus Amerika* (Berlin: Berlin Verlag, 2003). Translations of this text are all my own, since it has not been translated.

18. Cornelia Geissler, "Abgrund Erinnerung: Gedächtnisspuren in Prosa und Lyrik: Zwei neue Bücher aus und über Berlin," *Berliner Zeitung* 111 (May 14, 2003): 25; Reinhard Baumgart, "Ein Redeschlachtfest: Wie Susanne Riedel sich verrennt, verausgabt und verspekuliert," *Die Zeit* 27 (June 26, 2003): 42; Rolf-Bernhard Essig, "Die Freiheit, die Wahrheit zu finden: Susanne Riedels neuer Roman 'Eine Frau aus Amerika' nimmt den Kampf mit mächtigen Nationalgespenstern auf," *Badische Zeitung* 56 (March 8, 2003): IV; Petra Kohse, "Ach du bist es. Susanne Riedel hat eine tiefe Ahnung von der Traurigkeit des Paarlebens." *Frankfurter Rundschau*, 66 (March 19, 2003): 8; Brigitte Schwens-Harrant, "Völlig verkannt: Susanne Riedels Roman 'Eine Frau aus Amerika' ist deutsch, sehr deutsch," *Die Furche* 23 (June 5, 2003): 18; Martin Halter, "Moralkeule, gut durchgebraten: Susanne Riedel läßt die deutsch-amerikanische Beziehung scheitern," *Frankfurter Allgemeine Zeitung* 140 (June 20, 2003): 34; Andreas Nentwich, "Tagebuch der Entfremdung: Susanne Riedels Roman 'Eine Frau aus Amerika,'" *Neue Zürcher Zeitung* 153 (July 5/6, 2003): 37; Sibylle Cramer, "Auferstanden: Und nichts geht vorbei: Susanne Riedel lässt eine Tote sprechen," *Der Tagesspiegel* 18177 (July 13, 2003): 28.

19. Volker Mergenthaler, "'Der Turm stürzt ein': Warum Susanne Riedel den 11. September in ihren Roman 'Eine Frau aus Amerika' 'hineingequirlt' hat," *Literaturkritik.de* 9 (2011), http://www.literaturkritik.de/public/rezension.php?rez_id=15884&ausgabe=201109.

20. Reinhard Baumgart, "Ein Redeschlachtfest: Wie Susanne Riedel sich verausgabt, verspekuliert, verrennt." *Die Zeit* 27 (June 26, 2003): 42.

21. "Jo-Hannes steht auf, sein ganzer Körper schlenkert, die Gliedmassen einer Marionette" (Riedel, *Eine Frau aus Amerika*), 130.

22. "Nachdenklich massiert er sein Kinn, wo sich früher ein Bart befunden haben muss, als Kennzeichen erhöhter Spiegel männlicher Hormone. Die Leere, auf die er stösst, nimmer er irritiert zur Kenntnis" Riedel, *Eine Frau aus Amerika*, 124.

23. "'Diese schönenen Gefühle in deinem schönen Deutschland. Warum hast du dann einen Panamahut gekauft und das nächste Flugzeug genommen?'" Riedel, *Eine Frau aus Amerika*, 86.

24. "Was immer sie reitet, inzwischen geht es nur noch darum, dass ich ein Verbrecher bin" (Riedel, *Eine Frau aus Amerika*, 86), and later, "'Euer schönes Denkmal,' sagt sie, 'diese Mauer im deutschen Selbstverständnis. Gefühl kontra Verstand,' Aschenputtel denke ich, sage aber kein Wort" (Riedel, *Eine Frau aus Amerika*, 87).

25. See Robert Connell, *Gender and Power,* 184.

26. Pelligrini, "Interarticulations," 50.

27. This will be discussed in more detail in chapter 4.

28. Harry Brod, "The German-Jewish Hyphen: Conjunct, Disjunct, or Adjunct?" in Jerome, *Conceptions of Postwar German Masculinity*, 91–103. Brod argues convincingly that since Judaism is commonly associated with patriarchy, and feminist thought occasionally equates Nazism with patriarchy, the Jews are in this imagination ultimately responsible for the Holocaust since they are the original proponents of patriarchy (99).

29. Stuart Taberner, *German Literature of the 1990s and Beyond: Normalization and the Berlin Republic* (Rochester, N.Y.: Camden House, 2005), 170.

30. Schlink, "The Circumcision," 244.

31. Michael Kimmel, "Afterword," in Jerome, *Conceptions of Postwar German Masculinity*, 313–18, here 315.

32. Kimmel, "Afterword," 317.

33. Jeffrey Herf, *Divided Memory: The Nazi Past in the Two Germanys* (Cambridge, Mass.: Harvard University Press, 1997).

34. Schlant, *The Language of Silence*, 223.

35. On the common conflation of philo-Semitism and anti-Semitism, see Frank Stern, *The Whitewashing of the Yellow Badge: Antisemitism and Philosemitism in Postwar Germany* (Oxford: Pergamon, 1992).

36. Katharina Hacker, *Die Habenichtse: Roman* (Frankfurt: Suhrkamp, 2006).

37. Katharina Gerstenberger, "Fictionalizations: Holocaust Memory and the Generational Construct in the Works of Contemporary Women Writers," in Cohen-Pfister and Vees-Guliani, *Generational Shifts in Contemporary German Culture*, 95–136, here 107.

38. Monika Shafi, "'New Concept—New Life': Bodies and Buildings in Katharina Hacker's novel *Die Habenichtse*," *Seminar* 47, no. 4 (September 2011): 434–64.

39. Hacker, *The Have-Nots*, 232. German original: " Zwei nackte Männer im Park, und er als Spanner im Gebüsch, einem Gebüsch für Frauen" (Hacker, *Die Habenichtse*, 207).

40. George L. Mosse, *The Image of Man: The Creation of Modern Masculinity* (New York: Oxford University Press, 1996), 8.

41. Hacker, *The Have-Nots*, 231; German: "klein, zu klein für die kräftigen weissen Arme" (Hacker, *Die Habenichtse*, 206).

42. Sander Gilman, *The Jew's Body* (New York: Routledge, 1991), 199; and Frantz Fanon, "The Negro and Psychopathology," in *Black Skin, White Masks* (New York: Grove, 1967), 141–209.

43. Gilman, *The Jew's Body*, 234.

44. Sander Gilman, *Jewish Self-Hatred: Anti-Semitism and the Hidden Language of the Jews* (Baltimore: Johns Hopkins University Press, 1986), 12. Also important here is the recent approach by Paul Reitter, who shows convincingly that Jewish self-hatred has not always had a negative connotation: Paul Reitter, *On the Origins of Jewish Self-Hatred* (Princeton, N.J.: Princeton University Press, 2012).

45. Hacker, *Die Habenichtse*, 255–56, and 279–80 in *The Have-Nots*.

46. Hacker, *The Have-Not*, 212–3. German original: "Und gibt es ein deutsch-jüdisches Zusammenleben? Ich bin gar nicht sicher" (Hacker, *Die Habenichtse*, 189).

47. Hacker, *Die Habenichtse*, "Wer weiss schon dass ich jüdisch bin?" (189).

48. Hacker, *Die Habenichtse*. "Dass es Israel gibt, lässt mich hier ruhiger leben" (189).

49. Gerstenberger, "Fictionalizations," 102.

50. Gerstenberger, "Fictionalizations," 108.

51. Franck, *The Blind Side*, 423; German original: "Peter hatte den Fisch lange betrachtet, jeden Abend, er hatte ihn geöffnet und ihm in den Bauch geschaut, aber da war nichts, nur ein Hohlraum" (Franck, *Mittagsfrau*, 429).

52. Gerstenberger, "Fictionalizations," 104.

53. Gerstenberger, "Fictionalizations," 103.

54. LaCapra, *Writing History*, 48.

55. Franck, *The Blind Side*, 198; German: "Leontine liess ihn als kleinen Jungen erscheinen (. . .) seine Augen befanden sich auf ihrer Höhe, sein schmaler Körper war der eines Knaben" (Franck, *Die Mittagsfrau*, 204).

56. Franck, *The Blind Side*, 204; Franck, *Die Mittagsfrau*, 210.

57. Franck, *The Blind Side*, 205; Franck, *Die Mittagsfrau*, 211.

58. Franck, *The Blind Side*, 213; Franck, *Die Mittagsfrau*, 219.

59. Franck, *The Blind Side*, 206; "wie glatt der war, wie gut der duftete, ein Pelzkragen im Sommer. Martha arbeitet im Jüdischen Krankenhaus" (Franck, *Mittagsfrau*, 212).

60. Daniel Boyarin, *Unheroic Conduct: The Rise of Heterosexuality and the Invention of the Jewish Man* (Berkeley: University of California Press, 1997), 11.

61. Franck, *The Blind Side*, 399–400; German original: "Helene sah Martha in dem Viehwaggon, sie sah wie Martha's nackte Füsse auf den Exkrementen ausrutschten, wie sie Halt suchte, das Stöhnen der Gepferchten" (Franck, *Die Mittagsfrau*, 407), and later: "Helene wartete nicht . . . liess sich nicht aufhalten, sie setzte ihren Weg fort" (Franck, *Die Mittagsfrau*, 407).

Chapter 4

1. Thomas Hettche, *Woraus wir gemacht sind* (Cologne: Kiepenheuer & Witsch, 2006); translated by Shaun Whiteside as *What We Are Made of* (London: Picador, 2008); American edition: New York, MacMillan, 2010. My quotations are based on the 2008 UK edition. Here 204. German original: "Der Schwarze hatte einen muskulösen Hals mit stark ausgebildetem Adamsapfel, an dem fanden Kalfs Daumen Halt, und in einen schrillen Schrei hinein drückte er zu" (Hettche, *Woraus*, 212).

2. Peter Handtke, *Der kurze Brief zum langen Abschied* (Frankfurt: Suhrkamp, 1972); translated by Ralph Manheim as *Short Letter, Long Farewell* (New York: Farrar, 1974).

3. Thomas W. Kniesche delivers an important account of the German Jewish projections of America and meticulously traces the various and ambiguous roles that projections of America have played in the accounts of exile and more recent German Jewish literature. Thomas W. Kniesche, *Projektionen von Amerika: Die USA in der deutsch-jüdischen Literatur des 20. Jahrhunderts* (Bielefeld: Aisthesis, 2006).

4. For more recent scholarship on this issue, see Alexander Stephan and Jochen Vogt, eds., *America on My Mind: Zur Amerikanisierung der deutschen Kultur seit 1945* (Munich: Fink, 2006); and Alexander Stephan, ed., *Americanization and Anti-Americanism: The German Encounter with American Culture after 1945* (New York: Berghahn, 2005); as well as Alexander Stephan and Jochen Vogt, eds., *Das Amerika der Autoren: Von Kafka bis 9/11* (Munich: Fink, 2006).

5. Translation my own. Original: "Negativ finden sich in 'Amerika' die eigenen Verfallsängste gespiegelt, positiv werden Zukunftshoffnungen genährt. In ihrer Wirkung sind diese Bilder von langer Dauer; sie reichen aus der Vormoderne bis weit ins 20. Jahrhundert hinein." Dan Diner, *Feindbild Amerika* (Munich: Ullstein, 2002), 19.

6. For a more recent engagement with America as the location of utopian / dystopian space, see the many publications by Alexander Stephan and Jochen Vogt (in note 4), where many of the titles already reveal the dichotomy of love vs. hate.

7. Günter Kunert, *Der andere Planet: Ansichten von Amerika* (Berlin: Aufbau-Verlag, 1974). See on this and related binary projections: David Bathrick, "In weiter ferne so nah: Günter Kunerts Amerikabild," and Werner Jung, "'Let's Go, Man, Go!' Jörg Fauser und sein Amerika: Mit einem Seitenblick auf Rolf Dieter Brinkmann," in Stephan and Vogt, *Das Amerika der Autoren*, 311–21 and 323–36, respectively.

8. Hans Magnus Enzensberger, "William Carlos Williams," in *Einzelheiten IV* (Frankfurt: Suhrkamp, 1962), 273–89, here 289.

9. Hans Magnus Enzensberger, "Offener Brief an den Präsidenten der Weslyan University," in *Über Hans Magnus Enzensberger*, ed. Joachim Schickel (Frankfurt: Suhrkamp, 1968), 233–38, here 233.

10. Hans Magnus Enzensberger, "'Thriumphale Freude' über Saddams Sturz," *Frankfurter Allgemeine Zeitung*, April 14, 2003, http://www.faz.net/aktuell/feuilleton/irak-krieg-enzensberger-triumphale-freude-ueber-saddams-sturz-1101963.html.

11. Of the many texts that Karl May wrote, I will mainly reference his *Winnetou* trilogy, which is available in many editions. The English translation still available today is by Marlies Bugmann.

12. Katrin Sieg, *Ethnic Drag: Performing Race, Nation, Sexuality in West Germany* (Ann Arbor: University of Michigan Press, 2002). While the myth concerning "America" is, to a large extent, a West German projection, East German subversive fantasies were likewise celebrating Karl May.

13. Hartmut Lutz, "German Indianthusiasm," in *Germans and Indians: Fantasies, Encounters, Projections*, ed. Colin Gordon Calloway, Gerd Gemünden, and Susanne Zantop (Lincoln: University of Nebraska Press, 2002), 166–82.

14. Lutz, "German Indianthusiasm," 180.

15. Max Horkheimer, *Gesammelte Schriften in 19 Bänden*, vol. 14: *Nachgelassene Schriften 1949–1972: Nachgelassene Schriften 1949–1972* (Frankfurt: Fischer, 1988), 408. Also quoted in Diner, *Feindbild Amerika*, 34.

16. See Sander Gilman, *Jewish Self-Hatred*, on the othering of Jews by Houston Stewart Chaimberlain, as hybrids of blacks, and hence, an inferior race, 7–8.

17. Adam Sutcliffe, "Philosemitism," in *Antisemitism: A Historical Encyclopedia of Prejudice and Persecution*, ed. Richard S. Levy (Santa Barbara: ABC Clio, 2005), 2:544–45.

18. Jeffrey Peck, *Being Jewish in the New Germany* (Piscataway, N.J.: Rutgers University Press, 2006).

19. Schlink, *The Reader*, 211; German original: "Die Tochter lebte in New York in einer kleinen Strasse in der Nähe des Central Park" (Schlink, *Der Vorleser*, 200).

20. Schlink, *The Reader*, 218; German original, Schlink, Der *Vorleser*, 206–7. Ernestine Schlant also mentions this in *The Language of Silence*, 215.

21. Donahue, *Holocaust as Fiction*, 180–83.

22. Schlink, "The Circumcision," 204; German original: "'Er hat dir unsere Familiengeschichte erzählt, damit du weisst, mit wem du es zu tun hast.' Nach einer Weile fragte er: 'Warum wollte er nicht wissen, mit wem ihr es zu tun habt?' . . . [Sarah]: 'Was ist los? . . . Was sollen sie dich mit deiner Geschichte plagen? Dass du Deutscher bist, wissen sie'" (Schlink, "Die Beschneidung," 205–6).

23. Schlink, "The Circumcision," 243; Schlink, "Die Beschneidung," 242.

24. Jean Baudrillard, *America*, trans. Chris Turner (London: Verso, 1988); French original, Jean Baudrillard, *Amérique* (Paris: Grasset, 1986).

25. See Joyce Antler, ed., *Talking Back: Images of Jewish Women in American Popular Culture* (Hanover, N.H.: Brandeis University Press, 1998), especially Riv-Ellen Prell, "Cinderellas Who Almost Never Become Princesses," 123–38.

26. Roland Dollinger, "Interview with Henryk Broder," *German Quarterly* 76, no. 1 (2003): 1–10.

27. While Marwitz does not come across as American, she is clearly coded as Jewish, and her ironic diction is the main carrier for this inscription. When Susanne Rinner reads Marwitz's characteristics as "ironic distancing," then this is certainly true, but she misses the fact that ironic speech is an important anti-Semitic stereotype. Susanne Rinner, "From Student Movement to the Generation of 1968," in Cohen-Pfister and Vees-Gulani, *Generational Shifts*, 151.

28. Schneider, *Eduard's Homecoming*, 76.

29. Susanne Riedel, *Eine Frau aus Amerika*, 230. Translation from the German my own. "Sie ist eins von den deutschen Kindern, die keine Eltern mehr haben, weil aus ihren Eltern Seife gemacht wurde," and "das Entsetzliche daran ist, dass es alles ändert."

30. Riedel, *Eine Frau aus Amerika*, 230. Original: "Bis ich Amerika verliess, habe ich nicht gewusst, dass der Stillstand der Bilder keine Barmherzigkeit ist, sondern eine Schuld."

31. Anne Fuchs shows convincingly how, fifteen years after unification, a new surge of family memoirs and narratives are impacting the memory discourse in contemporary Germany. While I agree with most of her readings, the texts analyzed here indicate that Germans are also still employing strategies of repression, denial, and forgetting. Anne Fuchs, *Phantoms of War in Contemporary German Literature, Films, and Discourse: The Politics of Memory* (New York: Palgrave Macmillan, 2008).

32. See Diner, *Feindbild Amerika*, 70.

33. Andrea Bachner, "Thomas Hettche's Wound Ethics," *German Quarterly* 82, no. 2 (Spring 2009): 212–30.

34. See Thomas Steinfeld, "Der deutsche Dichter und sein Satan," *Süddeutsche Zeitung*, September 14, 2006; Volker Weidermann, "Der Herbst kann kommen,"

Frankfurter Allgemeine Zeitung, September 3, 2006; Heinrich Wefing, "Bitte werden Sie doch nicht sachlich," *Frankfurter Allgemeine Zeitung*, August 19, 2006, 34; Roman Bucheli, *NZZ*, September 12, 2006; Gerrit Bartels, *Die Taz*, September 16, 2006; Heribert Kuhn, *Frankfurter Rundschau*, October 4, 2006; Ulrich Greiner, *Die Zeit*, October 5, 2006.

35. Hettche, *What We Are Made of*, 286; German original: "Woraus war er gemacht? Er starrte Elsa Meerkaz an, bis ihm plötzlich eine Begegnung wieder einfiel, die er lange vergessen hatte. 'Anfang der neunziger Jahre, kurz nach der Öffnung der Mauer, fuhr ich zum ersten mal nach Auschwitz' " (Hettche, *Woraus wir gemacht sind*, 294).

36. Heide Fehrenbach, "Learning from America: Reconstructing 'Race' in Postwar Germany," in *Americanization and Anti-Americanism: The German Encounter with American Culture after 1945*, ed. Alexander Stephan (New York: Berghahn, 2005), 107–21.

37. The recent surge in generational studies attests to this. See Cohen-Pfister, Schaumann, McGlothlin, and so on.

38. Thomas Meinecke, *Hellblau* (Frankfurt: Suhrkamp, 2001). The English translation *Pale Blue* was released in August 2012, too recently to include the English translations here. For final revisions, the official authorized translation will be used.

39. Meinecke, *Hellblau*, 263. I am not including the English translation, since the language switch would be lost in an English version.

40. Florence Feiereisen, *Der Text als Soundtrack—der Autor als DJ. Postmoderne und Postkoloniale Samples bei Thomas Meinecke* (Würzburg: Königshausen und Neumann, 2011), 122. Also see Claudia Breger, "Postmoderne Inszenierungen von Gender in der Literatur: Meinecke, Schmidt, Roes," in *Räume der literarischen Postmoderne: Gender, Performativität, Globalisierung*, ed. Paul M. Lützeler (Tübingen: Stauffenburg, 2000), 97–125; and Charis Goer, "Cross the Border—Face the Gap: Ästhetik der Grenzerfahrung bei Thomas Meinecke und Andreas Neumeister," in *Pop-Literatur*, ed. Heinz Ludwig Arnold and Jörgen Schäfer (Text+Kritik, Sonderband X/03), 172–82.

41. Thomas Meinecke, "Ich als Text," *Neue deutsche Literatur: Zeitschrift für deutschsprachige Literatur* 48, no. 4 (2000): 183–89, here 185. Original: "Meine prophylaktische Arbeitshypothese lautet: Das autonome Subjekt ist abgeschafft."

42. Meinecke, *Hellblau*, 15.

43. Meinecke, *Hellblau*, 40. German original: "Vermilion fragt vorsichtig, ob vielleicht sie mir die Schramme am Oberschenkel, etwa mit den Fingernägeln, beigebracht haben könnte. Der Gedanke schien ihr zu gefallen. Amerikanerinnen lassen ihre Fingernägel ja länger wachsen als europäische Frauen."

44. Meinecke, *Hellblau*, 44–45.

45. Meinecke, *Hellblau*, 53. German original: "bei den Nazis habe aber doch der Supermaskuline Knecht regiert; bei den Nazis habe, ganz klar, der Körper über den Geist regiert."

46. See my essay "Sampling 'America'—Rolf Dieter Brinkmann and Thomas Meinecke's Poetics of Postmodernism," in *Literary Experiments*, ed. Christoph Zeller (Heidelberg: Winter, 2012).

47. Jeffrey Peck, *Being Jewish in the New Germany* (New Brunswick, N.J.: Rutgers University Press, 2006). When Peck suggests, in chapter 2, that the

American miniseries *Holocaust* had a significant impact on German audiences, he overestimates the extent to which this series was received in Germany. While it significantly contributed to America's understanding of and empathy towards Jewish Holocaust victims, the impact was much reduced in West Germany (which was, at the time, dealing with the aftermath of the *Deutscher Herbst*). Furthermore, Peck's study, while providing a useful overview of cultural history since 1989, uses terms such as "identity" and "Diaspora" somewhat haphazardly, and does not sufficiently differentiate between different Jewish groups' goals and interests.

48. Cecile Zorach, "Thomas Meinecke's German Fictions of Multicultural America: Model or Admonition?" *Transit* 1 (2004): 1–14.

49. Roland Barthes: "The Death of the Author," trans. Stephen Heath, in *Image—Music—Text* (New York: Farrar, 1977 [1968]), 142–48, here 146.

50. Matthias Politycki and Ulrich Wittstock began their call for a new German readability in 1992, starting a debate in which Politycki, proclaiming to be part of a new generation of '78ers (as opposed to '68ers), later modified his views that contemporary American novels are not at all desirable solutions to the problem of German literature being too remote, too much caught up in its own past, and too eclectic. See Tilman Krause, "Die 78er: Nur Maulhelden und Königskinder?" *Die Welt*, April 9, 1998, online, http://www.welt.de/print-welt/article625904/Die_78er_Nur_Maulhelden_und_Koenigskinder.html; Stuart Taberner, "A New Modernism or 'Neue Lesbarkeit'? Hybridity in Georg Klein's *Libidissi*," *German Life and Letters* 55, no. 2 (April 2002): 137–48; and Matthias Politycki, "The American Dead End of German Literature," in *German Pop Culture: How "American" Is It?* ed. Agnes C. Mueller (Ann Arbor: University of Michigan Press, 2004), 133–40.

51. The reviews by Ina Hartwig (*Frankfurter Rundschau*, October 10, 2001), Jochen Hörisch (*Neue Züricher Zeitung*, October 9, 2001), Reinhard Baumgart (*Die Zeit*, October 4, 2001), and Thomas Steinfeld (*Süddeutsche Zeitung*, September 22, 2001) all agree that *Hellblau* does not work as a novel, and that Meinecke disregards the reader in his monotone and lifeless depiction of characters, and due to the absence of a discernible plot. The only positive voice is that of Susanne Messmer (*Die Tageszeitung* September 3, 2001), who praises that Meinecke's texts invite the reader's participation in the reading process: http://www.perlentaucher.de/buch/7330 html.

52. "Meanwhile, it is not clear that Tillmann's grandfather is even remotely Jewish. . . . Probably there are few Germans in whose veins there isn't also some Jewish blood." Original: "Dabei ist gar nicht klar ob Tillmanns Grossvater auch nur im entferntesten jüdischer Abstammung ist. . . . Wahrscheinlich gibt es kaum Deutsche, in deren Adern nicht auch jüdischens Blut fliesst" (Meinecke, *Hellblau*, 30–31). Similar to Eduard's grandfather, Tillmann's grandfather is depicted as a "good German," who spoke out against Hitler when in the air bunker, and who might even have a Jewish ancestor (just like most Germans do).

53. Vamik Volkan, *Blind Trust: Large Groups and Their Leaders in Times of Crisis and Terror* (Charlottesville University of Virginia Press, 2004), 49.

54. A. Dirk Moses, "The Contradictory Legacies of German Jewry," in *The Future of German-Jewish Studies: Leo Baeck Institute Yearbook* 54 (2011): 3–56, here 37.

Epilogue

1. See Dan Diner, "Negative Symbiose: Deutsche und Juden nach Auschwitz," *Babylon* 1 (1987): 9–21.

2. See Goldhagen. *Hitler's Willing Executioners*. An international debate ensued, especially in Germany, where the consensus among scholars was that Goldhagen's statements were too generalizing to be of scholarly value. However, the debate itself raised important questions, especially in Germany. For an extensive summary, see Michael Schneider, *Die "Goldhagen-Debatte": Ein Historikerstreit in der Mediengesellschaft* (Bonn: Friedrich Ebert-Stiftung Library, 1998).

3. Whenever invoking writer identity, I am aware that there is some degree of paradoxical logic in my method of purposefully excluding one set of writers (i.e., Jewish German writers, writers residing outside of Germany, etc.) while claiming that writer identity is not at the center of my study. My aim is to focus on the public perception of the writers, rather than the writers themselves. I am interested in how contemporary Germans who are not Jewish view Jews. It is for this reason that German Jewish writers get—for the most part—excluded from this study, and it is for the same reason that writers residing outside of Germany (such as W. G. Sebald) are likewise not the focus of this study.

4. The reasons Stein invokes for changing his name to "Benjamin Stein" are indicative of this new emancipatory gesture: "It is not a personal achievement to be an heir to 'victims' nor is it a personal failure to be an heir to 'perpetrators.' I wanted to define for myself who I wanted to be—as a writer, as a person. I wanted to define that myself" (my own translation). "Es ist ebensowenig ein persönliches Verdienst, Nachkomme von 'Opfern' zu sein, wie es eine persönliche Schuld ist, Nachkomme von 'Tätern' zu sein. Ich wollte selbst bestimmen, wer ich sein würde—als Autor, als Mensch. Ich wollte selbst bestimmen." See Benjamin Stein's commentary on his biography from his blog *Turmsegler*, http://turmsegler.net/20100614/familiengeschichte/.

5. Benjamin Stein, *Die Leinwand* (Munich: Beck, 2010); translated by Brian Zumhagen as *The Canvas* (New York: University of Rochester Press, 2012).

6. Binyamin Wilkomirski, whose fraudulent autobiography was debunked by Swiss journalist Daniel Ganzfried, is clearly the nonfictional reference point for Schlink's novel. See Binyamin Wilkomirski, *Fragments: Memories of a Wartime Childhood*, trans. from the German by Carol Brown Janeway (New York: Schocken Books, 1996).

7. Of course, this title also references Schlink's short story "Girl with Lizard" where the canvas is the object of the narrator's projections and anxieties.

8. My next project will be entitled *Legacies of Despair and Hope: Jewish Writing in Today's Germany*. In it, I intend to show that the literary and artistic responses of Jews living in Germany today can teach us significant lessons about overcoming personal and collective trauma, and about living as a minority in a society where current sentiments range from hostility to indifference to concerted public efforts at redressing the crimes of the past.

9. Markus Flohr, *Wo samstags immer Sonntag ist* (Munich: Kindler, 2011).

10. Flohr, *Wo samstags*, 18: "'Hallo,' sagte Ruth. 'You are Jewish?' fragte Simson. 'No.' 'But your nose!'" This dialogue, in the way in which it inserts the original English, furthermore points to the cultural difference of the German who, in this setting, is clearly marked as the other.

11. Quote from Flohr, *Wo samstags*, 9, Friedrich speaking with the protagonist: "'It is the Germans who will never forgive the Jews that they have allowed them to gas them in Auschwitz. They go to Gaza and say 'Didn't the Jews learn from their history?' I'll say it again: If I were a Jew, I'd have enough from the Germans.'" German original: "'Diese Deutschen sind es doch, die den Juden niemals verzeihen werden, dass sie sich in Auschwitz haben vergasen lassen. Sie gehen nach Gaza und sagen 'Haben die Juden nichts aus der Geschichte gerlernt?' Ich sage es noch einmal: Wenn ich Jude ware hätte ich genug von Deutschen.'" This is exactly how Henryk Broder once quoted the Israeli psychoanalyst Zvi Rex: "Und Auschwitz, sagte mal ein kluger Israeli, 'Auschwitz werden uns die Deutschen nie verzeihen.'" Henryk M. Broder, *Der ewige Antisemit: Über Sinn und Funktion eines beständigen Gefühls* (Berlin: Berliner TB-Verlag, 2005), 158.

12. Flohr, *Wo samstags*, 167. "Es ist nicht so dass ich bei jedem Kuss davor Angst gehabt hätte dass du auch in einem kleinen Milimeter deines Kopfes einen Nazi sitzen hast. Ich habe auch nicht an den Holocaust gedacht, wenn wir uns trafen. Aber natürlich ist es immer da. . . . In jedem Menschen, der geboren wird, ist die Geschichte seiner Familie, seiner Verwandten, irgendwie auch der ganzen Menschheit, aufgehoben. Ich bin heute sicher dass kein Mini-Nazi in deinem Kopf sitzt und darauf wartet, hervorzuspringen. Doch ich will nicht eines Tages herausfinden, dass es Dinge an dir gibt, die ich nicht ertragen kann."

BIBLIOGRAPHY

Main Sources

Adelson, Leslie. "Opposing Oppositions: Turkish-German Questions in Contemporary German Studies." *German Studies Review* 17, no. 2 (May 1994): 305–30.

———. *The Turkish Turn in Contemporary German Literature: Toward a New Critical Grammar of Migration.* New York: Palgrave, 2005.

Adorno, Theodor W. *Kulturkritik und Gesellschaft.* Frankfurt: Suhrkamp [1962], 2003.

———. *Negative Dialektik.* Frankfurt: Suhrkamp, 1994.

Antler, Joyce, ed. *Talking Back: Images of Jewish Women in American Popular Culture.* Hanover, N.H.: Brandeis University Press, 1998.

Arnds, Peter. "On the Awful German Fairy Tale: Breaking Taboos in Representations of Nazi Euthanasia and the Holocaust in Günter Grass's *Die Blechtrommel*, Edgar Hilsenrath's *Der Nazi & der Friseur*, and Anselm Kiefer's Visual Art." *German Quarterly* 75, no. 4 (Fall 2002): 422–39.

Assmann, Aleida. "History from a Bird's Eye View: Reimagining the Past in Marcel Beyer's Kaltenburg." In *Debating German Cultural Identity Since 1989*, ed. Anne Fuchs, Kathleen James Chakraborty, and Linda Shortt, 205–20. Rochester, N.Y.: Camden House, 2011.

———. "On the (In)Compatibility of Guilt and Suffering in German Memory." *German Life and Letters* 59, no. 2 (April 2006): 187–200.

———. "Two Forms of Resentment: Jean Améry, Martin Walser and German Memorial Culture." *New German Critique* 90 (2003): 123–33.

Bachner, Andrea. "Thomas Hettche's Wound Ethics." *German Quarterly* 82, no. 2 (Spring 2009): 212–30.

Baer, Ulrich. "The Hubris of Humility: Günter Grass, Peter Schneider, and German Guilt after 1989." *Germanic Review* 80 (Winter 2005): 50–73.

Baker, Gary L. "The Middle Voice in Günter Grass's *Im Krebsgang*." *German Quarterly* 83, no. 2 (Spring 2010): 230–44.

Barthes, Roland. "The Death of the Author." In *Image—Music—Text*, by Roland Barthes, translated by Stephen Heath, 142–48. New York: Farrar, 1977 [1968].

Bartov, Omer. "Germany as Victim." *New German Critique* 80 (2000): 29–40.

Bathrick, David. "In weiter Ferne so nah: Günter Kunerts Amerikabild." In *Das Amerika der Autoren*, ed. Jochen Vogt and Alexander Stephan, 311–21. Munich: Fink, 2006.

Baudrillard, Jean. *America.* Translated by Chris Turner. London: Verso, 1988. French original: Jean Baudrillard. *Amérique*. Paris: Grasset, 1986.

Benz, Wolfgang. *Was ist Antisemitismus?* Munich: Beck, 2004.

Berman, Russell A. *Anti-Americanism in Europe: A Cultural Problem.* Stanford, Calif.: Hoover, 2004.

Bogdal, Klaus-Michael. "Literarischer Antisemitismus nach Auschwitz: Perspektiven der Forschung." In *Literarischer Antisemitismus nach Auschwitz*, eds. Klaus-Michael Bogdal, Klaus Holz, and Matthias N. Lorenz, 1–12. Stuttgart: Metzler, 2007.

Bordo, Susan. "Anorexia Nervosa: Psychopathology as the Crystallization of Culture." In *Feminism and Foucault: Reflections on Resistance*, ed. Irene Diamond and Renee Quinby. Boston: Northeastern University Press, 1988.

Boyarin, Daniel. *Unheroic Conduct: The Rise of Heterosexuality and the Invention of the Jewish Man.* Berkeley: University of California Press, 1997.

Boyarin, Daniel, Daniel Itzkovitz, and Ann Pelligrini, eds. *Queer Theory and the Jewish Question.* New York: Columbia University Press, 2003.

Breger, Claudia. "Postmoderne Inszenierungen von Gender in der Literatur: Meinecke, Schmidt, Roes." In *Räume der literarischen Postmoderne: Gender, Performativität, Globalisierung*, ed. Paul M. Lützeler, 97–125. Tübingen: Stauffenburg, 2000.

Brockmann, Stephen. "'Normalization?' Has Helmut Kohl's Vision Been Realized?" In *German Culture, Politics, and Literature into the Twenty-First Century: Beyond Normalization*, ed. Paul Cooke and Stuart Taberner, 17–30. Rochester, N.Y.: Camden House, 2006.

———. "Virgin Father and Prodigal Son." *Philosophy and Literature* 27 (2003): 341–62.

Brod, Harry. "The German-Jewish Hyphen: Conjunct, Disjunct, or Adjunct?" In *Conceptions of Postwar German Masculinity*, ed. Roy Jerome, 91–103. Albany: SUNY Press: 2001.

Broder, Henryk M. *Der ewige Antisemit: Über Sinn und Funktion eines beständigen Gefühls.* Frankfurt: Fischer Taschenbuch, 1986.

Bruhns, Wibke. *Nachrichtenzeit: Meine unfertigen Erinnerungen.* Munich: Droemer, 2012.

Butler, Judith. "Reflections on Germany." In *Queer Theory and the Jewish Question*, ed. Daniel Boyarin, Daniel Itzkovitz, and Ann Pelligrini, 395–402. New York: Columbia University Press, 2003.

Cohen-Pfister, Laurel, and Susanne Vees-Gulani, eds. *Generational Shifts in Contemporary German Culture.* Rochester, N.Y.: Camden House, 2010.

Connell, Robert (Raewyn). *Gender and Power: Society, the Person, and Sexual Politics.* Palo Alto, Calif.: Stanford University Press, 1987.

———. *Masculinities.* Cambridge, Eng.: Polity, 1995.

Cosgrove, Mary, and Anne Fuchs. "Germany's Memory Contests and the Management of the Past." In *German Memory Contests: The Quest for Identity in Literature, Film, and Discourse Since 1990*, ed. Anne Fuchs, Mary Cosgrove, and Georg Grote, 1–24. Rochester, N.Y.: Camden House, 2006.

Costabile-Heming, Carol Anne. "Berlin's Topography in Three Post-1989 Narratives," *German Life and Letters* 58, no. 3 (July 2005): 344–56.

Diner, Dan. *Feindbild Amerika—Über die Bestätigung eines Ressentiments.* Munich: Propyläen, 2002.

———. "Negative Symbiose: Deutsche und Juden nach Auschwitz." *Babylon* 1 (1987): 9–21.

Donahue, William Collins. *Holocaust as Fiction: Bernhard Schlink's "Nazi" Novels and Their Films.* New York: Palgrave, 2010.

———. *Holocaust Lite: Bernhard Schlinks "NS-Romane" und ihre Verfilmungen.* Bielefeld: Aisthesis, 2011.

———. "Revising '68: Bernhard Schlink's *Der Vorleser*, Peter Schneider's "Vati," and the Question of History." *Seminar* 40, no. 3 (September 2004): 293–311.

Donahue, William Collins, and Martha Helfer, eds. *Nexus: Essays in German Jewish Studies.* Volume 1. Rochester, N.Y.: Camden House, 2011.

Dückers, Tanja. *Himmelskörper.* Berlin: Aufbau, 2003.

Dye, Elizabeth. "'Weil die Geschichte nicht aufhört': Günter Grass's *Im Krebsgang.*" *German Life and Letters* 57, no. 4 (October 2004): 472–87.

Eigler, Friederike. "Beyond the Victim's Debate: Flight and Expulsion in Recent Novels by Authors from the Second and Third Generation (Christoph Hein, Reinhard Jirgl, Kathrin Schmidt, and Tanja Dückers)." In *Generational Shifts in Contemporary German Culture*, ed. Laurel Cohen-Pfister and Susanne Vees-Gulani, 77–94. Rochester, N.Y.: Camden House, 2010.

———. *Gedächtnis und Geschichte in Generationenromanen seit der Wende.* Berlin: Erich Schmidt, 2005.

Enzensberger, Hans Magnus. "Offener Brief an den Präsidenten der Weslyan University." In *Über Hans Magnus Enzensberger*, ed. Joachim Schickel, 233–38. Frankfurt: Suhrkamp, 1968.

———. "William Carlos Williams." In *Einzelheiten IV*, 273–89. Frankfurt: Suhrkamp, 1962.

Fanon, Frantz. "The Negro and Psychopathology." In *Black Skin, White Masks*, by Frantz Fanon, translated by Charles Lam Markmann, 141–209. New York: Grove, 1967.

Fehrenbach, Heide. "Learning from America: Reconstructing 'Race' in Postwar Germany." In *Americanization and Anti-Americanism: The German Encounter with American Culture after 1945*, ed. Alexander Stephan, 107–21. New York: Berghahn, 2005.

Feiereisen, Florence. *Der Text als Soundtrack—der Autor als DJ. Postmoderne und Postkoloniale Samples bei Thomas Meinecke.* Würzburg: Königshausen und Neumann, 2011.

Felman, Shoshana, ed. *Literature and Psychoanalysis: The Question of Reading: Otherwise.* Baltimore: Johns Hopkins University Press, 1982.

Flanzbaum, Hilene, ed. *The Americanization of the Holocaust.* Baltimore: Johns Hopkins University Press, 1999.

Flohr, Markus. *Wo samstags immer Sonntag ist.* Munich: Kindler, 2011.

Franck, Julia. *Die Mittagsfrau.* Frankfurt: Fischer, 2007. English translation: Julia Franck, *The Blind Side of the Heart*, translated by Anthea Bell. London: Vintage, 2009.

Friedlander, Saul, ed. *Probing the Limits of Representation: Nazism and the Final Solution.* Cambridge, Mass.: Harvard University Press, 1992.

Fritzsche, Peter. "What Exactly Is Vergangenheitsbewältigung? Narrative and Its Insufficiency in Postwar Germany." In *German Memory Contests: The Quest for Identity in Literature, Film, and Discourse Since 1990*, ed. Anne Fuchs, Mary Cosgrove, and Georg Grote, 25–40. Rochester, N.Y.: Camden House, 2006.

Fuchs, Anne. "'Ehrlich, du lügst wie gedruckt': Günter Grass's Autobiographical Confession and the Changing Territory of Germany's Memory Culture." *German Life and Letters* 60, no. 2 (April 2007): 261–75.

———. *Phantoms of War in Contemporary German Literature, Films, and Discourse: The Politics of Memory*. New York: Palgrave Macmillan, 2008.

———. "The Tinderbox of Memory: Generation and Masculinity in Väterliteratur by Christoph Meckel, Uwe Timm, Ulla Hahn, and Dagmar Leupold." In *German Memory Contests: The Quest for Identity in Literature, Film, and Discourse since 1990*, ed. Anne Fuchs, Mary Cosgrove, and Georg Grote, 41–65. Rochester, NY: Camden House, 2006.

———. "Towards an Ethics of Remembering: The Walser-Bubis Debate and the Other of Discourse." *German Quarterly* 75, no. 3 (Summer 2002): 235–46.

Fuchs, Anne, Kathleen James-Chakraborty, and Linda Shortt, eds. *Debating German Cultural Identity Since 1989*. Rochester, N.Y.: Camden House, 2011.

Fuchs, Anne, and Mary Cosgrove. "Introduction" to *German Memory Contests*, 1–21. Rochester, N.Y.: Camden House, 2006.

Fuchs, Anne, Mary Cosgrove, and Georg Grote, eds. *German Memory Contests: The Quest for Identity in Literature, Film, and Discourse Since 1990*. Rochester, N.Y.: Camden House, 2006.

Gehle, Holger. "Jüdischer Gott und deutscher Hiob: Über Martin Walser's Roman 'Tod eines Kritikers.'" In *Gerüchte über die Juden: Anti-Semitismus, Philosemitismus und aktuelle Verschwörungstheorien*, ed. Hanno Loewy, 301–26. Essen: Klartext, 2005.

Gerstenberger, Katharina. "Fictionalizations: Holocaust Memory and the Generational Construct in the Works of Contemporary Women Writers." In *Generational Shifts in Contemporary German Culture*, ed. Laurel Cohen-Pfister and Susanne Vees-Gulani, 95–114. Rochester, N.Y.: Camden House, 2010.

Gessler, Philipp. *Der neue Anti-Semitismus: Hinter den Kulissen der Normalität*. Freiburg: Herder, 2004.

Gilman, Sander. "Introduction" to *America in the Eyes of the Germans: An Essay on Anti-Americanism*, by Dan Diner, translated from German by Allison Brown, xi–xviii. Princeton, N.J.: Markus Wiener, 1996.

———. *Jewish Self-Hatred: Anti-Semitism and the Hidden Language of the Jews*. Baltimore: Johns Hopkins University Press, 1986.

———. "Jewish Writers in Contemporary Germany: The Dead Author Speaks." *Studies in Twentieth Century Literature* 13, no. 2 (1989): 218–19.

———. *The Jew's Body*. New York: Routledge, 1991.

———. "Male Sexuality and Contemporary Jewish Literature in German: The Damaged Body as the Image of the Damaged Soul." *Genders* 16 (Spring 1993): 113–40.

———. "Salome, Syphilis, Sarah Bernhardt, and the 'Modern Jewess.'" *German Quarterly* 66 (Spring 1993): 195–211.

Goer, Charis. "Cross the Border—Face the Gap: Ästhetik der Grenzerfahrung bei Thomas Meinecke und Andreas Neumeister." *Pop-Literatur*, ed. Heinz Ludwig Arnold and Jörgen Schäfer, 172–82. Text+Kritik. Sonderband X/03.

Goldhagen, Daniel Jonah. *Hitler's Willing Executioners: Ordinary Germans and the Holocaust*. New York: Knopf, 1996.

Grass, Günter. *Beim Häuten der Zwiebel.* Göttingen: Steidel, 2006. English translation: Günter Grass, *Peeling the Onion,* trans. Michael Henry Heim. Orlando, Fla.: Harcourt, 2007.

———. *Die Blechtrommel: Roman.* Neuwied: Luchterhand, 1959. English translation: Günter Grass, *The Tin Drum,* trans. Brean Mitchell. New York: Harcourt, 2009.

———. *Im Krebsgang: Eine Novelle.* Göttingen: Steidl, 2002. English translation: Günter Grass, *Crabwalk,* trans. Krishna Winston. Orlando, Fla.: Harcourt, 2002.

———. "Was gesagt werden muss." http://www.sueddeutsche.de/kultur/gedicht-zum-konflikt-zwischen-israel-und-iran-was-gesagt-werden-muss-1.1325809. Translation by Michael Kiefer and Nica Mintz. http://pulsemedia.org/2012/04/07/what-must-be-said.

Gray, Richard. "Fabulation and Metahistory: W. G. Sebald and Contemporary German Holocaust Fiction." In *Literarische Experimente: Medien, Kunst, Texte seit 1950,* ed. Christoph Zeller, 271–303. Heidelberg: Winter, 2012.

Hacker, Katharina. *Die Habenichtse.* Frankfurt: Suhrkamp, 2006. English translation: Katharina Hacker, *The Have-Nots,* trans. Helen Atkins. New York: Europa, 2007.

Handtke, Peter. *Der kurze Brief zum langen Abschied.* Frankfurt: Suhrkamp, 1972. English translation: *Short Letter, Long Farewell,* trans. Ralph Manheim. New York: Farrar, 1974.

Heffernan, Valerie. "Matria History and the Matrilineal Narrative: Julia Franck's *Die Mittagsfrau.*" In *Emerging German-Language Novelists of the Twenty-First Century,* ed. Lyn Marven and Stuart Taberner, 148–61. Rochester, NY: Camden House, 2011.

Heine, Heinrich. "Ludwig Börne: Eine Denkschrift: Viertes Buch." In *Heines Werke in fünf Bänden.* Vol. 5. Berlin: Aufbau, 1974.

Hell, Julia. "Eyes Wide Shut: German Post-Holocaust Authorship." *New German Critique* 88 (2003): 9–36.

Herf, Jeffrey. *Divided Memory: The Nazi Past in the Two Germanys.* Cambridge, Mass.: Harvard University Press, 1997.

———. "The 'Holocaust' Reception in West Germany: Right, Center, and Left." *New German Critique* 19 (1980): 30–52.

Hettche, Thomas. *Nox.* Cologne: Kiepenheuer & Witsch, 1995.

———. *Woraus wir gemacht sind.* Cologne: Kiepenheuer & Witsch, 2006. English translation: *What We Are Made of,* trans. Shaun Whiteside. London: Picador, 2008.

Hirsch, Marianne. *Family Frames: Photography, Narrative, and Postmemory.* Cambridge, Mass.: Harvard University Press, 1997.

Horkheimer, Max. *Gesammelte Schriften in 19 Bänden.* Volume 14: *Nachgelassene Schriften 1949–1972.* Frankfurt: Fischer, 1988.

Hutcheon, Linda. "Historiographic Metafiction: Parody and the Intertextuality of History." In *Intertextuality and Contemporary American Fiction,* ed. Patrick O'Donnell and Robert Con Davis, 3–32. Baltimore, Md.: Johns Hopkins University Press, 1989.

———. "The Postmodern Problematizing of History." *English Studies in Canada* 14, no. 4 (December 1988): 365–82.

Iser, Wolfgang. *Der Akt des Lesens: Theorie ästhetischer Wirkung*. Munich: Fink, 1976.

Jauss, Hans Robert. *Ästhetische Erfahrung und literarische Hermeneutik*. Munich: Fink, 1977.

Jerome, Roy, ed. *Conceptions of Postwar German Masculinity*. Albany: SUNY Press, 2001.

———. "Introduction" to *Conceptions of Postwar German Masculinity*, ed. Roy Jerome, 3–12. Albany: SUNY Press, 2001.

Jung, Werner. "'Let's Go, Man, Go!' Jörg Fauser und sein Amerika: Mit einem Seitenblick auf Rolf Dieter Brinkmann." In *Das Amerika der Autoren: Von Kafka bis 9/11*, 323–36. Munich: Fink, 2006.

Kimmel, Michael S. "The Kindest Un-Cut: Feminism, Judaism, and My Son's Foreskin." In *The Gender of Desire: Essays on Male Sexuality*, 175–84. Albany: SUNY Press, 2005.

Kniesche, Thomas W. *Projektionen von Amerika: Die USA in der deutsch-jüdischen Literatur des 20. Jahrhunderts*. Bielefeld: Aisthesis, 2006.

Kolmar, Gertrud. *Die jüdische Mutter*. Frankfurt: Suhrkamp, 2003. Re-edition of Gertrud Kolmar. *Eine Mutter*. Munich: Kösel, 1965.

Körte, Mona. "Erlkönigs Kinder." In *Jahrbuch für Anti-Semitismusfoschung 11*, ed. Wolfgang Benz, 295–310. Berlin: Metropol Verlag, 2002.

———. "Judaeus ex machina und 'jüdisches perpetuum mobile': Technik oder Demontage eines Literarischen Anti-Semitismus?" In *Literarischer Anti-Semitismus nach Auschwitz*, ed. K.-M. Bogdal, Klaus Holz, and Matthias N. Lorenz, 59–74. Stuttgart: Metzler, 2007.

Kosta, Barbara. "Väterliteratur, Masculinity, and History: The Melancholic Texts of the 1980s." In *Conceptions of Postwar German Masculinity*, ed. Roy Jerome, 219–224. Albany: SUNY Press, 2001.

Krause, Tilman. "Die 78er: Nur Maulhelden und Königskinder?" *Die Welt*, April 9, 1998.

Kunert, Günter. *Der andere Planet: Ansichten von Amerika*. Berlin: Aufbau, 1974.

LaCapra, Dominick. *Writing History, Writing Trauma*. Baltimore: Johns Hopkins University Press, 2001.

Levi, Primo. "The Memory of the Offense." In *The Drowned and the Saved*, by Primo Levi, trans. Raymond Rosenthal, 23–35. New York: Summit Books, 1988.

Levy, Richard S., ed. *Antisemitism: A Historical Encyclopedia of Prejudice and Persecution*. 2 vols. Santa Barbara, Calif.: ABC Clio, 2005.

———. "Forget Webster." *German Studies Review* 24, no. 1 (February 2006): 145–46.

Loewy, Hanno, ed. *Gerüchte über die Juden: Antisemitismus, Philosemitismus und aktuelle Verschwörungstheorien*. Essen: Klartext, 2005.

Lorenz, Matthias N. "Auschwitz drängt uns auf einen Fleck." In *Judendarstellung und Auschwitzdiskurs bei Martin Walser*. Stuttgart: Metzler, 2005.

———. "'Political Correctness' als Phantasma: Zu Bernhard Schlink's 'Die Beschneidung.'" in *Literarischer Antisemitismus nach Auschwitz*, ed. K.-M. Bogdal, Klaus Holz, and Matthias N. Lorenz, 219–42. Stuttgart: Metzler, 2007.

Lustiger, Gila. *So sind wir: Ein Familienroman*. Berlin: Berlin Verlag, 2005.

Lutz, Hartmut. "German Indianthusiasm." In *Germans and Indians: Fantasies, Encounters, Projections*, ed. Colin Gordon Calloway, Gerd Gemünden, and Susanne Zantop, 166–82. Lincoln: University of Nebraska Press, 2002.

Margalit, Gilad. "Grass und das jüdische Alter Ego." In *Literarischer Anti-Semitismus nach Auschwitz*, ed. Klaus-Michael Bogdal, Klaus Holz, and Matthias N. Lorenz, 159–69. Stuttgart: Metzler, 2007.

———. *Guilt, Suffering, and Memory: Germany Remembers Its Dead of World War II*. Trans. Haim Watzman. Bloomington: Indiana University Press, 2010.

May, Karl. *Winnetou I-III*. Munich: Bertelsmann, 1964. English translation by Marlies Bugmann. Independently published, Australia, 2008.

McGlothlin, Erin. *Second-Generation Holocaust Literature: Legacies of Survival and Perpetration*. Rochester, N.Y.: Camden House, 2006.

Metz, Joseph. "'Truth Is a Woman': Post-Holocaust Narrative, Postmodernism, and the Gender of Fascism in Der Vorleser." *German Quarterly* 77, no. 3 (Summer 2004): 300–323.

Mitscherlich, Margarete, and Alexander Mitscherlich. *Die Unfähigkeit zu trauern: Grundlagen kollektiven Verhaltens*. Munich: Piper, 1967. English translation: *The Inability to Mourn: Principles of Collective Behavior*, trans. Beverly R. Placzek. New York: Grove, 1975.

Moses, A. Dirk. "The Contradictory Legacies of German Jewry." In *The Future of German-Jewish Studies. Leo Baeck Institute Yearbook* 54 (2011), 3–56.

———. *German Intellectuals and the Nazi Past*. Cambridge, Eng.: Cambridge University Press, 2007.

———. "The Non-German German and the German German: Dilemmas of Identity after the Holocaust." *New German Critique* 101 (34.2; Summer 2007): 45–94.

Mosse, George L. *The Image of Man: The Creation of Modern Masculinity*. New York: Oxford University Press, 1996.

Mueller, Agnes C. "Forgiving the Jews for Auschwitz? Guilt and Gender in Bernhard Schlink's *Liebesfluchten*." *German Quarterly* 80, no. 4 (Fall 2007): 511–30.

Niven, Bill. "Bernhard Schlink's Der Vorleser and the Problem of Shame." *Modern Language Review* 28 (2003): 381–96.

———. *Facing the Nazi Past: United Germany and the Legacy of the Third Reich*. London: Routledge, 2003.

Partouche, Rebecca. "Der nüchterne Blick der Enkel: Wie begegnen junge Autoren der Kriegsgeneration? Ein Gespräch mit Tanja Dückers." *Die Zeit* 19 (April 30, 2003): 42.

Peck, Jeffrey. *Being Jewish in the New Germany*. Rochester, N.Y.: Rutgers University Press, 2006.

Pellegrini, Ann. "Interarticulations: Gender, Race, and the Jewish Women Question." In *Judaism Since Gender*, ed. Miriam Peskowitz and Laura Levitt, 49–55. New York: Routledge, 1997.

Peskowitz, Miriam, and Laura Levitt, eds. *Judaism Since Gender*. New York: Routledge, 1997.

Politycki, Matthias. "The American Dead End of German Literature." In *German Pop Culture: How "American" Is It?* ed. Agnes C. Mueller, 133–40. Ann Arbor: University of Michigan Press, 2004.

Prell, Riv-Ellen. "Cinderellas Who Almost Never Become Princesses." In *Talking Back: Images of Jewish Women in American Popular Culture*, ed. Joyce Antler, 123–38. Hanover, N.H.: Brandeis University Press, 1998.

Prinz, Jessica. "Jewish Mothers: Types, Stereotypes, and Countertypes." In *Mommy Angst: Motherhood in American Popular Culture*, ed. Ann C. Hall and Mardia J. Bishop, 197–226. Santa Barbara, Calif.: ABC-Clio, 2009.

Prüver, Christina. "Interview mit Martin Walser am 16. 07. 2003." In *Auschwitz drängt uns auf einen Fleck*, by Mattias N. Lorenz, 495–503.

Ravits, Martha A. "Comedy and Controversy in American Popular Culture." *MELUS* 25, no. 1 (Spring 2000): 3–31.

Reich-Ranicki, Marcel. *Mein Leben*. Stuttgart: Deutsche Verlagsanstalt, 1999. English translation: Marcel Reich-Ranicki. *The Author of Himself: The Life of Marcel Reich-Ranicki*, with an introduction by Jack Zipes. Translated from the German by Ewald Osers. Princeton, N.J.: Princeton University Press, 2001.

Reitter, Paul. *On the Origins of Jewish Self-Hatred*. Princeton, N.J.: Princeton University Press, 2012.

Riedel, Susanne. *Eine Frau aus Amerika*. Berlin: Berlin Verlag, 2003.

Rinner, Susanne. "From Student Movement to the Generation of 1968: Generational Conflicts in German Novels from the 1970s and the 1990s." In *Generational Shifts in Contemporary German Culture*, ed. Laurel Cohen-Pfister and Susanne Vees-Gulani, 139–60. Rochester, N.Y.: Camden House, 2010.

Riordan, Colin. "German-Jewish Relations in the Works of Peter Schneider." In *Jews in German Literature Since 1945*, ed. Pól O'Dochartaigh, 625–36. Amsterdam: Rodopi, 2000.

Rohr, Susanne, and Sophia Komor, eds. *The Holocaust, Art, and Taboo: Transatlantic Exchanges on the Ethics and Aesthetics of Representation*. Heidelberg: Winter, 2010.

Santner, Eric. "History beyond the Pleasure Principle." In *Probing the Limits of Representation: Nazism and the Final Solution*, ed. Saul Friedlander, 143–54. Cambridge, Mass.: Harvard University Press, 1992.

———. *Stranded Objects: Mourning, Memory and Film in Postwar Germany*. Ithaca, N.Y.: Cornell University Press, 1990.

Schaumann, Caroline. *Memory Matters: Generational Responses to Germany's Nazi Past in Recent Women's Literature*. Berlin: Walter de Gruyter, 2008.

Schlant, Ernestine. *The Language of Silence: West German Literature and the Holocaust*. New York: Routledge 1999.

Schlink, Bernhard. "Das Mädchen mit der Eidechse." In *Liebesfluchten: Erzählungen*, 7–54. Zurich: Diogenes, 2000. English translation: Bernhard Schlink, "Girl with Lizard," in *Flights of Love. Stories*, trans. John E. Woods, 3–51. New York, Vintage, 2002.

———. *Der Vorleser*. Zurich: Diogenes, 1995. English translation: *The Reader*, trans. Carol Brown. New York: Pantheon, 1997.

———. "Die Beschneidung." In *Liebesfluchten: Erzählungen*, 199–256. Zurich: Diogenes, 2000. English translation: Bernhard Schlink, "The Circumcision," in *Flights of Love: Stories*, trans. John E. Woods, 197–255. New York, Vintage, 2002.

———. *Die Heimkehr*. Zurich: Diogenes, 2006.

———. *Liebesfluchten: Erzählungen*. Zurich: Diogenes, 2000. English translation: *Flights of Love: Stories*, trans. John E. Woods. New York, Vintage, 2002.

Schmitz, Helmut. *On Their Own Terms. The Legacy of National Socialism in Post-1990 German Fiction*. Birmingham: University of Birmingham Press, 2004.

Schneider, Peter. *Eduards Heimkehr*. Berlin: Rowohlt, 1999. English translation: Peter Schneider, *Eduard's Homecoming*, trans. John Brownjohn. New York: Farrar, 2000.

———. *Paarungen*. Berlin: Rowohlt, 1992.

———. *"Und wenn wir nur eine Stunde gewinnen . . ." Wie ein jüdischer Musiker die Nazi-Jahre überlebte*. Berlin: Rowohlt, 2001.

Schödel, Kathrin. "Martin Walser's Ein springender Brunnen (A Gushing Fountain)." In *The Novel in German Since 1990*, ed. Stuart Taberner, 108–22. Cambridge, Eng.: Cambridge University Press, 2011.

Schütte, Wolfram. "Der Sommer der Ressentimentalisten." *Newsletter zur Geschichte und Wirkung des Holocaust: Informationen des Fritz-Bauer-Instituts* 23 (Fall 2002): 10–14.

Sebald, W. G. *Austerlitz*. Munich: Hanser, 2001. English translation: W. G. Sebald, *Austerlitz*, trans. Anthea Bell. New York: Random House, 2002.

———. *Luftkrieg und Literatur*. Munich: Hanser, 1999.

Şenocak, Zafer. *Gefährliche Verwandtschaft*. Munich: Babel, 1998. English translation: Zafer Şenocak, *Perilous Kinship*, trans. Tom Cheesman. Swansea: Hafan Books, 2009.

Shafi, Monika. "'New Concept—New Life': Bodies and Buildings in Katharina Hacker's novel *Die Habenichtse*." *Seminar* 47, no. 4 (September 2011): 434–64.

Shell, Marc. "The Holy Foreskin; or, Money, Relics, and Judeo-Christianity." In *Jews and Other Differences: The New Jewish Cultural Studies*, ed. Jonathan Boyarin and Daniel Boyarin, 345–59. Minneapolis: University of Minnesota Press, 1997.

Sieg, Katrin. *Ethnic Drag: Performing Race, Nation, Sexuality in West Germany*. Ann Arbor: University of Michigan Press, 2002.

Silverman, Kaja. *Male Subjectivity at the Margins*. New York: Routledge, 1992.

Stein, Benjamin. *Die Leinwand*. Munich: Beck, 2010.

Steinecke, Hartmut. "Die Shoah in der Literatur der 'zweiten Generation.'" In *Shoah in der deutschsprachigen Literatur*, ed. Norbert Otto Eke and Hartmut Steinecke, 135–53. Berlin: Erich Schmidt, 2006.

Stephan, Alexander, ed. *Americanization and Anti-Americanism: The German Encounter with American Culture after 1945*. New York: Berghahn, 2005.

Stephan, Alexander, and Jochen Vogt, eds. *America on My Mind: Zur Amerikanisierung der deutschen Kultur seit 1945*. Munich: Fink, 2006.

———. *Das Amerika der Autoren: Von Kafka bis 9/11*. Munich: Fink, 2006.

Stern, Frank. *The Whitewashing of the Yellow Badge: Antisemitism and Philosemitism in Postwar Germany*. Oxford: Pergamon, 1992.

Sutcliffe, Adam. "Philosemitism." In *Antisemitism: A Historical Encyclopedia of Prejudice and Persecution*, ed. Richard S. Levy, 2:544–45. Santa Barbara, Calif.: ABC Clio, 2005.

Swales, Martin. "Sex, Shame and Guilt: Reflections on Bernhard Schlink's *Der Vorleser* (*The Reader*) and J. M. Coetzee's *Disgrace*." *Journal of European Studies* 33 (2003): 7–22.

Taberner, Stuart, ed. *Contemporary German Fiction: Writing in the Berlin Republic*. Cambridge, Eng.: Cambridge University Press, 2007.

———. *German Literature of the 1990s and Beyond: Normalization and the Berlin Republic*. Rochester, N.Y.: Camden House, 2005.

———. "A New Modernism or 'Neue Lesbarkeit'? Hybridity in Georg Klein's Libidissi." *German Life and Letters* 55, no. 2 (April 2002): 137–48.

Taberner, Stuart, and Karina Berger, eds. *Germans as Victims in the Literary Fiction of the Berlin Republic*. Rochester, N.Y.: Camden House, 2009.

Taberner, Stuart, and Frank Finlay, eds. *Recasting German Identity: Culture, Politics, and Literature in the Berlin Republic*. Rochester, N.Y.: Camden House, 2002.

Theweleit, Klaus. *Männerphantasien 1 und 2*. Frankfurt am Main: Stroemfeld, 1977/78. English translation: Klaus Theweleit, *Male Fantasies*, 2 vols. Minneapolis: University of Minnesota Press, 1987.

Valman, Nadia. "La Belle Juive." *Jewish Quarterly* 205 (Spring 2007), http://www.jewishquarterly.org/issuearchive/articlee2fe.html?articleid=263.

Volkan, Vamik D. *Blind Trust: Large Groups and Their Leaders in Times of Crisis and Terror*. Charlottesville: University of Virginia Press, 2004.

Volkov, Shulamit. *Germans, Jews, and Antisemites: Trials in Emancipation*. Cambridge, Eng.: Cambridge University Press, 2006.

Walser, Martin. *Ein springender Brunnen*. Frankfurt: Suhrkamp, 1998.

———. *Erfahrungen Beim Verfassen Einer Sonntagsrede: Friedenspreis des Deutschen Buchhandels 1998*. Frankfurt: Suhrkamp, 1998.

———. *Tod eines Kritikers: Roman*. Frankfurt: Suhrkamp, 2002.

Weigel, Sigrid. "'Generation' as a Symbolic Form: On the Genealogical Discourse of Memory Since 1945." *Germanic Review* 77, no. 4 (2002): 264–77.

Weininger, Otto. *Sex and Character: An Investigation of Fundamental Principles*. Trans. Ladislaus Löb; ed. Daniel Steuer and Laura Marcus. Bloomington: Indiana University Press, 2005.

Welzer, Harald, Sabine Moeller, and Karolina Tschuggnall. "Opa war kein Nazi." In *Nationalsozialismus und Holocaust im Familiengedächtnis*. Frankfurt: Fischer, 2002.

Zorach, Cecile. "Thomas Meinecke's German Fictions of Multicultural America: Model or Admonition?" *Transit* 1 (2004): 1–14.

Reviews of Contemporary Texts

Aufferman, Verena. "Der wunde Punkt: Neue Erzählungen des 'Vorlesers' Bernhard Schlink." *Süddeutsche Zeitung* 35 (January 29, 2000): 21.

Baumgart, Reinhard. "Ein Redeschlachtfest: Wie Susanne Riedel sich verausgabt, verspekuliert, verrennt." *Die Zeit* 27 (June 26, 2003): 42.

Bucheli, Roman. "Auf eigene Faust und Rechnung. *Woraus wir gemacht sind*—Thomas Hettches Roman ist auch eine Liebeserklärung an Amerika." *Neue Zürcher Zeitung* 211 (September 12, 2006): 25.

Cramer, Sybille. "Auferstanden: Und nichts geht vorbei: Susanne Riedel lässt eine Tote sprechen." *Der Tagesspiegel* 18177 (July 13, 2003): 28.

Geissler, Cornelia. "Abgrund Erinnerung: Gedächtnisspuren in Prosa und Lyrik: Zwei neue Bücher aus und über Berlin." *Berliner Zeitung* 111 (May 14, 2003): 25.

Greiner, Ulrich. “Im Abgrund der Bilder: Kleine Verteidigung des neuen Romans von Thomas Hettche gegen seine großen Kritiker.” *Die Zeit* 41 (October 5, 2006): 59.

Haberl, Tobias. “Tanja Dückers—eine sinnliche Geschichtsschreiberin: Tanja Dückers im Porträt.” *Titel—Kulturmagazin.* February 20, 2004. http://www.titel-magazin.de/artikel/19/466.html.

Halter, Martin. “Moralkeule, gut durchgebraten: Susanne Riedel läßt die deutsch-amerikanische Beziehung scheitern.” *Frankfurter Allgemeine Zeitung* 140 (June 20, 2003): 34.

Kohse, Petra. “Ach du bist es: Susanne Riedel hat eine tiefe Ahnung von der Traurigkeit des Paarlebens.” *Frankfurter Rundschau* 66 (March 19, 2003): 8.

Krekeler, Elmar. “Deutsch in der Fremde: Es spukt: Thomas Hettche wird erwachsen in Amerika.” *Die Welt* 39 (September 30, 2006): 6.

Maidt-Zinke, Kristina. “Ein Macho wie die Axt im Walde: Julia Franck hat sich mit ihrem Roman *Die Mittagsfrau* ganz dem historischen Genre verschrieben. Nur warum?” *Süddeutsche Zeitung* 223 (September 27, 2007): 22.

Moritz, Rainer. “Marfa ist nicht Frankfurt am Main: Thomas Hettches Roman *Woraus wir gemacht sind*.” *Stuttgarter Zeitung* 229 (October 4, 2006): III.

Nentwich, Andreas. “Tagebuch der Entfremdung: Susanne Riedels Roman ‘Eine Frau aus Amerika.’ ” *Neue Zürcher Zeitung* 153 (July 5/6, 2003): 37.

Partouche, Rebecca. “Der nüchterne Blick der Enkel: Wie begegnen junge Autoren der Kriegsgeneration? Ein Gespräch mit Tanja Dückers.” *Die Zeit* 19 (April 13, 2003): 42.

Reents, Edo. “Das kalte Herz: Julia Franck’s Roman *Die Mittagsfrau* rührt an eine Schicksalsfrage unserer Gesellschaft.” *Frankfurter Allgemeine Zeitung* 235 (October 10, 2007): L1.

Richter, Steffen. “Utopie in der Prärie: Der Hauch des amerikanischen Imperiums: Thomas Hettches Roman *Woraus wir gemacht sind*.” *Der Tagesspiegel* 19294 (August 28, 2006): 24.

Steinfeld, Thomas. “Der deutsche Dichter und sein Satan: Ein Liebling der Kritik: Thomas Hettches Roman *Woraus wir gemacht sind*, ein Produkt der Schwerarbeit an der Leichtigkeit.” *Süddeutsche Zeitung* 212 (September 14, 2006): 20.

———. “Und ewig singen die Sehnen: Ein Fall von Gefühlspolitik: Peter Schneider bleibt gern daheim.” *Frankfurter Allgemeine Zeitung*, July 2, 1999, 45.

Wefing, Heinrich. “Im Inneren des Imperiums: Liebe und Absturz in Amerika: Thomas Hettche erzählt die Geschichte einer Entführung.” *Frankfurter Allgemeine Zeitung*, August 19, 2006, 34.

Weidermann, Volker. “Der Herbst kann kommen: Zwischen Heimat und Hollywood: Selten war die deutschsprachige Literatur so welthaltig wie heute: Ein Ausblick auf die neuen Bücher.” *Frankfurter Allgemeine Zeitung* 230 (September 3, 2006): 17.

Wirtz, Thomas. “Immer nur lebenslänglich: Bernhard Schlink verhängt Liebesstrafen.” *Frankfurter Allgemeine Zeitung* 36 (February 2, 2000): 5.

INDEX